PUBLIC ACCOUNTABILITY AND THE SCHOOLING SYSTEM
A SOCIOLOGY OF SCHOOL BOARD DEMOCRACY

WILLIAM BACON

Harper & Row, Publishers

London   New York   Hagerstown   Sydney
San Francisco

First published 1978
Harper & Row Ltd
28 Tavistock Street
London WC2E 7PN

British Library Cataloguing in Publication Data

Bacon, William
    Public accountability and the schooling system.
    1. School management and organization — England
    2. Educational accountability — England
    3. School boards — England
    I. Title
    301.5'6   LB2901

ISBN 0-06-318082-0

Designed by Richard Dewing, 'Millions'
Typeset by Preface Ltd, Salisbury
Printed by Butler & Tanner Ltd, Frome and London

Contents

Preface

In this book I have aimed to shed a little more light on the ways in which current moves to democratize our schooling system, including the kinds of proposals recently advocated by the Taylor Committee Report, are likely to work out in practice. In pursuing this aim I have of necessity looked both at present distributions of power and at those factors which promise to make our schools more responsive to the wider society. However, this is not intended to be simply another book about educational theory for, since this is such a badly neglected field which is redolent with pious statements of good intent, but weak on substantive data or basic research, I have also found it necessary to provide my readers with a good deal of original material about how things actually work out in practice.

In the course of this exercise, I have not only examined the responses of headteachers, administrators, and politicians towards school board democracy, but have also thought it right that I balance this interest in the powerful with an equal concern for the powerless. Thus, I have spent a good deal of time examining the reactions of students, parents, rank-and-file teachers, the man in the street, and the community at large to school board democracy. In the course of this exercise I have constantly attempted to address what seems to me to be the key issues in the current debate on the Taylor Report, namely, 'Who gains?' and 'Who loses out?', by this kind of participatory initiative.

A good deal of my material is concerned with an 'in-depth' study of the workings of the Sheffield school board system. This is simply because this particular authority has been in the forefront of the current move to democratize school managing and governing bodies, and I see it very much as a critical case study in the sense that its present democratized school board system clearly anticipates many of the major recommendations of the Taylor Report.

The kind of readers I have in mind include the busy professional administrator, the teacher, the concerned parent, and the diligent, but typically overburdened, student of the educational system. Because I am aware at first hand of the very limited amount of time which is typically available to all of these people, I have purposefully aimed to write about what is after all a complex subject in a simple and direct manner, which will I hope make it relatively easy for them to explore those social factors which will make our schools more democratic in character, and accountable to the wider society.

The increased teaching and administrative load in British universities in the last decade has meant that it has not always been easy to find the time needed for the kind of reflection and analysis which must necessarily underpin a book of this nature. I am, therefore, indebted to those of my colleagues who have found the time and energy to exchange ideas with me, particularly Trevor Noble. My debt to my students is a heavy one, especially the seven hundred or so members of the various school manager training and study groups I have taught over the past six years. My thanks also to Mrs. Betty Engelsöy and Mrs. Mary Wells who did the bulk of the work of typing my manuscript. Above all my acknowledgements to my wife Ann, who provided a constant source of encouragement at all stages of my work. Finally, thanks to the Editorial Board of *Sociological Review* who gave their permission for some material published in the paper "Parent Power and Professional Control", to be included in Chapter 6 of this book.

CHAPTER 1

NEW APPROACHES TO SCHOOL GOVERNMENT AND MANAGEMENT

Introduction

During the last decade the many social and cultural changes taking place in British society have led to a wide-ranging reassessment of the present nature of managerial authority within the nation's school system. Today, the twin issues of 'Who controls the schools?' and 'How shall schools be governed or managed?' have once more emerged as contentious political issues, and there seems to be a widespread agreement that all of the various institutions of what is a highly labour intensive and costly industry ought to be made more accountable to the public interest in general, and also run in a manner which is more consistent with the democratic values of the wider society. In short there seems to be a growing consensus, both within educational circles themselves and in the wider society, that 'something is missing', from the nation's present school system. Public attitudes to education are changing and teachers, administrations, and politicians all feel that there is a need to question the continued efficiency of traditional representative models of democracy, and in turn espouse the cause of participation in an attempt to seek a wider community-based support for their policies.

Largely as a result of all these developments, during the last ten years there has been a slow but steadily growing recognition that many schools have become too isolated from the communities they were built to serve. They needed to be 'shored up' by the creation of a new series of local consultative, or participatory, structures, which might not only serve to act as an 'interface', between the school and the local society, but would also help to negotiate between and ultimately conciliate many estranged local interests. This new awareness has probably been the driving force which, in the early 1970s, led many educational authorities, particularly those located in the larger urban areas to experiment with more democratized schemes of school management and government. These initiatives have typically involved the establishment of individual boards for each school with wide-ranging responsibilities in such fields as teacher appointments and promotions, premises and lettings, finance, the curriculum, internal school organization, and so on. At the same time a concerted attempt has been made to democratize these new bodies and closely involve representatives of the parents, teachers, nonteaching staff, school pupils, and people from the surrounding community in the running of their own local school affairs. The evident success of these local participatory initiatives in such places as Sheffield, Humberside, Bristol, and some London boroughs has in turn stimulated a strong national and all-party movement in favour of the further democratization and reform of school boards.

The Taylor Committee

Largely in response to this pressure for a more democratic and open system of school government and management, the late Wilson government decided to initiate a formal inquiry into the whole situation. Thus, in the House of Commons on 27 January 1975, Mr. Reginald Prentice, the then Secretary of State for Education and Science, announced the proposal to establish an inquiry into the management and government of schools in England and Wales. Later in the year it transpired that this investigation was to be conducted by a twenty-four-strong committee under the chairmanship of Mr. Tom Taylor, leader of Blackburn Council. The Taylor Committee, as it was generally referred to, contained representatives and assessors from a variety of concerned agencies and interests including the universities, colleges of education, trade unions, the churches, educational administration, teachers, parents, and the Department of Education and Science, and worked to the following terms of reference:

> To review the arrangements for the management and government of maintained primary and secondary schools in England and Wales, including the composition and functions of bodies of manager and governors, and their relationships with local education authorities, with head teachers and staffs of schools, with parents of pupils and with the local community at large; and to make recommendations.

In the course of their investigations over the next two and a half years the members of the Taylor Committee were, largely because of the wide-ranging nature of their brief, able to engage in a widespread inquiry and discussion. Their substantial report, *A New Partnership for our Schools*, appeared in the latter half of September, 1977, and contains a comprehensive examination of the relevant law and history of school government and management, and also a review of developments in recent years. It also contains a series of quite radical proposals which effectively aim to consolidate those innovations which started taking place in Sheffield, Bristol, Humberside, and so on in the early 1970s, in order to create a new, and universally applicable, kind of democratic structure which would help to make schools more responsive to and accountable to the local community they serve. In particular, Taylor recommended that every school, big or small, should have its own governing body to look after its own interests, and that this board should consist of equal numbers of local authority representatives, school staff, parents (with pupils where appropriate), and representatives of the local community.* These new governing bodies would have a wide variety of duties, including general responsibility for the schools curriculum, the appointment of its staff, financial matters, admission and expulsion, and the community use of school premises. Indeed, from one point of view, the work of the Taylor Committee, like so many other officially sponsored inquiries such as the Newsom, Plowden, and Bullock reports, has in a very real sense served to place a seal of official approval on developments which have already been taking place in an ad hoc manner at the grass roots of the educational service.

Moreover, although some of Taylor's recommendations, particularly those concerned with the governors' control of the curriculum and responsibility for drawing up the schools' financial estimates, have met

---

* For the sake of brevity I shall where possible follow the style of the Taylor Report and use the term governor to refer both to managers who generally look after primary schools and governors who generally look after secondary schools.

with some harsh criticism from representatives of teachers' organizations and educational administrators respectively, there seems every likelihood that most major items within the report will be implemented quite quickly. Thus, for example, in the debate on the Queen's speech in November, 1977, Mrs. Shirley Williams, Secretary of State for Education and Science stated, in the course of a general debate on educational matters that,

> The government, as did the Liberal Party, wanted to improve the system of school government and in particular increase the involvement of parents and teachers and to make schools more open to the community. They had recently received the report of Mr. Tom Taylor's committee on the management and government of schools.

> Some of the recommendations were controversial but on others there was sufficient basis of agreement to allow them to act.

and she went on to say,

> We believe each school should have its own governing body and that representatives of parents, teachers and the community should have a statutory right to membership of that governing body.

> This would in no way diminish the professional responsibility of the teacher or the statutory right of the local authorities but it would create the kind of forum for discussion, explanation and consultation which would enable them to open up the relationship between schools and the community.

Although, as the Taylor Report itself makes very clear, there are no significant legal obstacles to implementing all of its recommendations at once, and no reason therefore why local authorities who accept the main principles of the report should not put them into effect immediately, nonetheless, to require local authorities to establish democratic governing bodies on this basis is a different matter and needs government action. In particular, legislation would be needed to end the practice of the grouping of governing bodies, to implement equal parental, teacher, community, and local authority representation, and to give effect to the Taylor Committee's recommendations on suspension and explusion. At present the government's proposals on the Taylor Committee's recommendations are the subject of consultation with the teachers, local authority associations, and others, and time for a bill to implement the relevant legislation rests with the House of Commons. However, if, as seems likely, simply because there is a broad all-party agreement on the desirability of implementing the main tenants, if not all the controversial details of, Taylor's proposals, then the recent trend towards a more open and participatory style of educational decision making will be formalized in statute and become commonplace. In other words, by the early 1980s it seems likely that the structure of school administration and local educational politics will be radically different in character from that which existed in much of the country up until the late 1960s. Instead of a centralized and tightly politically controlled system of management, each of the nation's schools will be provided with it's own individual and representative governing body. This board will enjoy quite wide powers over the curriculum, staff appointments, the community use of buildings, admission policies, behavioural problems, and so on, and will thus, in turn, be able to exert a considerable influence upon the future development of the schools they are appointed to serve.

The need for research

However, although all of these initiatives appear to be exciting and seem to offer the promise of fundamentally altering the balance of power within the nation's schooling system, at the same time most of the successful local developments within this field have proceeded in what has often been a largely ad hoc and experimental manner. They have largely been the combined product of the work of pressure groups, teachers, parents, innovating administrations, and often a new generation of local politicians believing passionately in the merits of participatory democracy. However, they have not, as yet, been extensively reviewed, within the context of a wider historical experience; nor have they been critically examined in the light of, or related to, a substantive body of sociological theory. Perhaps even more surprisingly, in view of national moves which now seem imminent in this field, is the fact that much of our existing knowledge about these new developments stems from the advocates of change and reform themselves. Moreover, this gap was not filled by the work of the Taylor Committee, for this body neglected to commission independent and basic research into this field and rather chose to rely for the source of much of its evidence upon the views of people who were either professionally employed by, and in the main held positions of power within, the existing educational system, or alternatively were the representatives of pressure and interest groups seeking to change it. In other words, this is a subject which is redolent with pious hopes and good intentions, but is surprisingly lacking in either substantive theory or even any significant amount of empirical work about how newly democratized managing or governing bodies work in practice.

Quite obviously this situation will not last forever and what follows will be but one of many attempts to illuminate this little-researched field through attempting to answer such critical questions as, 'What is the long-term impact of the major recommendations of the Taylor Committee likely to be?'; 'What are the main advantages and disadvantages of participatory styles of school administration?'; 'What impact will democratized governing bodies have upon existing structures of power?'; and perhaps most important of all, 'Who benefits and who eventually loses out through the introduction of these new participatory systems of control?'

However, before I proceed to provide my readers with a descriptive account of how one radically democratized school board system actually works out in practice, I want to place present-day developments within a wider sociological context which will pay due attention both to contemporary events and to the largely Victorian antecedents of our present educational system. This initial review will, I hope, provide my readers with a series of guidelines allowing them to place present developments into a wider historical perspective and also serving as a convenient introduction to a detailed study of the ways in which one of the most radically democratized school board systems in the country actually works in practice. Since many features of the latter structure — the Sheffield system of managing and governing its schools — clearly anticipate some of the major features of, though obviously not all the details of, the major recommendations of the Taylor Committee, I trust that when my task has been completed my readers will be in a better position to then find their own answers to the following key questions. 'Who benefits from democratized school boards?'; 'Who loses out?'; 'What is democratic participation for, and whose interests does it serve?'

School boards in Victorian society

Like so many other major features of life in present-day British society many of the major institutions of the present-day educational system can trace their antecedents directly back to mid-Victorian society, but often no further. The major steps taken by the Victorians to reform the nation's educational system are codified in such major documents as the Clarendon Report of 1864 and the Taunton Report of 1868, and in such great statutes as the Endowed Schools Act of 1869, Forster's Act of 1870, and finally Balfour's great Act of 1902. All of these measures helped to build the foundations of a highly organized and socially segregated schooling system, which has with some slight modifications remained intact for much of the twentieth century. Thus, the public schools were reformed during the 1860s and then flourished as exclusive, residential establishments preparing the sons of Britain's unique 'agro-industrial' aristocracy for their future dominating role in society. The grammar schools, particularly after the infusion of public funds at the turn of the century, also prospered and were largely patronized by the middle classes. Their curriculum — the liberal-classical syllabus, and their institutional peculiarities of houses, prefects, uniforms, and so on — offered parents a watered-down, if inexpensive, version of the type of education the public schools were providing for their betters. Finally, the elementary schools were developed to provide a basic, but necessarily inexpensive education for the children of the working classes. Their restricted syllabus, poor facilities, harsh discipline, and rote teaching methods all tended to crush the child's spontaneity and imagination, and helped to mould the type of obedient, differential personality structure which many educational reformers thought was entirely appropriate for members of what was after all seen as the subordinate strata in Victorian society.

The Victorians also took good care to provide the newly reformed public or grammar schools and the newly created state elementary schools with efficient and effective forms of management or government. They were very concerned about, and thus gave particular attention to, such key issues as the need to define precisely the role of the headteacher, deciding who was to hold the ultimate responsibility for overall control of the school's curriculum, finances, and buildings, and finally and perhaps most important of all, what was the best way in which effective lay control of the school could be linked to the continued day-to-day efficiency of the educational process itself.

However, since as we have seen the Victorian school system was tripartite in structure, and since the answer to the question, 'What is the most effective form of controlling a school?', might thus be given differently in respect to grammar schools, public schools, or elementary schools, then it is hardly surprising to find that the Victorians did not create a uniform national system of school management or government. Rather there were considerable variations in the powers, duties, and responsibilities of school boards in different parts of the school system and in different parts of the country. Nonetheless, if a generalization is to be attempted, then we may distinguish, with many exceptions, between the governing body system adopted by the public schools, and later, like so much else of its institutional fabric, copied by the grammar schools and the very different school management system developed in the remaining elementary sector of either voluntary or state-provided education.

School governors and public schools

Many of the hundred or so public schools established in the country by the turn of the century originated as local grammar schools and their founders intended them to provide a subsidized education for the sons of local farmers and tradesmen, and a free education for poor, if promising, scholars. However, by the middle of the nineteenth century many of these schools had fallen into decay, while others were being transformed into quite different national and residential institutions. This latter process of regeneration was greatly facilitated by the Endowed Schools Act of 1869. This legislation not only allowed the newly emerging public schools to use their ancient endowments for new purposes, but also enabled them to change the narrowly local composition of their governing bodies, and recruit new members of high esteem and great influence. Thus, in the latter half of the nineteenth century, we find that the newly emerging public school no longer needs to recruit its school governors from the ranks of the local farmers or tradesmen; rather it can attract new members from the ranks of the nation's aristocracy including high church dignitaries, Members of Parliament, representatives from Oxford and Cambridge, senior army officers, and even princes, earls, and dukes.[1]

This new generation of cosmopolitan governors naturally tended to support the policies of such entrepreneurial headmasters as Harper of Sherborne, or Thring of Uppingham, who were not only building up their school's national reputations, but were also developing a new and exclusive type of residential education. These new governors were not only able to act as national advocates of their schools, but could also protect them from any local interference or the restrictive control of the rapidly growing state educational bureaucracy. Perhaps one of the best examples of this protective function occurred in the late 1860s when W. E. Forster attempted to include within the Endowed Schools' bill proposals to facilitate much greater state control over public schools.

Naturally many headmasters violently opposed this policy and elicited the support of their governors in their fight to amend the bill. One headmaster, E. W. Benson of Wellington School, played a particularly notable role in organizing this resistance, and his governing body, which included a number of particularly influential princes, earls, and dukes, exerted such an authoritative influence in the corridors of power that Forster's initial bill was withdrawn and replaced with a less offensive draft.[2]

Although governors sometimes worked hard to protect their schools from local interference or state control, it would be unwise to imagine that this insulating role was their prime or sole function. Most Victorian governors also took an active interest in the internal affairs of their schools, and often made a substantial contribution to the development of their own particular ethos. They were also usually powerful enough to prevent their schools falling totally into the hands of either an idiosyncratic or incompetent headteacher. Although this danger was unlikely to occur, since both the headmaster and his staff were recruited from the same social strata as the governors and generally shared a set of basic assumptions about their social world, nonetheless the Victorians usually thought it necessary to be quite explicit about the relative powers and functions of governors and teachers.

In most cases, the constitution of the newly developing public school boards followed the suggestions made by the commissioners examining the revenue and management of the nine original public schools, who included their recommendations in the Clarendon Report of 1864.[3] Their document made a clear distinction between the authority of the governors acting in a general lay, or public, interest and the authority of the headteacher acting within the terms of a narrow but well-defined academic tradition.[4] The commissioners acknowledged that the responsibilities of the governors were very large and suggested that they

> . . . should include, at the least, the management of the property of the school, and of its revenue, from whatever source derived; the control of its expenditure; the appointment and dismissal of the Headmaster, the regulation of the boarding houses, of fees and charges, of Masters' stipends, of the terms of admission to the school, and of the times and length of the vacations; the supervision of the general treatment of the boys, and all arrangements bearing on the sanitary condition of the school.

The commissioners went on to suggest that the powers of governing boards should not only be limited to such administrative questions as finance, admission procedures, or the management of school property, but should also include an overall authority to decide the vital issue of what was to be taught within the school. Their explicit recognition of the central role of governing bodies in this critical policy-making field, and their concern to distinguish this form of authority from the proper professional and technical concerns of the headteacher, was made very clear in the following passage of their report.

> The introduction of a new branch of study or the suppression of one already established, and the relative degrees of weight to be assigned to different branches, are matters respecting which a better judgement is likely to be formed by . . . men conversant with the requirements of public and professional life and acquainted with the general progress of science and literature, than by a single person, however able and accomplished, whose views may be more circumscribed and whose mind is liable to be unduly pressed by difficulties of detail. What should be taught, and what importance should be given to each subject, are therefore questions for the Governing Body; how to teach is a question of the Headmaster.

However, although the commissioners were anxious to stress the ultimate supremacy of the principle of lay control, their recommendations also gave headmasters virtually unlimited powers over the daily lives of their teachers and pupils, and as we can see from the following statement were instrumental in legitimizing a particularly authoritarian view of the headteacher's role, which was in turn to be widely disseminated throughout all sectors of the English school system.

> Details, therefore, such as the division of classes, the school hours and school books, the holidays and half-holidays during the school time, belong properly to him, the headmaster, rather than to the Governing Body; and the appointment and dismissal of Assistant Masters, the measures necessary for maintaining discipline, and the general direction of the course and methods of study, which it is his duty to conduct and his business to understand thoroughly, had better be left in his hands.

School managers and the voluntary school movement

In contrast with the public schools, the task of providing some form of educational provisions for the mass of the people was left to local initiatives. In the rural counties and expanding manufacturing towns, groups of clergymen, landowners, manufacturers, and other community notables, acting under the general guidance of two great national voluntary educational societies, the National Society and the British and Foreign School Society, gradually built up the rudiments of a national elementary school structure. These developments did not always meet with universal approval: many of the more conservative elements in society remained suspicious of mass education, and saw it as a subversive activity which not only taught people to become dissatisfied with their lot but which might in the long run lead to the dissolution of the existing social order. However, the advocates of public education for the masses generally took a different view of their work. The more evangelical amongst them argued passionately that a basic instruction in religious and rudimentary skills would not only make the industrial labour force more efficient but would also enable it to withstand sin and sedition. The more sophisticated reformers also recognized that mass education might have more subtle long-term effects upon England's social structure. This was because the very routine and discipline of the educational process would inevitably come to play a significant part in moulding the character of future generations of industrial workers. At an early and impressionable age they would learn to implicitly accept the rightness and goodness of a routine, time-tabled and work-centred way of life. In other words they suggested that a universal elementary educational system was likely to provide society with a new kind of maleable labour force, which would more readily accept its subordinate lot in life.

This inherently political function of mass educational provision was, of course, not only appreciated by the more subtle members of the reform movement; it was also as we can see from the following extracts well recognized by many radical critics of this development. As one of them pointed out early in the century,

> When government interferes, it directs its efforts more to make people obedient and docile, than wise and happy. It desires to control the thoughts, and fashion even the minds of its subject; and to give into its hands the power of educating the people, is the widest possible extension of that most pernicious practise which has so long desolated society, of allowing one or a few men to direct the actions and control the conduct of millions. *Men had better be without education*, than be educated by their rulers; for their education is but the mere breaking in of the steer to the yoke; the mere discipline of the hunting dog, which, by dint of severity, is made to forego the strongest impulse of his nature, and instead of devouring his prey, to hasten with it to the feet of his master.[5]

Similarly another critique of these developments commented,

> Some simpletons talk of knowledge making the working classes more
> obedient, more dutiful — better servants, better subjects and so on, which
> means making them more subservient slaves and more conducive to the
> wealth and gratification of idlers of all descriptions. But such knowledge
> is trash; the only knowledge which is of service to the working people is
> that which makes them more dissatisfied, and makes them worse slaves.
> This is the knowledge which we shall give them.[6]

The first school managers

In spite of the suspicion of radical movements and the sometimes
violent opposition of conservative interests, the movement to provide
some form of rudimentary elementary education for the working classes
developed strongly, and in 1833 the first state grant ever was made by
Parliament to support this work. This intervention by central government into what had previously been a predominantly local and
voluntary movement also stimulated the growth of a recognizable
system of school management. A number of things contributed to this
development. Firstly, as we have already seen, education for the masses
was a contentious issue, and many people were unhappy with the idea.
Consequently, in view of their concern, it was thought desirable to
place the control of each school in the hands of an appropriate lay body
representing the dominant sentiments of the community. In the second
place, the personal views of the Secretary of Education, Kay
Shuttleworth, also encouraged the development of school managing
bodies. He was anxious to engineer a wider lay involvement in the work
of schools, and remove the effective day-to-day control of their affairs
from the hands of ministers of religion. Finally, and perhaps in the long
run most influential of all, a number of administrative exigencies
stimulated the growth of a fairly uniform national school board system.
The officials, who had the job of dispensing grants to schools, found it
difficult to negotiate with large numbers of individuals and local
voluntary bodies. They pressed for the introduction of a more uniform
system of local school administration with properly elected managing
committees and a more precise delineation of the duties of the
managers. As a result of all these pressures we find that from 1840
onwards the committee of the Council on Education was drawing up
specimen trust deeds and suggesting their adoption in schools applying
for state grants. By 1847 this principal of uniformity was so far advanced
that the state was able to make it a condition for the acceptance of grant

aid that schools should have properly consituted boards of managers. However, although in principle lay control was widely accepted by the mid-nineteenth century, and all schools receiving state grants possessed, in theory at least, properly constituted boards of managers, in practice for much of this period effective day-to-day control, particularly of Church of England schools, remained with the local clergy. This was mainly because these people had the time, ability and spiritual motivation to take up the often onerous and routine administrative matters which are inevitably involved in the management of schools. This situation was well illustrated by a report from the Reverend J. P. Norris who inspected church schools in the counties of Cheshire, Shropshire, and Staffordshire in 1858. Norris wrote that, in each area he visited, 'those who are willing to make themselves responsible for the pecuniary maintenance of schools become its de facto managers'; and he went on to give the following interesting analysis of the extent to which the clergy remained dominant in the management of the schools he visited.[7]

37% of schools managed entirely by the clergy, the management committee being inactive or not in existence.

43% of schools managed by the clergy in concert with a management committee.

9% managed by the clergy and the local squire.

5% managed entirely by the local squire or his family.

3% managed by a local industrialist.

3% managed by a lay committee.

The powers of voluntary school boards, whether exercised entirely by a local clergyman or an active group of laymen, were considerable and in many ways were more extensive than those enjoyed by the governors of the great public schools. This was mainly because the voluntary schoolteacher was perceived in very different social terms from those applied to a public schoolmaster. He was not seen as a well-qualified professional academic, working within the limits of his particular specialism, but as an employee possessing a certain limited competence and craft-type skills, and as such he was thought to require, like all other working men, close supervision or management. As a result of this view of the elementary teaching process, we find that voluntary school managers performed an essentially different social function from their public school counterparts. They were not only concerned with such general policy directed issues as financial accountability, oversight of the curriculum, maintenance of the school fabric, and the appointment of headmasters, but also with a host of more localized and detailed issues. They often took a close interest in the spiritual well-being, social welfare, and discipline of their school's children. They were often personally involved in the teaching process, particularly of religious affairs, and they sometimes exercised a close supervision over both the quality and the content of their teachers' work and social conduct.

School managers and the state elementary schools

However, although the number of school places rose rapidly in the first half of the nineteenth century and by 1850 nearly two million children were receiving some form of elementary education, the voluntary societies were still unable to provide enough school places for all children. In view of this short fall the state was reluctantly forced to intervene, and in 1870 Forster's Education Act made provision for a universal, though not as yet compulsory, elementary school system. One of the most important items in Forster's Act was the creation of an entirely new unit of educational administration, the school board system; and these new bodies were given the task of filling in the gaps left by the great national school societies. These boards were quite small, but probably for that reason effective bodies, and consisted of not less than five and not more than fifteen members. They were elected by the ratepayers of the parish or borough concerned, served for a three-year period, and were given considerable financial powers to raise their own funds from the local community. Apart from their mandatory fiscal powers, most of the remaining powers of these new boards were broadly similar to those already enjoyed by governors or managers in the private, or voluntary, sectors of the educational system. They had a general duty to maintain the fabric of their schools, appoint and dismiss teachers, take general responsibility for the curriculum, and take a close interest in the daily lives of their schools. Although the new board system had a number of similarities both with existing school management systems, it also owed much to the American experience where locally elected school boards had been long in existence. The American boards had tended not only to make their schools very responsible to local community interests but, since they were tax-levying bodies, had generated a local awareness of educational issues amongst people who did not customarily concern themselves with this matter.

However, although Forster's legislation introduced the idea of local democratic control of education into England and Wales, it unfortunately did not provide the means to establish either a relatively uniform or coherent board system throughout the country. In part this was because the administrative units on which the boards were based were not standardized. Under the provisions of the act, in rural areas the parish was chosen as the appropriate area for a board to work, but in urban areas the much larger borough was chosen for the same purpose, and London was treated as an entirely separate entity. This decision not only inevitably meant that too many boards were created (and by 1902 there were some 2544 of them) but also that they differed widely in size and responsibility. At one extreme one could find the small board of Mallerstang in Westmorland, where five elected members and a paid clerk looked after the needs of seventeen children; at the other extreme one might take the case of the fifteen-strong Sheffield board, which had broadly similar powers, but looked after the educational needs of a city of some 400,000 people.[8]

Moreover, the ways in which school boards developed was also far from uniform, and further added to the heterogeneity of this late Victorian system.

This was mainly because boards could either choose to retain or to delegate some or many of their powers to local school managers. In some places, and particularly in the larger English commercial cities, the ideal of local communal management and involvement in schools was so strong that a quite remarkable devolution of power took place. Consequently, it is possible to distinguish, particularly in the larger urban boards, two radically different systems of educational administration developing coterminously in the 1870s and 1880s.

In the first of these we can include boards such as Hull, Salford, Leeds, Bradford, and Sheffield, who decided early on in their life as a general matter of policy not to delegate their powers to local school managers. These 'centralist authorities' developed strong unitary systems of administration, and all customary managerial functions were looked after in theory by the full board. However, since a single body couldn't possibly look after the details of inspection, appointments, fabric maintenance, curriculum development, and so on involved in the management of literally hundreds of schools, we find in practice that, within these unitary systems, the clerk to the board and a team of officials gradually take over many of the day-to-day functions customarily exercised by a school's managers — the appointment of

teachers, letting and maintenance of the school building, and supervision of the curriculum. In short, by the end of the Victorian period in
many urban areas, lay control was rapidly giving way to professional
supervision, and in many large cities the most expensive and important
institution in the local community was no longer closely controlled by
the locality, but by a relatively distant and impersonal bureaucratic
machine.

However, the move towards centralized administrative systems was not
a unilateral development, and a number of boards, the most notable
being Liverpool, Bristol and London, decided, again at an early stage in
their development, to delegate many of their powers to local managers
looking after the interests of particular schools. This development had
a number of advantages; it made it easier for schools to build up their
own specific ethos, and discouraged the growth of a supervisory
bureaucracy. It also enabled communities to participate in the running
of their own schools, and encouraged people, who would otherwise not
have become involved, to take up voluntary work on behalf of the educational advancement of local children. However, although such
devolved administrative systems as that developed by the Liverpool
school board were warmly praised by the Cross Commission in its
report on the working of the 1870 Act, these early attempts to create a
local participatory educational system also had a number of
weaknesses. This was because they increased the chances of a potentially
damaging conflict breaking out between a central board and a local
group of managers, and also because they depended for their success
upon the help of large numbers of people willing to devote themselves
to the routine of school administration. Although there was generally
no lack of willing volunteers for this work in such large commercial
towns as Bristol, Liverpool, and London, which all possessed a large,
leisured 'rentier class', this was not always the case elsewhere. There was
less likelihood of finding sufficient volunteers in such predominantly
proletarian cities as Leeds, Sheffield, or Bradford, where most people
were industrial workers and could not simply afford to take time off
work to look after the daily life of their local school. Consequently, it is
precisely in these northern cities that one first notices that the functions
of school managers are gradually being subsumed by a full-time corps
of officials who not only take over responsibility for curriculum
development, teacher appointment, and the school fabric, but are also
the inadvertent instruments of an inexorable alienative process in
which decisions about, 'how and when to educate children' are no

longer taken locally, and by a representative committee composed of parents, or people in the local community, but by a distant group of professional administrators.

Urban and Rural Boards

The great differences which existed between centralized and devolved, and parish and borough board systems, were further accentuated by particular local reactions to the 1870 Act. In general it seems that boards in rural counties were less enthusiastic about education than their counterparts in the towns and cities. This was partly because church schools were already strongly established in many villages and there was less work for them to do. It was also due to the dominance of the squirearchy and clergy in local politics. They were often suspicious of giving village people too much education, since they feared, as we have seen earlier, that it would not only create unrealizable expectations, but might also create too many village agitations.

The Reverend J. Fitzgram made this point quite explicitly in his work, *Hints for the Improvement of Village Schools*, published in 1859; he wrote that:

> I am no advocate of any 'high pressure' system of education. It seems to me to be of the utmost importance to keep each class of society in its proper place; and with this view, to give to each child such a measure of instruction as its station in life is likely to require, and no more. For is it not right that the farmer should be better educated than the labourer, and the gentleman better than the farmer? Are we not in danger of doing much mischief, if we educate highly the class of labourers, while we neglect the classes immediately above them?[9]

Largely as a result of the economic and political power of landlords, farmers, and the established church, in most villages education was merely defined as a contentious issue, and there was a general pragmatic acceptance that the local board school should not only be cheap and confine itself to elementary instruction, but at certain key periods it should give way to the imperatives of the local economy and let its children go harvesting or potato picking. The following account by the Reverend G. H. Aitkin, of his experience on the Mary Bourne school board in Hampshire was probably not untypical of the generally in-different attitudes many rural boards took towards their school.

> The Board was composed, before I joined it, entirely of farmers and small shopkeepers. Their ideas was to spend not a penny that could be avoided.

Before I left I persuaded them to pass a resolution in favour of lighting the school with oil lamps and also in favour of getting an additional teacher who was sorely needed. Both these resolutions were rescinded at the first meeting after I left the parish and for all I know the school works on still in darkness through the winter afternoons.[10]

However, if publicly provided education was not a matter which stimulated great excitement in the countryside, the same was not true of urban England, and in many towns and cities the triennial school board elections were often bitterly fought. The roots of this conflict lay in a quite fundamental disagreement about the basic structure and long-term aims of public educational provisions. In the first years of their existence this conflict centred on purely religious issues, and the basic split occurred between dissenters, who approved of the board schools, and the Anglicans and Roman Catholics, who did not. The roots of their disagreement centred on the allocation of responsibility for school building costs. Until 1870 all of the voluntary schools had been developed and paid for by the major religious bodies. However, the churches were finding it increasingly difficult to fund the development of new schools from their own resources, and argued that public moneys should be used to subsidize their development programme. They naturally opposed secular schools and attempted to secure places on local boards. Unfortunately, once they were established in these bodies, they usually adopted attitudes which were virtually indistinguishable from obstruction, and consequently generated considerable animosity amongst their generally nonconformist board members. However, it was not only religious matters which galvanized school board politics, and as we shall see later in this chapter new secular issues emerged to divide them towards the close of the century, as people with quite new ideas about the purpose and aims of public education were elected to the places on the board.

Although school boards developed in a chaotic manner, which was not always viewed sympathetically by state officials who tended to favour a more orderly and regulated system for the public, if not for the private, sector of education, they were at their best healthy and lively democratic institutions. They were not only capable of working hard and building up their own schools systems, but they also generated a tremendous local interest in educational affairs. They made their communities feel that education was not a distant process, but was something in which lay people could either be involved indirectly as local managers, or indirectly as electors deciding general policy-related issues. Many of the more progressive boards also made a systematic attempt to train their managers so that they would be able to play a more effective role in the local educational process. Consequently, one finds that, as early as 1880, the Liverpool board published a handbook, *Suggestions to the Managers of Public Elementary Schools* and the London board followed closely behind publishing its own *School Managers Manual* in 1885. These tracts not only encouraged managers to visit their schools regularly and familiarize themselves with their work, but also contained many useful and practical hints about what to look out for in a classroom situation. For example, managers were asked to notice if their teachers wandered about the classroom while they were talking and thus distracted the children, and they were warned about teachers who were content to allow a few bright, responsive children to answer all their questions. However, managers were not only asked to adopt a quasi-inspectorial role. The London board manual, for example, also expected them to be active in integrating their schools into the surrounding community, and suggested they promote community entertainments in their schools as a means of encouraging better informal personal relationships between parents, teachers, and children.

Although the urban boards were generally imaginative, and at their best were providing a democratically organized system of education responsive to local needs and aspirations, this development also gradually estranged many of the dominant forces in English society and led to a reaction which not only led to the abolition of the school board system, but also to the gradual downgrading of the role of the school managers and the increasing dominance of the local authority and state official in the public, if not the private, sectors of education. However, in order to understand why this reaction against local community control of education took place, it is now necessary to look at some of the developments taking place in the last years of the nineteenth century.

The school board system at the turn of the century

In the just over thirty years of their existence the school boards encountered, and in the main successfully overcame, a great number of problems. Indeed, in many areas their achievements were surprising for they not only suffered from a chronic shortage of money, which inevitably meant their schools suffered from overcrowding, poor pupil-staff ratios, and a limited range of equipment, but their freedom of manoeuvre was often quite seriously limited by central government. This was mainly because the Education Department insisted on the imposition of the Revised Code and an associated system of 'payment by results'. These regulations were first introduced into voluntary schools in 1862 and were to last with some modifications until the 1890s. They were extremely unpopular and not only encouraged teachers to concentrate on routine methods of learning, but also tended to stifle the child's natural imagination and initiative and facilitate the growth of a passive, dependent type of personality structure.[11]

However, in spite of these weaknesses, the democratic and highly localized educational system created by Forsters's Act also gave people the opportunity to become involved in the administration of their local schools and facilitated the development of a grassroots movement which successfully modified the structure of public elementary education in many parts of England. By the 1880s many people — parents, liberals, radicals, socialists, and trade unionists — were not only becoming increasingly critical of the overcrowding, rote learning, and inflexibility of their local board schools, but also of their limited curriculum and relatively early leaving age. As a result of this concern, during the 1880s and 1890s large numbers of people stood for election, and gained places on school boards, because they wanted to change their school's curriculum and expand the educational opportunities available for local children.[12]

This reform movement was particularly strong in urban areas and led to many changes in the local elementary school system. As a result, some boards actively encouraged their schools to develop a wider curriculum and were particularly influential in introducing the study of technical and scientific subjects. A number of boards also attempted to provide more facilities for able children, and in such cities as Sheffield, Manchester, and Leeds these pupils were no longer forced to leave school at thirteen, but were encouraged to carry on their studies in newly established central or higher board schools until it was time for them to enter the ancient professions or universities. In short, then, by the turn of the century the more progressive boards were not only providing their children with a more scientific and technically orientated curriculum, but were also gradually building up a ladder of educational opportunity for the able but poor scholar. The following remarks by a member of the Sheffield board not only made this meritocratic policy quite explicit, but is also a good example of the way in which this issue was perceived by one radical board member as early as 1879.

> If a gap were allowed to remain between the primary elementary schools and Firth College, then the education of the children of the working classes must stop where the primary elementary schools leave it, however great the ability and industry of the pupils may be. If, on the other hand, the Board supplies to them what I have called secondary elementary education, a straight course to the very highest educational advantages which the country can offer — I mean, of course, to the Universities — will be open, not only to the children of the wealthier classes, but also to those children of other classes who show extraordinary ability.

> He added that without the scheme which the board had already in hand (the central school) 'a rung will be wanting in our educational ladder'.[13]

However, although these developments were popular in most of the larger urban boroughs, they were viewed with reservations elsewhere. In part this was because some boards placed great emphasis upon the development of a technical-scientific curriculum, and this was seen as potentially threatening to the hegemony of the literary-classical culture dominating the curriculum of both grammar and public schools. In part these reservations were also stimulated by the new types of further educational provision which were being developed in new higher grade or central schools. These institutions were placed in an 'end on' relationship with the existing elementary schools, and were not, as later occurred, part of an entirely separate and segregated secondary school system. As a result, in some parts of the country an able child was able to proceed in an uninterruped sequence, from the lowest to the highest part of the elementary school system. In other words, an uninterrrupted and meritorcratic ladder of advancement was created, and the able child could stay within the culture of one school system until it was time for him to leave and go on to the university or professions. He was not, as later, forced to leave his peers at eleven or twelve years of age and enter the strange, radically different ethos of the selective and largely middle-class grammar school. Finally, these reservations were reinforced by what many people assumed to be the typical elementary teacher insularity, and lack of a finer appreciation of the dominant liberal-classical culture. This was partly because most board teachers were recruited from amongst the most able elementary school children and given a form of 'on the job' craft training during their period of apprenticeship as a pupil-teacher. They were not, as later occurred, recruited from amongst selective, or grammar school, pupils and trained in the confining environment of a residential college. Although the pupil-teacher system had many disadvantages, it did mean that most school board teachers had experienced the same kind of social and learning environment as their pupils, and were not, as was to occur in the twentieth century, to become both socially and culturally distanced from their charges.

It was hardly surprising in view of all these developments that the school boards were seen by many people to be centres of anarchy or radicalism. This was not only because they were adopting policies which offered a comprehensive alternative to the rigid tripartite system the Victorian ruling classes had planned for the three great social orders, but was also because, at their best, they were producing a new kind of imaginative, technically able pupil, whose very way of thinking represented a potential challenge to the stability of the existing social order. In short, by the end of the century, some of the most progressive boards were adopting policies which simply confirmed some of the worst suspicions of people who had never been in favour of any but the cheapest and meanest form of public education for the mass of the people.

Although this general criticism of the boards was quite widespread, it was most frequently resonated amongst the leaders of the Conservative Party, the Anglican Church, rural society generally, and those permanent officials responsible for guiding the educational policy of the state. This heterogeneous group quite obviously differed on many detailed issues, but was generally agreed that it was desirable to abolish school managers and the school board system, greatly strengthen the grammar schools and maintain them as the sole providers of secondary education, and, above all else, place all elementary education under an effective system of central governmental supervision.

Balfour's Education Act

The campaign to remodel the educational system, and in so doing effectively make it more uniform and less responsive to local community needs and interests, followed many complicated and bitterly fought stages, and it is clearly impossible to itemize all of these in this short review of nineteenth-century developments. Consequently, what I want to do in the concluding part of this chapter is simply to delineate some of the major features of a campaign which not only reduced the amount of democratic control people were able to exercise over the education of their children and the use of their local schools, but which, perhaps axiomatically, led to the increasing bureaucratization of the educational service and the inexorable growth in power both of the teaching profession and of the educational official.

The first steps in this campaign were largely taken on the initiative of Sir John Gorst, the Conservative Party's spokesman for education in the House of Commons, and took the form of an extensive examination of the existing regulations governing the powers and the duties of school boards. This review led not only to a series of administrative measures, such as those designed to deny board schools the science and art department grants allowing them to develop advanced courses. It also encouraged legal action, and in June, 1899, a case was brought by a school of art in London which complained of competition from evening classes run by the school board. The resulting Cockerton judgement, which was seen by many to be the educational equivalent of the first Taff Vale judgement, disallowed expenditure from the rates on the running of science and art classes, and effectively brought into question all of the advanced, higher, or secondary education going on in the school boards.

The next stages of the struggle were more overtly political and involved the formation of alliances, the development of specific politics, and the mounting of a concerted and skilled political campaign which culminated in Balfour's Education Act of 1902. This new legislation was bitterly opposed by nonconformist, liberal, radical, and trade union organizations. This was partly because it placed church schools on the rates and removed the burden of supporting them from the local squire or parson, partly because it effectively limited local control over education, and severely curtailed some of the most pioneering curriculum developments taking place in the higher elementary schools, and partly because it reinforced the divisions within a tripartite system of education, which seemed to many people to be designed to maintain the strength of the existing social order.

However, although this opposition was both vocal and powerful, it was not sufficiently influential to prevent the successful passage of Balfour's Act in 1902. This legislation quite simply abolished the school boards and transferred their responsibilities to the recently established local county or borough councils. These new bodies were not only generally larger than the old school boards, but were also expected to be, and generally proved to be, less enthusiastic advocates of the popular educational cause. This was partly because local councillors were not elected on specifically educational issues, but on a wide and quite often diffuse party programme which might include plans for the development of such local services as the highways or sewage systems. Consequently, it was more difficult to crystallize a specific educational issue in a local council election than had been the case under the board system. At the same time, many of the day-to-day administrative responsibilities previously exercised by the directly elected school boards were now taken over by a subcommittee of the full borough or county council. This committee not only contained many coopted members who were not directly responsible through the ballot box to the local electorate, but it was also not a final decision-making body, since all its proposals had to be ratified by the larger council, which might include many people who were more interested in saving their ratepayers' money than advancing the people's education. Finally, many of the new councils were generally less radical than the school boards. This was partly because their franchise was restricted and, for example women, who had often been extremely active in school board politics, could neither stand for office nor vote in local council elections. It was also due to the great influence of the conservative rural interest in many counties, and as a result, in many parts of England, Balfour's Act meant that local education was once more firmly under the control of the parson and squire.

The local county, county borough, or borough councils who were given the task of administering Balfour's Act were not allowed, even if they had wished to do so, to develop in the flexible and experimental manner so characteristic of the work of the larger urban, if not the smaller rural, school boards. They were tightly bound both by the general provisions of the act and the wealth of administrative regulations that consolidated its main characteristics in the first years of the twentieth century. Moreover, the new system also tended to be less responsive to local community interests and requirements, and gave people less opportunity to become involved in the day-to-day management of their local schools. This was mainly because Balfour's Act only prescribed managing or governing bodies for secondary and voluntary schools, and in the case of the public elementary schools the newly established educational authorities could decide for themselves whether or not they wished to establish, retain, or dispense with individual school boards. Some authorities simply decided on the latter course, others gave their managers the most trivial of powers. However, in London, where managers had always been strongly established, they were given quite wide powers of local control and not only empowered to inspect the school premises and equipment, but also to draw up an annual report, check the school records, investigate complaints against teachers and advise on staff appointments.

In contrast, in the case of church schools, managing bodies remained mandatory, since it was recognized that they formed an effective means of ensuring that these institutions continued to follow the sectarian aims of their founders. Following the provisions of the 1902 Act, these bodies were required to include one-third representation from the local authority, while the remainder, who invariably included the local vicar, were representative of the religious interest. Church school managers were given complete control over all religious instruction in their schools and also had great influence over the appointment and dismissal of teaching staff. However, as was generally the case with the remainder of the nonsectarian elementary schools, the local education authority was given wide powers of control over their financial affairs, teacher supply, salaries, curriculum, and other details of school administration. These functions were usually exercised by a growing body of full-time education officers, who, as we have seen, had already gained an influential position in such urban school board systems as Leeds and Sheffield, which had chosen to develop a strictly centralized form of educational management and had not, as was the case with Liverpool and Bristol, devolved some of their powers to individual managing bodies. Consequently one finds, as the new local educational authorities establish themselves and strive to provide a better, more efficient, and centralized service, that they gradually come to employ more and more officials, and the opportunity for local people to participate in or control the day-to-day management of their own schools in particular, or to gradually become involved in educational affairs in general, slowly diminishes as the twentieth century progresses.

Grammar school boards

One of the great paradoxes of the years following Balfour's Act, and a clear indication of the dual standards applied to different parts of the nation's tripartite educational system, was seen in the very different attitude Sir Robert Morant, the first secretary of the Board of Education, took towards the governors of grammar schools and the managers of elementary schools.

Traditionally the grammar schools had been autonomous bodies responsible for their own administrative, financial, and educational affairs, and they had usually possessed strong governing bodies composed of influential members of local society. However, under the 1902 Education Act, the new county councils or county borough councils were given responsibility for the general administration of secondary education and, as a result, the question then arose of, 'How far was it desirable for the grammar schools to be controlled by these new education authorities?'

As we have already seen, in the case of the public elementary school this question was not considered to be a relevant one to ask. It was assumed that they would remain under a tight local and central administrative control. However, Sir Robert Morant was worried about this happening to the grammar schools. This was partly because he wanted these schools to retain their freedom from zealous local authority officials, who naturally wanted to incorporate them into a tidy local administrative structure with clearly defined lines of authority and responsibility. It was also because Morant wanted to insulate these schools from the influence of local politicians who, particularly in urban areas, were critical of the practical utility of the traditional liberal-classical grammar school curriculum. These fears were not of course peculiar to Morant, but were generally resonant of a point of view which saw the public schools as one of England's most cherished possessions, and which also wanted their ethos to permeate all forms of secondary education. The permanent officials of the Board of Education, who were in the main educated at public schools and the ancient universities, were naturally suspicious of the practical, nonsectarian culture found in so many provincial communities. They despised its concern with the concrete and its bias towards an instrumental and utilitarian type of education. They want to protect the grammar schools from the provincial cultural influences and provide them with strong governing bodies, so that they could continue to play their traditional role and transmit the ideals and aspirations associated with the liberal-classical culture to future generations of the middle classes.

These tactics were not of course new ones. In the previous century the establishment of strong and independent governing bodies for the public schools has allowed these institutions to slough off local control, adopt independent policies, and establish national reputations. Clearly the Board of Education intended governing bodies to perform much the same function in the case of the newly expanding secondary schools. This policy was stated very clearly by Robert Morant in the following extract from the Secondary School Regulations of 1904:

> . . . . the Board attach importance to direct communications with the Governing Body, and to preserving for the Governing Body as much responsibility, independence and freedom of action as is consistent with effective control of educational policy and educational provision, by the Local Authority in its own area, and by the Central Authority in all areas.[14]

And in the Regulations for the next year, Morant went further and took the view that:

> . . . . shall have such powers and be so constituted as to ensure living interest in the School on the part of the Governors, a real supervision by them of the conduct and progress of the School, and ready access to them by the Headmaster.[15]

In spite of these instructions many education authorities were reluctant to sanction the development of strong secondary school boards. Consequently, the Board of Education reluctantly decided to make its views quite explicit, and in the Secondary School Regulations for 1909 it required that all secondary schools must have properly constituted governing bodies if they were to continue to receive public grants for their maintenance.

This policy was strongly opposed by many local authorities, who simply refused to set up independent governing boards for each of their grammar schools. This was partly because some local councillors had little sympathy with what they saw as the individual idiosyncrasies, or personal ambitions, of grammar school headmasters, and partly because many local authority officers were struggling to build up an efficient local system of administration and did not want their plans obstructed by the creation of powerful new intermediary bodies between them and what they increasingly saw as their authorities' schools.

Although this opposition was widespread in the larger urban authorities, Graham, the director of education for Leeds, took the initiative in opposing Morant's policies. He took the view that Parliament had not intended this form of check to be established on the local educational authorities' powers, and argued that the Board of

Education was in effect not only dictating their committee structure, but was also seeking to make grammar school headmasters virtually independent of local authority control.

The departure of Morant from the Board of Education, the increasing power and confidence of the newly developing local authority officers, and the decision to appoint directors of education as de facto clerk to grammar school governing bodies, all tended to discourage the independence of grammar school governing boards, and as a result these institutions did not in the main develop the independence enjoyed by their public school counterparts, but were more tightly controlled by the local authority. Consequently, whether or not a secondary school possessed a strong governing body came to depend in part upon past history, in part upon local educational policy, and sometimes upon sheer accident. In the main, in the country areas, which tended to be served by the older endowed foundation schools, governing bodies were better established and more active than in the larger cities, where they were often totally incorporated into the committee structure of the local authority.

In short, in the case of the grammar schools as in the case of the remainder of the educational system, the growth of a new and centralized local authority school service slowly tended to subsume many of the important functions which once gave local people the opportunity to participate in the management of their own local schools. The local educational service gradually took over all of the tasks which had once been performed by lay managers, and at the same time built up large specialized teams of professional workers who were given special responsibilities for inspecting schools, advising teachers, maintaining the good order of the school fabric, appointing staff, and initiating new developments. In general, the administrators who controlled these new, developing school systems remained unsympathetic to school managers or governors. This was because they worried that influential and independent school heads might not only challenge their own position, but might also hinder their attempts to create a uniform, efficiently administered, local educational service, and might ultimately undermine the effective operation of the democratic processes themselves.

Teachers and school boards

These centralizing trends were often tacitly, if not always explicitly, supported by the majority of teachers working within the state system.

Most of them tended to support the viewpoint that lay people, including parents as well as locally recruited governors or managers, ought to be tactfully discouraged from taking too close an interest in the day-to-day work of the school. This assumption in part reflected the growth of a new kind of professionalism amongst teachers. This view tended at first hesitatingly and then in an increasingly strident manner to make the claims that the whole of the educative process, including of course the day-to-day management of schools, was the legitimate and particular occupational concern of teachers, and no one else.

However, the teachers concern to insulate their schools as effectively as possible from local control, or lay influence, was also in part stimulated by the narrow and peculiar nature of their own educative experiences. Most people working in Britain's schools have followed what may be called a conventional 'teacher career trajectory', in the sense that they have spent some fourteen years at school, two or three years at a teacher training college, and they have finally returned to the classroom, there to reside for the remaining forty years of their working lives. Furthermore, the phasing out of the pupil-teacher system at the turn of the century, and the adoption of a deliberate policy of selecting prospective teachers from amongst able grammar school pupils, meant that the social experiences of teachers, both within the educational system itself, and also in relationship to their local community, were a peculiar kind.

During their formative years at school, they not only received a selective type of schooling, which effectively isolated them from the social and cultural experiences of the bulk of young people of their generation, but also received an education which attempted to replicate the public school and emphasize the value of a distant metropolitan 'liberal high culture'. Moreover, for many teachers, their professional training often merely served to reinforce this disdain of the local and the commonplace. They typically spent some of the most formative years of their young adult lives in residential, semimonastic, total institutions, which were not only effectively cut off from the world of industry and commerce, but which actively encouraged students to adopt a view of the remainder of their society which was elitest in perspective, as well as evangelical in content. Consequently, early on in their careers many teachers learnt to assume an implicit semimissionary role, and saw their life task either as one of leavening the broad 'middle brown culture' of suburbia, or simply acting as a restraining and civilizing influence on the more hedonistic impulses of the working classes. It was perhaps almost inevitable that teachers adopting this view of their 'life task' not only tended to support the 'centralist' policies advocated by the educational administrators, but were also equally unhappy if lay people sought to take too active an interest in the day-to-day affairs of their schools. In general, most teachers seemed to have been happiest working in situations where school boards effectively did not exist, while in those authorities where this was not the case, teachers took a generally cautious attitude towards their managers and governors and generally discouraged them from visiting schools except, of course, on those several ritual occassions — speech day, sports day, and open day — when the institution and its staff and pupils were officially on display.

Local and central school systems

In short then, it seems that the amount of effective local involvement in the affairs of the school has altered considerably over the last century. At times local respresentative managers or governors have been able to exercise a close control both over the school's curriculum and its internal affairs. However, in the twentieth century, we have seen a gradual decline in the availability of opportunities for this kind of lay participation, and a seemingly inexorable drift of power towards the administrator and the teaching profession. While there are obviously some exceptions to this broad generalization, my readers may find it convenient to relate these changing patterns of community involvement to the following simple theoretical model of school board-community relationships. The first horizontal axis of this model examines the amount of control local people are able to exercise over the policies and internal affairs of their schools. As we can see, this control might be total, it might be partial, in the sense that it was shared with teachers or the local authority, or it might simply not exist, in the sense that the local community had no say in either what went on in the local school or the way its resources were allocated.

The second vertical axis of the model examines the degree of local participation in school board affairs. Again this might be total, it might be partial, or it might not exist at all, in the sense that the school board had become redundant.

Generally, we can place many Victorian communities in section 'A' of the above model, for, as we have already seen, under the nineteenth-century school system the local manager was not only often democratically elected, but also enjoyed quite wide powers of control over his

A model of school and community relationships

Degree of Local Participation	Degree of Control over Policy		
	Total (+)	Partial (0)	None (−)
Total +	A	B	C
Partial 0	D	E	F
None	E	H	I

school's curriculum, staff, financial affairs, and internal organization. In striking contrast, by the mid-twentieth century, most school systems, and particularly those to be found in the larger metropolitan areas of Britain, may be placed in the double negative section 'I' of our model. In places such as Sheffield, Manchester and Birmingham, no effective mechanisms remained to facilitate local involvement or control of the day-to-day affairs of schools, and education was in the main perceived by its clients as a commodity which was provided for them by an efficient, if remote and impersonal, administrative machine.

Moreover, the recent spate of local government reorganization has tended to exacerbate this situation in the sense that the number of local, democratically elected, educational authorities has been substantially reduced. Thus, from the point of view of the layman, nothing but 'officialdom', seems to stretch from the school to county hall. The new local government structures, particularly those in the metropolitan areas, serve quite large numbers of people, and can only by their nature address issues of general policy. Moreover, the number of democratically elected councillors has diminished, and those that remain must look after enlarged constituencies and serve on an ever-expanding number of committees. As a result of this increase in the burden of their work, many of them no longer have sufficient time to take a detailed interest in the needs of individual schools or intersts of particular small communities. As a result, most effective policy making at the local school level, that is, the social level which is most prominent both in the daily consciousness of the lay public in general, and parents and children in particular, is effectively monopolized by full-time educa-tion officials and senior members of the teaching profession. In other words, in contrast with the late Victorian situation, there is no longer any effective formal means of effectively institutionalizing local involvement in the contemporary school system, and in many parts of Britain most of the vital choices about the use of the most expensive public investment in the community — the local school buildings and equipment — moral questions about the type of education one's child ought to receive, and social questions about the involvement of children, parents, and other lay people in the educational process, are all taken by full-time professional workers.

The revival of the school board

Largely because of the disquiet they felt about this increasingly alienating situation, many politicians, teachers, administrators, and also members of the general public have, in recent years, set about the task of reexamining the way we presently organize our educational system. As we saw at the beginning of this chapter, this reassessment has formed part of an ongoing and exploratory process in which people are asking themselves how they can best help to effectively reintegrate the school into, and at the same time make it more accountable to, the wider local society.

This process has, perhaps naturally, generated a variety of short-, and long-term proposals for the reform of the state school system. These have included voucher schemes aiming to give people a greater degree of consumer choice,[16] administrative reforms suggesting a stricter definition of educational aims and objectives,[17] managerial innovations primarily concerned with involving a wider cross-section of people in the execution of policies, and finally structural change aimed at the reform and redevelopment of the school board system itself.[18] These latter proposals primarily seek to widen the composition of school governing and managing bodies, so that client groups such as pupils and parents, user and interest groups in the wider community such as the trade unions, neighbourhood groups, and employers, and teachers and ancillary staff can all participate more fully in directing the affairs of their own schools.

To date, as we have already seen, the latter kind of reforms have received the most enthusiastic support from local and national politicians, the leaders of teachers' organizations, educational pressure groups such as CASE and NAGM, and the public at large. In many parts of the country, including Sheffield, Bristol, Humberside, Stockport, and so on, many interesting attempts have been made to establish individual managing or governing bodies for each school, to increase their accountability at the community level, and above all to make this more representative of the various interest and user groups concerned with the local educational system.

Moreover, as we have already seen, these developments have also been endorsed in principal by the recent report of the Taylor Committee, and are as a result likely to be formalized in statute. Indeed, from one point of view the work of the latter committee has, like so many other official inquiries, merely tended to place a stamp of official recognition and approval on the kind of developments already taking place in many parts of the country. These have all, in a variety of ways, been attempting to alter the balance of influence and power within the local school system along the lines now officially approved by the Taylor Committee. The pace of this change has, in turn, accelerated sharply in the last ten years. Thus, for example, when Baron and Howell reported in 1968 on the first full-scale national survey of the constitution and membership of school managing and governing bodies, only nine counties and eleven county boroughs had formal representation of parents on governing boards.[19] By 1975 a survey conducted by the National Association of Governors and Managers showed that over 80 percent of the local authorities taking part in this study had made some provision for parents on their school boards, and it is probable that the pace of change has been equally dramatic in the case of the inclusion of representatives of teaching, auxiliary staff, student, community, and other interested local parties.[20]

The need for research

However, although most first-hand impressions indicate that these newly reformed school board systems are working well, surprisingly little is known about the people currently serving on these newly democratized bodies, or of their impact upon the traditional roles of teachers, headteachers, councillors, or administrators. Moreover, most of our existing knowledge about these new developments stems from the statements of those people, or interest groups, who are passionate advocates of change, and who have been closely associated with the movement to democratize the local school system. In short, from a social scientist's point of view this is a badly underresearched field, which is redolent with pious hopes and statements of intent, but is woefully lacking in empirically grounded studies which show us 'how things work out in day-to-day practice'. Largely as a result of their lack of basic research data, we know surprisingly little about who participates in the newly established or reformed school boards, nor do we know why people want to participate in this kind of activity. In the same way we know very little about the impact of these changes on the existing structure of the school system; thus we don't really know whose interests are advanced by these new kinds of local participatory structures, nor, perhaps even more surprisingly, do we really know who loses out by them.

In view of this situation, it is now perhaps time for me to conclude this largely historical introductory chapter and move on to a study of the world of school board politics as it exists today in the late 1970s. In order to do this I am going to move on in the next chapter to look in detail at some of the pressures which led one large educational authority, Sheffield, to introduce in 1970 the first stages of what remains at the time of writing one of the most radically democratized school board systems in the country, and which clearly anticipates, within the obvious constraints of the 1944 Education Act, some of the main recommendations of the Taylor Committee. In the course of this review I shall look in some detail both at the social pressures which led the Sheffield City Fathers to reform their school board system and also at the impact of this decision upon the work of its politicians, administrators, and teachers, and also, of course, upon the prospective parents, pupils, and other members of the local society.

The experiences of Sheffield cannot, of course, speak for or hope, in any way, to be entirely representative of the rest of the nation. Nevertheless, for the purpose of this inquiry, the city does offer something of a critical case study. This is not only because the city's educational authority serves the needs of over 500,000 people, and therefore may be thought of as a convenient 1 percent sample of the country as a whole, but also because Sheffield is a predominantly working-class community with a long history of democratic centralist styles of administration. This latter tradition goes well back into the nineteenth century, and tended, as we have already seen, to discourage a close local involvement in the affairs of schools, as well as to leave effective power in the hands of head-teachers, officials, and a small group of politicians. It was then the local educational equivalent of the 'great leap forward', when Sheffield decided, in the late 1960s, to break with its traditional centralized system of school administration and to pioneer a new participatory form of school management and government. This innovation in turn stimulated a great amount of interest in a large number of local authorities, and was so self-evidently successful that many of them introduced similar schemes into their own school systems. However, from the point of view of this analysis, what is perhaps even more pertinent is that the new Sheffield system clearly anticipates some, if not all, of the major proposals implicit in the Taylor Committee's recent report on the management and government of schools. Thus, I hope the following pages will give my readers a clearer understanding not only of the way in which the Sheffield system works at the moment, but also some idea of the ways in which participatory democratic theories are likely to effect the development of the nation's educational service in the latter half of this century.

Notes and references

1.   B. Simon, *Education and the Labour Movement*, Lawrence and Weshart, 1965, pp. 101-102.

2.   B. Simon, op. cit., pp. 105-106.

3.   Quoted in G. Baran and D. A. Howell, *The Government and Management of Schools*, The Athlone Press, 1974, p. 20.

4.   Public Schools Commission Report, pp. 5 and 6.

5.   T. Hodgskin, *Mechanics Magazine*, 11 October 1834.

6.   B. O'Brian, *Destruction*, 7 June 1834.

7.   Quoted in P. Gordon, *The Victorian School Manager*, Woburn Press, 1974, p. 10.

8.   P. Gordon, op. cit. p. 113.

9.   Quoted in P. Hollis, *Class and Conflict in the 19th Century*, Routledge & Kegan Paul, 1973, p. 340.

10.   P. Gordon, op. cit., p. 114.

11.   For an extended discussion of this point, see B. Simon, op. cit., pp. 121-162.

12.   B. Simon, op. cit., pp. 156-158.

13.   Quoted in J. H. Bingham, *History of the Sheffield School Board*, Northend, 1949.

14.   Regulations for Secondary Schools, 1964.

15.   Regulations for Secondary Schools, 1905.

16.   Alan Maynard, *Experiments with Choice in Education*, Institute of Economic Affairs, London, 1975.

17.   B. Taylor, *Combe Lodge Report*, Volume 7, No. 15, 1974, Further Education Staff College, Combe Lodge, Bristol.

18.   In many publications of the National Association of Governors and Managers, in particular Policy Papers Nos. 1 to 4 and discussion papers 1 to 4.

19.   G. Baran and D. N. Howell, op. cit.

20.   *School Managers: Some facts and figures*, NAGM publications, London, 1975.

CHAPTER 2

SOCIAL CHANGE AND ADMINISTRATIVE INNOVATION

Introduction

Sheffield's experiments with a new participatory system of individual managing bodies for each of its many schools was a relatively recent innovation and formed a striking contrast, both with its past practices and with traditional attitudes to school boards and community politics. In the late nineteenth century the city's educational authority had, in common with those in many other large northern boroughs, consciously decided to opt for a strictly centralized form of administration and did not, as was more commonly the case in Liverpool, Bristol, and London, choose to substantially devolve its powers and thus establish a complex network of influential local managing bodies. This preference for a rigidly centralized style of government remained dominant in Sheffield for much of the twentieth century and, largely as a result of this choice, the city leaders were extremely reluctant to implement the spirit of, if not the letter of, the law associated with the relevant five clauses of the Education Act of 1944 which specifically referred to school managing or governing bodies.

The 1944 Act had not only provided that every primary and secondary school, county or voluntary, should have its own body of managers or governors, but at the time of its passage through Parliament it was also generally agreed that these committees would be clearly recognizable bodies and would be closely identified with the work of the schools they served. In particular, the then Minister for Education, Mr. Rab Butler, made it very clear that he did not want Section 18 of the act, the part which gave local authorities the power to group school boards, simply to become a tool of administrative convenience which would effectively destroy the spirit behind the act. For, if this were to occur, and, say, several schools were allocated to one board, then this might operate both to destroy the individuality and effectiveness of the boards themselves and ultimately the independence of the schools they were designed to serve.

However, in spite of the sentiments of the national Parliament, the local civic leadership in Sheffield remained loyal to its centralist tradition and continued to question both the wisdom and practicality of establishing individual managing or governing bodies for each of its many schools. This of course was not a unique situation, rather it reflected the kind of response commonly found in many other large midland and northern education authorities and in turn reflected the exigencies of the local political and social situation. Thus it seems that, certainly in the older urban-industrial, if not the suburban or rural areas of England, there was little incentive for politicians to introduce this kind of change in the sense that there was no widespread 'grassroot' public demand for the introduction of this type of administrative structure into the local school system. Moreover, it seems probable that in Sheffield, as elsewhere in England and Wales, many civic leaders worried that the creation of a large number of entirely new administrative bodies would place an additional and perhaps intolerable burden on what was already an extremely strained series of resources. This was not only because they would generate fresh administrative work and thus calls upon public expenditure, but also because their presence would inevitably place additional demands on the time and energies of those officers, inspectors, and politicians who would naturally be expected to attend, or service, their meetings.

At the same time, and apart from these many practical difficulties, many civic leaders also questioned the wisdom of establishing individual school managing bodies on purely political grounds. This was mainly because they realized that this type of innovation might well facilitate the development of a new form of instability and perhaps ultimately conflict, in the sense that some boards might seek to establish them-selves as powerful, independent bodies, advocating educational policies which ran counter to those practised by the local, democrati-cally elected councils. This latent refractory tendency was particularly worrying for some of the leaders of those Labour councils, which perhaps inevitably tended to dominate the large northern and midland cities. These people were extremely reluctant to implement the spirit of the 1944 Act and establish a large number of individual managing bodies for each of their many schools, since they saw that this embryonic participatory system might ultimately work to their own disadvantage. In particular, it might, especially in the middle-class and largely conservative dominated suburban residential districts, facilitate the gradual development of a series of powerful local boards which might seek to run the local schools in the interests of a sectional, not a publicly approved, policy. At the same time, and in other parts of the city, particularly in the more deprived inner urban areas, the reverse process might occur in the sense that it would be extremely difficult to find sufficient numbers of local people with either the time, interest, or knowledge to serve effectively on these bodies.

Finally, and apart from these very serious practical and political objections, it seems probable that in the years immediately following the passage of the 1944 Act many people simply worried that, despite the rhetoric of good intention, managing bodies were simply one more 'talking shop' serving to waste both busy people's time and the public's money. In practice they seemed to achieve very little, apart from behaving in an unpredictable manner and threatening to disrupt the uniformity of the educational service the authority wished to provide for the children in its charge.

In short then, in many urban and industrial areas of England the proposals implicit in the 1944 Act, that is, to create individual managing or governing bodies for each school, were still viewed with a good deal of suspicion. School boards were still seen by many people as administrative devices which had been inherited from a nineteenth-century elitist tradition of education and which had little relevance for urban schools in the mid-twentieth century. They were not self-evidently desirable in theory, tended to become basically middle-class pressure groups in practice, and might, if allowed to, facilitate the growth of significant differences between schools serving different social classes, religious groups, or different regions of the city.

School boards in Sheffield 1945-1970

It seems probable that all of the factors implicit in the foregoing appraisal exerted a great deal of influence upon the policies adopted by Sheffield's political leaders in the immediate postwar years. Thus the City Fathers continued to remain loyal to the democratic centralist administrative traditions which had served them so well and in fact decided to pay only a nominal lip service to the legal requirements implicit in, if not the spirit of the debate associated with, the passage of the 1944 Act. In order to facilitate these aims, they established a system of school management and government in the city which seemed specifically designed to effectively negate these bodies and guard against any possibility that they might grow into powerful and independent institutions, which might not only sponsor the growth of an independent ethos within each school, but might also seriously disrupt the uniform system of school administration prevailing in the city.

In the case of the city's many primary schools, the objective of maintaining a relatively tight party control was simply achieved through the legal fiction of nominating a subcommittee of the education committee as the de jure, though purely nominal, managing body for over 150 schools. This administrative stratagem tended to leave effective day-to-day control of these schools in the hands of a relatively small corps of full-time inspectors and officials. In other words, the city's many primary headteachers were directly responsible for their work not to an individual school board containing representatives of the parents and the local community, but to the local authority inspectorate, and through them to the elected representatives and coopted members sitting on the city's education committee.

In the case of the city's secondary schools, although a number of the City Fathers evidently thought it might be desirable to create a number of publicly recognizable governing bodies, they again thought it necessary to maintain an effectively centralized and overtly political control over the working of these new bodies. These objectives were achieved in two ways: firstly, the membership of these bodies was severely restricted so that the majority of places were filled by members of the education committee, while the remainder were filled by people acceptable to and then appointed by the same committee. Secondly, and in order to ensure that the relatively small number of active politicians in the city retained an effective degree of control over all the city's many secondary schools, a grouping system was implemented under Section 18 of the 1944

Education Act and in this way several schools shared the services of one joint school board dominated by local politicians or their direct nominees. Thus, in the first constitution adopted for the city's secondary schools in 1947, six grouped boards were established to serve thirteen institutions. Each of these boards was, as the relevant instrument said, to consist of thirteen persons, that is to say,

> Two ex-officio Governors being the Chairmen for the time being of the Education Committee and the Secondary Education Sub-Committee appointed in accordance with the provisions of Part II of the First Schedule of the Education Act, 1944; and seven Governors who shall be members of the Education Committee, to be appointed by the Education Committee; and four Co-optative Governors, being persons who have special interests in and/or knowledge of educational affairs, to be appointed by the Education Committee but who need not be members of the Education Committee.

Each of the governors was to serve for a term of three years and the director of education, or his nominee, was to act as a clerk to the board. However, no explicit recognition was made of the parental interest, and the managerial prerogative of the administration was strongly defended in the sense that the instruments specifically stated that, 'No master or other person employed for the purposes of the School shall be a Governor.'

This basic structure continued in force for the next twenty-three years; during this period the system was modified from time to time both to cater for the growth in the number of secondary schools in the city and also to further reduce the independence of each governor, and in this way maintain an even tighter control over their behaviour. Thus in 1953 the instruments were slightly revised and now specified that the governors should only hold office for one year before seeking reelection or reappointment. At the same time provision was made for the six boards of governors which had been established in the city to take on the responsibility for the oversight of no less than 34 schools. Further modifications occurred in 1955 when the then 47 secondary schools in the city were provided with a governing system reorganized into ten groups. In 1960 the composition of each group was again slightly modified and finally in 1964 the existing instruments and articles of government of secondary schools were revoked in favour of a new scheme which continued in operation until 1970. This final version of the 'grouped system' sought to return to the post-1945 system, for the number of boards was reduced from ten to seven, though at the same time the growth in school numbers meant that these seven governing bodies were theoretically responsible for looking after the interests of no less than 47 schools.

Obviously one of the perhaps not unintended consequences of these constitutional limitations was that the few governing bodies which existed in Sheffield had little capacity to grow into the kind of active and effective organizations which might have taken a close interest in the work of a school and facilitated the development of a particular institutional ethos. In contrast these boards were extremely formal and often nominal organizations. Most of their members belonged to the majority party in the city, and were not only kept under a tight party discipline, but were also expected to remain loyal to the decisions taken by the party caucus. At the same time most governors were either councillors or active in local political or voluntary activities and the burdens of these responsibilities inevitably meant that they found it difficult to find sufficient time to devote to the day-to-day affairs of the six or seven schools they were nominally responsible for. Largely as a result of this situation, Sheffield schools lacked any kind of effective liaison structure which could not only reflect local communal or client interests, but could also act upon and influence the decision-making processes at a neighbourhood level. Thus, in the case of secondary, as in primary education, apart from matters of general policy, effective control remained in the hands of the full-time officials and inspectors employed by the authority.

However, this is not to suggest that governing bodies were not unimportant to local politicians. This was mainly because they represented one of the few sources of political patronage available and consequently a place on a school board was a useful way of publicly acknowledging the services of a loyal relative or faithful party worker's efforts in the long, heartless, grinding routines of delivering literature, organizing rummage sales, stewarding party meetings, in short in maintaining the vitality of the lifeblood of English local politics. For these people, becoming a school governor might not only give them a prestigious position in the social hierarchy of their own local community, but also gave them the trappings, if not realities, of power. Indeed, in some cities local political activists found the annual routine of presenting prizes, appearing on platforms, inspecting school premises, and receiving differential abasements from headteachers such an intoxicating mixture that they collected school board places as others might collect stamps. The following extract from a report on the Wolverhampton situation is indicative of a situation which was not peculiar to the black country.

> Some Councillors and non-Councillors held as many as 6 or 7 appointments; endearingly, the husbands of women Councillors and the wives of men Councillors sat on several boards of schools in the same wards; a considerable number of failed council candidates and former Councillors held posts; no parents or teachers were represented per se. A request for reform was turned down by the Conservative Education Committee in the Spring of 1971.[1]

As a result of all of these developments it was hardly surprising that many teachers viewed these often nominal lay bodies with a general cynicism and at times veiled contempt. One Sheffield head made this quite clear when he told me,

> Before 1971 I shared a governing body with 5 other schools. All of the heads for a group used to wait together in one room, waiting to be called in one at a time, like bad boys to give our reports. It was an extremely humiliating formality, and as you can imagine many of the reports were cursory in the extreme.

Social change in Sheffield 1960-1970

However, although this reluctance to implement the spirit of the 1944 Act and provide each of the city's schools with its own individual managing or governing body may be criticized in retrospect, nonetheless the evidence does seem to suggest that the quite rigid and centralized system of educational administration which existed in the city in the postwar years was widely supported. This was mainly because it resonated well with the political philosophy of, and social programmes adopted by, the leaders of the dominant party whose power in turn rested upon the solidaristic class-based loyalties of what was still a relatively homogeneous and proletarian society. Thus, within the general guidelines laid down by the city council and its education committee, a body of full-time professional workers was able to gradually provide the city with the kind of sophisticated and comprehensive educational service their political masters required and which in turn reflected the wider public's faith in, and concern with, the educational venture.

However, although this quite rigid system of political control was well suited to a society in which a widespread concern for educational progress was clearly articulated through a dominant political party, the evidence tends to suggest that it was gradually becoming less effective in the very different social and political climate which emerged in Britain in the late 1960s. Although many of these changes have been referred to in general terms in the last chapter, I shall now look at them in a little more detail for it seems reasonable to assume that many of the clearly recognizable social, economic, and educational developments taking place in Sheffield in the late 1960s gradually influenced the views of many politicians and led them to question the efficacy of maintaining the rigid style of administration traditionally associated with the democratic-centralist philosophy.

Changes in education

In Sheffield, as in the rest of the country, the educational system had expanded rapidly in the postwar years and had rapidly grown into an elaborate organization which was not only one of the largest employers of labour in the city, but also one of the biggest spenders of public money. However, perhaps inevitably as a result of all these developments, the school system had become more socially if not geographically distant from the people and communities it served. Many of the city's schools had grown into complex, large institutions drawing on a very wide catchment area. Within each school the increasing professionalization of the labour force, the ever-increasing elaboration of the division of labour, the introduction of a more sophisticated curriculum, and a complex associated assessment and examination system, all combined to facilitate a new situation in which local people felt they no longer understood what was going on within their schools. This state of what many people might well define as a sense of estrangement or alienation from the state schooling system was perhaps further exacerbated by the fact that in the postwar years success within the educative system has become the major and publicly accepted means through which people are allocated to their respective places in the labour market. In other words, in Sheffield, as in the rest of England and Wales, most people's life chances are now significantly determined by their initial degree of success or failure within a state schooling system which is growing more socially distant from the community it serves. Today there is much less chance than there was, say, even twenty-five years ago for people who were failures at school to 'get on in the world' without some formal and socially acceptable ticket of certification or accreditation.

Largely as a result of all these kinds of developments, education has become, as never before in our society, a topic of common everyday private concern and public interest. Most families now maintain a very close interest in the educational careers of their children, their progress through the various stages of the local school system, and the factors which may facilitate their ultimate success within the examination system. However, this being said, it seems probable that in many areas this public 'pressure' upon the local school system has been further raised by the ways in which the educational service has been consciously used by politicians as a tool to create a more democratic and egalitarian society. These new policies were adopted mainly because the system of selected secondary education which existed in Sheffield until the mid-1960s, and which still struggles to survive in other parts of the country, was seen to be a key factor in the maintenance of an inegalitarian class-stratified society. Thus both in Sheffield and in most other parts of England and Wales local politicians fought hard to abolish the grammar school and introduce a comprehensive system of education which it was hoped would provide more equality of opportunity and facilitate the development of a more egalitarian and just society.

Naturally, it is not my intention in a book which is primarily concerned with school boards to discuss the merits and disadvantages of these types of reforms. Rather in referring to them my purpose is to draw my readers attention to the fact that, certainly in the case of Sheffield as happened elsewhere in the country, the abolition of grammar schools and the implementation of a seemingly more meritocratic structure of secondary education created many tensions both amongst the local professional middle classes and those who aspired to emulate their ways of life.[2] These groups of often highly articulate and politically conscious people were often highly critical of educational policies which seemed from their point of view to threaten to destroy good and long-established schools and replace them with large and anonymous comprehensive structures. Ironically, in Sheffield the latter structures found it difficult to defend themselves against this type of criticism or to relate themselves effectively to the local community they served, precisely because they continued to function within a democratic-centralized tradition of administration, which effectively denied them their own individual governing boards.

Changes in the social structure

These developments in the nature of the city's educational system were naturally complimented by a number of deeper and more fundamental changes taking place in the social structure of urban Britain. In Sheffield, as in the rest of Western industrial society, the advance of technology, the development of public spending programmes, and the growth of the service sector of the economy have all facilitated the development of an increasingly sophisticated division of labour. The economy no longer requires large pools of unskilled and semiskilled manual workers who in the past have all tended to share a common series of life experience and have been conscious of and owed a strong allegiance to their particular class as well as closely identifying themselves with the geographic area within which they both commonly worked and spent the remainder of their lives. In Sheffield in the mid-1970s the social structure is no longer best thought of in terms of a simple and rigid class system in which the middle classes, the respectable working classes, other workers and the poor each possess their own distinctive types of value systems, social relationships, economic characteristics, and tribal territories. In contrast, in modern Sheffield, as elsewhere in England, although social inequality exists and it is still possible to distinguish broad social strata, at the same time the former neat Victorian class system is breaking down and giving place to a complex multibonded society in which the balance between different categories of workers is slowly changing.

At the same time as the nature of the labour force is changing, it is also gradually losing its once monolithically proletarian character in the sense that the working class in urban English society is often seriously divided both in terms of race and the type of housing tenure it enjoys, as well as each group's specific wage rates in the labour market. All of these changes are, perhaps quite naturally, reflected in the composition and fortunes of the dominant Labour Party in Sheffield. This organization is now far less of a class-based proletarian party in the sense that the proportion of blue-collar workers maintaining an active interest in its affairs is slowly declining, while the influence of people working in white-collar occupations and the professions is gradually increasing. This new generation of Labour Party recruits may trace their antecedents back to the old middle or working classes, or even from amongst the poor. However, their social origins are largely irrelevant to their present social role as teachers, foremen, managers, welfare officers, planners, social workers, and so on; moreover, their life style does not tend to facilitate the growth of a tightly knit series of specific and localized social relationships. Rather they typically belong to a kaleidoscope of interlocking interests and groups which bring them into close personal contact with people from many different sectors of society. Paradoxically, and largely because their work has encouraged the development of capacities found useful in leadership — the ability to think abstractly, make decisions rapidly, disseminate information and so on — they often tend to assume a dominant role in many of the groups or organizations they join, be it a community association, sports club, religious institution, or, of course, the Labour Party. This is not to imply that blue-collar workers are inactive in this organization, rather it is simply to record the inevitability that they may find it more difficult to execute the kinds of tasks which are associated with the leadership role.

Now quite obviously a political party which is gradually changing its social character in this manner and becoming much more a loose coalition of interest groups headed up by a generally middle-class and progressive leadership may find it needs to review its system of decision making. Its leaders will find it difficult to maintain the type of close, often fierce, discipline over the membership which it was possible to operate within a more homogeneous and proletarian organization. There is a need for more flexibility, the open acknowledgement of differences, and the absorption of public controversy. In turn, the politicians who must work within the parameters of this new social structure are no longer in the position of tribal leaders who can rely upon the unquestioning class-based loyalties of their followers. In the political climate of the late 1960s, they could no longer assume a tacit, if taken-for-granted consensus, for their policies; rather they often found fierce local opposition on such key issues as planning developments, housing, welfare, or education.

All of these new developments were by chance highlighted in a perhaps classical form in the case of Sheffield by the violent 'grassroots' opposition which was rapidly mobilized amongst its council house tenants in order to campaign against the councils proposals to introduce a rent rebate scheme into the city. This new system effectively meant that a tenant would have to disclose his income in the course of applying for rent rebate. Naturally, in such a large industrial area as Sheffield, this proposal stoked up bitter folk memories of the 'means test' administered to the unemployed in the interwar years, and in turn led to the formation of a new kind of mass working-class organization, the tenants' association, which was not only independent of the Labour Party, but also campaigned passionately against its policies. The deep antagonisms which this issue raised amongst Labour's traditional supporters was made very clear in the following comments from one respected Labour Party pioneer in the city, published in the form of an open letter, and included in the October, 1967, edition of *Sheffield Forward*, the local party newspaper,

> Rising costs of commodities; increased rents and cuts in social services cause resentment, but normally little action. I believe this has caused the majority of the Sheffield City Council's Labour Group to make a terrible miscalculation. They have become accustomed to patronising tenants and to issuing orders that they accepted responsibility for administering traditional policy without calculating the effect on the people concerned.

> A demand for extortionate increases in rent brought spontaneous reaction to refuse to pay these increases. This is tantamount to a strike situation on the industrial field. The worm has turned. For the first time in my experience it is possible in this situation to equate community power with industrial power. It is a new experience for our labour leadership. Will they react like nineteenth century employers, or will they see the full implications inherent in the situation and come to a reasonable settlement before the logic of the situation takes full effect?

Partly as a result of this extensive level of 'grassroot' disaffection with their policies, partly as a result of the national unpopularity of the government, and partly due to organizational weaknesses within the local party machine, Labour lost control of the city in 1968, for only the second time since they gained power in 1926. This defeat was obviously a salutory experience for many party members, and in an article in the local party newspaper for July, 1968, headed 'The Fight Back Begins', one party member commented on the general national situation in the following terms,

> For Labour there is a spine-chilling element in the local government defeat. It is plain everywhere. The old loyal solid working class vote is no longer there for the asking.

> Not just the cloth cap vote. The worker's vote, the skilled engineering draughtsman, instrument maker, computer programmer, technician and manager — all these, as well as the new mechanised labourer and big machine minder.

They are no longer deeply conscious, class-conscious, that Labour is their party. They were ours in 1964; they were ours exultantly in 1966. Now they are sullen and even marginally hostile.[3]

Naturally enough, in a time of defeat, a local party leadership enjoys the time, and has been sufficiently stimulated by its loss of office, to review the efficacy of its past policies and practices, including, of course, in the case of Sheffield, the extremely closed system of local administration associated with it's democratic-centralist theories of politics. In other words, the local party leadership had the opportunity to examine its past practices, examine new ideas, and consider whether it ought to adopt a more open and participatory style of conducting local affairs.

It soon became clear that during the course of this evaluation, many councillors were willing to consider the practicability of experimenting with new, more open forms of local government. They were gradually moving towards a position within which they started to think about the best ways in which they might gradually build up a new type of local governmental structure, which would ultimately reach out to a wide variety of concerned groups, including those operating within, as well as outside, the formal structure of their party. One of their leaders, Alderman Harold Lambert, well illustrated the flexibility of mind and imaginative innovation which was required in adopting this entirely new approach to local politics, when he wrote:[4]

Participation's ultimate form is at the moment obscure. . . . Our experience in the city has shown a different approach by different groups, bout out of these experiences will grow a greater liaison between the local authority and citizens and a new role for the elected representative. The surgeries of the councillor for dealing with personal problems must continue but the contact with the electors, as envisaged by the old ward meetings, is diminishing and to replace this one can see emerging a more broader based meeting of electors in wards, with the elected representative as liaison officer.

This kind of thorough reevaluation which was taking place in Sheffield, must not, however, be seen as a purely isolated phenomenon which was largely confined to one large industrial city in South Yorkshire. Rather, it was part of a wider, total, national examination of the sort of local governmental structure which might be considered most appropriate for the complex, multibonded, plural society, which was developing in postwar Britain. Although the boundaries of this debate were far from clear, there seemed to be a general agreement that, as Carole Pateman suggested, writing in 1970, that our democratic institutions and people could no longer be considered in isolation from one another.[5] Rather, each of these forces interacts continuously with the other through an ongoing nextwork of complex relationships. Largely as a result of this situation, the process of effective local government can't work within, as is implicit in the democratic centralist theories of democracy, a system in which the local electorate simply chooses its decision makers and then leaves power in their hands for the next half a decade. In other words, there was, in the late 1960s, a growing recognition, both locally and nationally, that England needed a more open style of local government in which the existence of local interests and pressure groups was formally acknowledged, in the sense that new participatory structures were created to provide an avenue through which people could be consulted about those decisions most effecting their everyday world, about the nature of the local school, the local road system, planning, their environment, housing, medical services, and so on.

Obviously, it is not my purpose within the limits of this chapter to examine all aspects of what is a complex, and still developing, subject. However, perhaps these general trends are best summarized in the influential Skeffington Report, which, though it is not specifically concerned with education, does look at the ways in which people can be encouraged to participate in public affairs at a level, and in a form, which is most meaningful for their own lives. Thus, the authors of this document point out that:

> It may be that the evolution of the structures of representative government which has concerned western nations for the last century and a half is now entering into a new phase. There is a growing demand by many groups for more opportunity to contribute and for more say in the working out of policies which affect people not merely at election time, but continuously as proposals are being hammered out and, certainly as they are being implemented. Life, so the argument runs, is becoming more and more complex, and one cannot leave all the problems to one's representatives. They need some help in reaching the right decision, and opportunity should be provided for discussions with all those involved.[6]

Similarly, and within the context of a specific study of Sheffield politics in the late 1960s, William Hampton, a local university don and member of the Labour Party, argued strongly that traditional local representative bodies, such as the Sheffield Education Committee, could no longer effectively combine the twin functions of, firstly, initiating a policy and then controlling it's executive, and then, secondly, at the same time, attempting to facilitate a close, local involvement in community affairs. He argued that precisely because of this situation the local council would need to create a completely new network of single-purpose bodies, such as, in the case of schools, individual managing and governing bodies, whose primary aim and functions would be to support and monitor the activities of the local representative.[7]

Certainly all of these developments had a marked impact on Labour Party thinking in Sheffield, and in their manifesto for the municipal elections of 1970 they made it clear in a section labelled, appropriately enough, 'Participation' that,

> Labour is pledged to give more say to people in our local affairs. It has started by appointing boards of governors for every school, by public meetings and help to residents' associations at Darnall, Walkley and Mosborough. The Advisory Committee with Tenants' Associations has met regularly, and Works Consultative Committees have been set up in Corporation departments to involve employees at all levels.[8]

Participatory democracy and the school system 1970-1977

In the case of schools, the adoption of this new participatory approach to local government soon meant a rapid move away from the old centralized traditions, which, as we have already seen, had effectively cut off parents, teachers, ancillary staff, students, and local people from any significant level of involvement in the key decisions which were taken about their school's affairs. The Labour Party's open commitment to new forms of public involvement in the affairs of schools was made very clear in the party's manifesto, 'Put Labour Back' which they prepared for the 1969 municipal elections; it said:

> Labour wants to promote the widest participation in the running of schools by parents, teachers, trade unionists, people from all walks of life. When full details are announced it will be amongst the most ambitious attempts at local democracy ever attempted in a large city.

The new school management system which was finally introduced into the city in 1970 was largely consistent with these promises, and was at the time one of the most radical experiments in this field in the whole country. This structure was the final result of wide discussions both within the party caucus itself and with senior administrators, representatives of teachers' organizations, and local pressure groups. It now fully implemented the spirit, as well as the precise letter, of the 1944

Act, and in doing so, gave each Sheffield school its own representative managing board, so constituted that it would be flexible and sensitive to local needs and interests. The chairman of the Education Committee commented at the time, 'These proposals could transform the involvement of the community in education at every level, and lead to a better understanding and more real concern for the part the future generation can in turn play in the life of the community.'[9]

Thus, while the new school boards maintained a minority of committed political activists appointed by the education committee, they also contained elected representatives of the parents, teachers, and non-teaching staff; in addition representatives came from local community, religious, and voluntary organizations. Each board was also given the power of cooption, and in some large secondary schools this also enabled senior pupils to attend managers' meetings.

The participatory democratic philosophy generating this quite radical departure from Sheffield's previously dominant centralized tradition of school administration was well summed up by one prominent member of the city's political establishment when he wrote the following comments on the city's decentralized system of managing boards,

> The emphasis will more and more be on partnership rather than edicts being handed down from on high. It will be exhilarating, exciting and interesting to see every school with local knowledge of both needs and abilities, engaging in a democratic process of helping the children to integrate in an expanding, interdependent social grouping. Thousands of people who have always wanted to play some role in education and who have felt that they could never do so, will now have their chance. In Sheffield alone this will involve up to some two thousand citizens and throughout the country, some hundreds of thousands. This is, indeed, a landmark in the development of education.[10]

Scale of reform

Naturally this reform involved a tremendous upheaval in terms of traditional habits of mind, customs, and administrative practices. A new department was set up within the education offices to deal with the administration of nearly 300 new bodies, and, in turn, the very presence of these brand new institutions inevitably placed fresh demands upon the time of those administrative staff, councillors, headteachers, and advisors who were required to attend their meetings.

Contrary to the pessimistic assumptions of those centralists who had opposed this 'brave new experiment' in local democracy, the City

Fathers found little difficulty in recruiting sufficient numbers of people wanting to be governors or managers of their own local schools. The chairman of the Education Committee made this very clear when he wrote,

> There has been a splendid response to the request to wards and unions to suggest names of people willing to be considered for the new boards of governors and managers to start in the summer term 1970.
>
> So far over 200 names have been put forward from the labour movement in Sheffield. In addition to these, several hundred other names have been sent in by other organisations to the Education Office, including 70 from the Polytechnic staff alone.[11]

Indeed, simply in terms of sheer numbers, the quantity of people who were now brought into the service of education by the new participatory system was quite spectacular. Thus, up to 1970, only seven governing bodies, each with 13 places, had existed in the city, and thus only just over 100 places were theoretically available for those people who wanted to serve as school governors. However, following the reforms of 1970, simply because each of the city's schools now had it's own governing body, the number of places available rose quite dramatically to 2750. One year later, when the special school boards were established, this figure rose to 3300, and, in the next year, largely as a result of the extension of the city boundaries following local government reorganization, the number of places again rose to 3500. Finally, at the time of writing, and following the further democratization of the school boards in 1975, when additional places were made available for the elected representatives of the parents and teachers, the number of places has again risen and now stands at nearly 5000. If one considers that most managers and governors are popular and prominent people, who are active within their schools, or have their feet firmly placed in the local community in the sense that they are members of local ward parties, community associations, neighbourhood groups, parents' associations, and so on, then certainly it seems reasonable to assume that the initiatives taken by the city council seem to offer a most effective means of breaking down the isolation of the school and involving an influential network of local people in the activities and concerns.

The new school boards

Moreover, Sheffield's Education Committee made it very clear from the start that it wanted the new school boards to be active and effective bodies taking a lively interest in the affairs of the schools they served. In order to facilitate this kind of involvement, the committee produced a small, concise, and extremely helpful booklet for all new managers. This document explained in simple terms the general educational policies which had been adopted by the committee and which were now in force in all of the city's schools. It contained guidance on such key issues as the appointment of teaching staff, admission policy, the role of the advisory service, financial assistance to pupils, and so on. For example, in the case of letting the school buildings, a topic which may be of great concern in many communities where the school premises may be the only source of suitable available accommodation for voluntary community or neighbourhood activities, the governors were remained that Sheffield's policy was as follows:

Lettings

The Education Committee wish to make their schools and playing fields available as much as possible to community and tenants associations, adult groups, youth clubs and sports clubs. This policy may lead to difficult problems regarding the possible over-use of facilities, and the cleaning and caretaking of buildings which are heavily used, but the Education Committee are most anxious that these difficulties should be overcome and should not be impediments to the community use of schools.

Later in the booklet this specific point was referred to in more general terms in the course of a concluding paragraph which attempted to inform the new managers what 'the Education Committee have planned for the overall development of education in Sheffield', it said:

The Committee are anxious that all their schools should be open and used by the community, and they have made a particular point of developing some of the secondary schools as campus schools. Campus schools will have various special facilities, a full-time head of adult education centre, in most cases a youth leader, where appropriate a sports centre manager, and a single head of campus responsible for co-ordinating the use of the campus. Where campus schools exist, the governors are responsible for promoting the development of the adult and youth activities as well as the school.

Apart from containing a section referring to the general policy of the authority, the booklet also contained the newly appointed governors formal terms of reference, namely, the instruments dealing with the composition of the boards and the articles dealing with their powers on such matters as the curriculum, teacher appointment, complaints against teachers, pupil admission, and so on. Both of these quite radical documents had been carefully designed to take account of 'changing patterns of education', and were the formal and legal implementation of a reform which was also important nationally, because for the first time every school had its own governing body with staff, parent, and community representation.

Finally, apart from informing the new governors about their formal terms of reference and the Education Committee's general policy for Sheffield, the booklet also contained a set of explicit recommendations about the ways in which people could set about learning to become really effective in their new office.

Apart from reminding them that they must regularly attend meetings, the new managers were also told to 'Find out as much as you can about the local and national systems of education, and the radical changes which are going on in our schools and colleges today.'

In other words they were being invited to actively concern themselves with what their schools were teaching to children, and in this way the Education Committee was implicitly endorsing a type of approach which assumed that lay governors had a legitimate interest in, and a right to discuss, their school's curriculum, and ought not to eschew this area, simply because the teachers claimed it as their own specific and professional area of responsibility.

In the same way, the instructional booklet also reminded the new governors that they could also promote their schools development by supporting, '. . . . any functions such as concerts, plays, open days and sports days which your school arranges. Offer to help with school activities. Please answer promptly any correspondence from the school.'

However, the Education Committe also made it very clear from the start that it did not want its new governors to simply concern themselves with the annual rituals of institutional display or marginal fund-raising activities. It also made it very clear that they ought to take a close interest in what are, perhaps, more central educational concerns, namely, what the schools are trying to achieve in theory and what they are doing in practice. Thus, the committee reminded its governors that,

> You will learn a great deal about education by visiting your school, and this will help you to understand what the school is trying to achieve. Visit your school informally though the headteacher would appreciate you fixing a mutually convenient time beforehand. Let the headteacher know

you will be glad to accept further invitations. Make a point of getting to know the staff, too.

In other words, the new governors were being reminded in the most tactful of ways that they had a duty to represent the public interest and develop their function as a forum of accountability at the neighbourhood level. For, if local people are encouraged to ask teachers questions about, and find out more about, what was being taught in their own community schools, then this very social process of exploration might well help to facilitate a greater degree of professional communication with, and ultimate accountability to, those they served. Moreover, and perhaps as one more extension of this general theme of local accountability, the Education Committee also saw fit to remind its new governors that it saw that one of their prime functions would be to 'try to strengthen the links between your school and the local community, between school and home, and between associated primary and secondary schools.'

In other words, the new governing bodies were also requested to assume a 'bridge-building role' in the sense that they were to help break down the many social barriers which effectively isolated so many schools from the communities they theoretically served. However, the Education Committee evidently did not see this as being a totally one-way process, for it's booklet also reminded its governors that, 'If you wish to pursue any complaint you hear about the school refer it first to the headteacher. If you still feel uneasy get in touch with the Chairman of Governors, who may suggest that the question should be raised with the Chief Education Officer.'

Training new governors

Finally, and in addition to the helpful advice contained in its booklet, the City Fathers also made a serious effort to provide some training opportunities for its new generation of governors. This was because many of them took the view that it was not sufficient simply to reform the formal structure of school government, without, at the same time, attempting a parallel programme of adult education which would attempt to give people the skills, confidence, and knowledge to take a more helpful and active part in the affairs of their local schools. One of the results of this kind of appreciation was that the local authority approached the extramural department of the local university and the two bodies agreed to pool their resources and cooperate in a joint endeavour which would aim to provide a series of relevant training courses for Sheffield's new governors.

The first of these courses was organized in the autumn term of 1972 and attracted over 40 students. In the subsequent four years up to the end of 1977, another 14 courses have been held in different parts of the city, and over 700 students have attended them. The students evident motivation and keenness has been constantly reflected both in a relatively high rate of attendance and in the fact that they have usually reported to fellow governors that they found the course a useful and interesting one, and in this way the demand for places on new courses remained consistently high.

The training courses provided in Sheffield typically consist of ten consecutive weekly meetings, each of which lasts for two hours. Each session is designed to give the students the maximum opportunity to study and assimilate complex, unfamiliar information, and at the same time apply it to their own school situation. To this end, formal lectures are typically disposed of and lecture notes are circulated to all students well in advance of each meeting. This procedure gives the new governors some time to reflect and relate new ideas to their own peculiar experiences, so they can, in turn, ask meaningful and relevant questions and explore new avenues with other members of their class. The syllabus of each course is extremely flexible, in the sense that it may well be modified to meet the needs of a particular group of students, or the exigencies of a particular social situation; however, this being said, most of the training courses attempt to deal with at least the following basic topics.

1   The structure of the educational system.

2   The powers of school managers or governors.

3   Finance and budgeting.

4   Modern educational philosophy.

5   School and the local community.

6   Educational management.

7   Politics and education

8   Educational policy in Sheffield.

The lecturers on the training course have included from the university, a sociologist, a psychologist, and a social administrator; and from the local authority, the deputy chief education officer, the chairman of the Education Committee, and a senior finance officer. The students have also come from a variety of backgrounds and have included parents, school auxiliary staff, trade unionists, members of voluntary organizations, and teachers. Generally, the evidence suggests that most people's reaction to the courses has been favourable in the sense that most of the dropouts have been caused by illness, business pressures, or the constraints of alternative voluntary or familial commitments. However, perhaps the best indication of the relatively successful nature of this initiative may be found in the following remarks, which appeared in the newsletter of the National Association of Governors and Managers and which had been written by a local member and officer who had recently attended a training course:

> My impression is that the organisers have largely achieved their aims and are to be congratulated. I believe too that it is important that the structure of this couse should continue to be responsibility of some other body than the L.E.A.[12]

Conclusions

It seems then that in the case of Sheffield, the Local Educational Authority has in recent years made a complete volte-face, both in its traditionally suspicious attitude to school governing bodies and to participatory democratic theories. This 'great leap forward' may, of course, in retrospect be seen as a belated response to some of the deeper social and political trends we have looked at in the chapter. However, whatever the verdict of later historians, these recent developments in Sheffield are also of great interest and importance from a national point of view. This is partly because, in terms of their powers and constitutions, the new school boards are now some of the most radical in the country, and partly because the thinking behind these new structures clearly anticipates some of the major recommendations within, though obviously not all the detailed proposals contained in, the recent report of the Taylor Committee.

Largely as a result of this situation, the Sheffield school boards have already aroused a widespread interest in many other Local Educational Authorities and some of these have, in turn, introduced similar systems into their own school management structures. In turn, Sheffield's leaders have been so pleased with their own experiments in community politics that they have decided to further modify their original system and thus, in 1975, they provided for additional parental, student, and community involvement.

However, in spite of all these quite exciting developments, surprisingly little is known about the work of these new bodies. Most of our existing knowledge about the work of democratized school boards, both locally and nationally, is derived from the reports of people who have been clearly pressing for school board reform themselves or have been closely involved in the establishment of new participatory systems. Thus, we know very little about how these new initiatives tend to work out in practice. For example, we don't know how far the ideals of the participatory democrats are aborted by 'the exigencies of daily life', 'administrative convenience', 'traditional professional attitudes', or simply the 'human frailty of the new generation of managers'. In other words, there is in this, as in many other fields of education, a need for more objective and independent research. Although our first and often extremely superficial impressions may lead us to the conclusion that the new systems are all working well, in practice, as I pointed out in Chapter 1, little of detail is known about the people serving on the new boards or in turn about the impact of these new bodies on existing structures of power.

In short, the field of school board politics remains a badly under-researched field. We know surprisingly little about who gains or who looses by participation, or indeed the effect of participation itself upon the traditional roles of teachers, administrators, headteachers or councillors, or upon the day-to-day behaviour and perspectives of children, parents, or local people in general. However, it seems to me that these questions are important ones to ask at the present juncture in time, for if, as seems likely, the Taylor Committee's recommendations to introduce individual and thoroughly democratized school boards are generally implemented throughout the country, then both the general public and its political leaders should be as fully informed as possible about how these developments are likely to work out in practice.

In view of this situation, I decided, as soon as I heard that national changes were likely to occur in the powers, constitution, and position of school managing and governing bodies, to conduct an ongoing investigation into the day-to-day working of the new Sheffield school boards. This interest was partly sparked off by my own professional interest in the subject of decision making in education, and partly by my own close personal involvement as a member of Sheffield University staff, in the joint university/local authority-sponsored training courses for governors I have already referred to in this chapter. However, as I hope to make clear in the next chapter, this project which initially started as what I thought in 1974 would be quite a simple and straightforward research exercise, gradually led me into a landscape which was relatively uncharted, and where I found it necessary to construct new bridges and pathways. Thus, in what follows, my readers will find that, in order to bring some light into the world of school board politics, I have been forced to question commonplace conventional assumptions, both about the current nature of the sociology of education, as well as about such terms as participation, community, or democracy. This process has naturally been an uncomfortable one. However, I hope that in following the route I have hacked out, my readers will both be able to learn from my mistakes and also come to a deeper appreciation of the role of democratized school boards within the nation's educational system which is evolving in the late 1970s.

Notes and references

1. NAGM Newsletter, March 1973.

2. 'In a survey by the Conservative Party in a district of West Sheffield, more than a quarter of people questioned said they were positively against comprehensive schools. Only 9% were in favour.' Quoted in the *Daily Mail*, 2 November 1976.

3. *Sheffield Forward*, July 1968.

4. Quoted by William Hampton in 'Popular Participation in Local Democracy', one of a number of papers published in the *Fabian Tract, Towards Participation in Local Services*.

5. C. Pateman, *Participation and Democratic Theory*, Oxford University Press, 1970.

6. Ministry of Housing and Local Government, Report of the (Skeffington) Committee on Public Participation in Planning, People and Planning, HMSO, 1969, p. 11.

7. William Hampton, *Democracy and Community*, Oxford University Press, 1970.

8. *Sheffield Forward*, May 1970.

9. P. Horton, writing in an article, 'The End of the Forties', *Sheffield Forward*, 1970.

10. John Ball, in an article, 'Democratisation of Schools', *Sheffield Forward*, July, 1969.

11. P. Horton, op. cit.

12. NAGM Newsletter, March 1973.

CHAPTER 3

RESEARCHING SCHOOL BOARDS

Introduction

In the course of my work in Sheffield I decided to spend the bulk of my time assessing both the role of the newly appointed or elected governors[1] and also the reaction of local people in general to these new experiments in participatory democracy. I spent much of my time talking to people I met in the course of my daily activities and I also asked my students, some of whom were governors themselves, and others community workers in the more deprived areas of the city, to undertake a similar exercise and to report their findings to a number of research groups I established. At all times I guided my discussions towards an exploration of people's perceptions of the organizations and structure of decision making within their own local school system, and at suitably appropriate occasions asked my respondents such questions as:

What are managing bodies?

Who sits on your school managing board?

If your child is having problems, who would you go and see about it?

I then supplemented the considerable amount of information I received through this basic fieldwork exercise with a conventional questionnaire survey of Sheffield governors and managers. This more formal exercise in data collection contained two parts, the first of these involving an extended questionnaire which is reproduced in Appendix B of this book. This document was filled in by twenty members of the local Sheffield branch of the National Association of Governors and Managers, and by 45 governors attending a training course organized jointly by the Local University and Education Authority. The second part of the survey involved a shorter version of the questionnaire and this is reproduced in Appendix A of this book. This document was distributed at the meeting of 53 school boards, and 279 successfully completed returns were made. In addition, and in order to balance any inbuilt biases towards the keen, literate, or articulate board member, I also supplemented this survey material with some 60 extended personal interviews and a content analysis of the minutes of some 30 boards.

At all stages in this work I was fortunate to receive the very ready cooperation both of the local authority itself and of its senior officers and other employees. I was allowed a ready access to records, documents, and committee and school board minutes and, in this way, was able to build a clearer picture of the social processes at work within the city. I also spent many happy hours talking to leading politicians, senior officers, and teachers about the advantages and disadvantages of the new school board systems and, in this way, was able to attempt some dialogue between the theoretician and the practitioner. These relationships were undoubtedly greatly facilitated both by my own strong personal sympathies with the participatory ideals so consistently advocated by many of Sheffield's leaders and also our common membership of, and allegiance to, its dominant political party.

However, in spite of this excellent record of cooperation, I also found from an early stage in this investigation that I was entering a field which was difficult to research in an objective and dispassionate manner and which contained a number of challenging if, from a professional point of view, also extremely interesting problems. The sources of those perplexing dilemmas stemmed partly from the nature of the subject matter itself and partly from my professional role as a sociologist working within the magnetic orbit of Sheffield's educational system.

The subject matter

In the first place, I soon found that a number of difficult conceptual problems arose simply because in the course of my work I was forced to examine such generalized and diffuse terms as 'community', 'participation', and 'democracy'. These words not only reflect widely held sentiments and are liable, therefore, to evoke a varied series of images in different people's minds, but at the same time they are remarkably difficult to define in a precise and readily operational form. In the case of the term 'community' alone sociologists have already expanded a great deal of effort in trying to define the term, without reaching any appreciable degree of consensus. Thus, for example, Hillary in 1955 reported that he had reviewed 94 definitions of the concept and found that, beyond the recognition that 'people are involved in the community', there was little common agreement in the use of the term.[2] Obviously, similar difficulties exist in the case of the terms 'participation' or 'democracy'. These concepts not only evoke a wide range of images, but they are also typically used in a purposefully emotive way to describe states of government, both in the present-day world and in a number of postulated ideal societies.

These conceptual problems were exacerbated by the fact that the doctrines which characteristically employ these terms are rarely constructed in a social vacuum, but are constructed within the confines of a society and are typically used to legitimate the interests or policies of those who use them. Thus, in the case of Sheffield, I soon found out that these words did not simply exist within a 'nebulous limbo'; rather they had also become incorporated into some of the official doctrines and policies of the city's largest and most expensive public organization, its educational service. Thus, in attempting any form of critical analysis of such words as community, participation, or democracy, I was not simply concerned with the type of arid theoretical exercise which simply reviews mutually exclusive definitions of these terms; rather I was forced to examine quite elaborate statements of intent. These ideas were not only constantly utilized to justify the educational service's claim upon scarce public resources, but also its officers daily actions in a publicly emotive field where judgements were constantly being made about the type of education children shall receive.

Moreover, these ideas are not articulated within a static, one-dimensional framework, but within the dynamic social milieux of a complex, expensive, publicly funded educational service employing many thousands of people. This large organization is best thought of not in static terms but rather as an extremely flexible instrument which is constantly adapting itself to new problems and developments. This process inevitably involves large numbers of people and takes place within the context of a long corporate tradition and a series of institutional constraints. Consequently, I found it useful to think of this particular educational system as a dynamic conditioning field which had built up a life tradition of its own. These forces, which might be articulated through informal personal contacts, or in more formal group situations, not only inevitably tended to shape the behaviour of Sheffield's teachers, officials, and auxilliary staff but might also, unless explicitly acknowledged, act to subvert the aims and objectivity of such people as myself attempting to research within their orbit.

Research into education

These difficulties were further compounded by the ambiguous nature of the research process itself. As my work in Sheffield gradually progressed, I soon came to realize that, apart from those questions of personal independence and objectivity I have already referred to, there was also in this field, as in much of the rest of sociology, the problem of understanding what the researcher purported to explain. The reasons for this situation are complex; however, in part, they may be explained if one looks closely at the financial nexus linking the person or interest which sponsors a large-scale investigation and the specialist research worker or team which carries out the project. In part, it seems reasonable to argue that the social sciences have expanded rapidly in the last two decades precisely because their practitioners are expected to help solve complex human and social problems in such fields as housing, medicine, race relations, industrial relations, and so on. In short, the growth has been in those areas which have been seen to be of direct and practical help to society, and thus other areas such as the sociology of literature, leisure, or religion have been seen as marginal to these wider societal aims and have been badly neglected by those who fund large-scale research enterprises.

Largely because of this system of financial sponsorship, many research programmes tend, perhaps inevitably, to be sympathetic to the managerial perspective in the sense that they address themselves to those social phenomena conceived to be problematic by the leaders of agencies directly funding, or indirectly facilitating, their work. This productive locale tends to induce a curious bias in much contemporary research in the sense that the research worker never addresses the totality of his subject, but rather tends to concentrate upon those subsystems or elements within it which are of interest to those sponsoring his work. Thus, largely as a result of this situation, much of what has been labelled as industrial sociology had been funded by management and has been concerned with finding out ways in which the worker can be fitted more adequately into his job, so that, in this way, the efficiency and profitability of the enterprise may be increased. The converse, and perhaps in the long term more useful question, 'How to fit the job to meet the natural biological rhythms, or innate social, or intellectual interests of people working in industry?', has until recently been badly neglected by research workers, if not always by 'idealogues' concerned with the ideals, if not the practical technological structure, of an alternative society. In the same way, much of what is currently taken for political sociology, with its plethora of opinion polls and survey enquiries, is funded either by the press or para-statal agencies and tends to give a misleadingly one-dimensional view of its subject matter in that it suggests that electoral choices are the only legitimate areas of political activity and other types of action are invalid.

In the same way, similar pressures are obviously at work within the field of education in the sense that most large-scale research is conducted either directly by the state or by a state-funded agency and has in the main been concerned with improving the efficiency of, or, as in my case, assessing the impact of, a structural change in organization within a publicly funded and controlled service. Thus, much energy has been expended collecting what remains in essence a vast amount of fragmented and disparate data on isolated subunits of the educational system, on the efficiency of various types of selection processes, on individual school success and failure, on teaching methods, and on the curriculum. However, little empirical work has been done from a position which is not only independent of the educational system itself but also sees the latter's organization and function as problematic within our society. This type of alternative perspective might well be concerned with an examination of the total structure of formal education, both publicly and privately funded, its value system, rituals, and functions within what many people believe to be a highly inegalitarian, class-stratified, capitalist society.

In short then, in the course of my work in Sheffield, I came to the conclusion that, in the case of the study of education, just as in the case of medicine or industrial relations or politics, one may usefully distinguish between what may be seen from a theoretical point of view as two different types of work: namely, studies which may be categorized as a 'Sociology in Education', and those which attempt, despite all the difficulties contingent upon objectivity and funding, to be a 'Sociology of Education'. Although in practice these two categories are not always exclusive and contain a number of overlapping elements, nonetheless this distinction is useful in that it helps to alert us to the fact that different research locales and different research perspectives can produce different research strategies and surprisingly contradictory research results.

Thus, to return to the subject matter of the present study — school boards — a 'Sociology in Education' might well address itself to the type of 'middle-range' topics currently of interest to those administrators and politicans who wish to involve a wider cross-section of the public in the management of schools. These might include:

The social class of governors.

Length of service and links with the community.

Previous educational experience and knowledge of the local school system.

The work of school boards; which topics are discussed and which are neglected?

Naturally, research on all of these topics would be useful and of great help to those people who were interested in improving the efficiency of the present school board system; however, it would not offer the kind of perspective implicit in a true 'Sociology of Education'. The latter study might well proceed from a vantage point which saw the entire school management system as problematic and its field of concern might include:

Power and control within the school system.

The values of providers and of clients.

School boards and school rituals.

The legitimization of the decision-making process.

Naturally, the results of the latter type of study might not always be perceived as of direct use or practical benefit to the present generation of politicians and administrators currently looking after the public's school system. Indeed, it might be directly construed as 'threatening' to their present position. However, it might also stimulate change in the sense that it questions established conventions, and in this way helps people to think more critically about the nature of the society they live in at present and the one they might wish to live in in the future.

The production of knowledge

In general, the evidence suggests that the type of study which may be categorized as a 'Sociology in Education' is likely to be produced when one, or a combination of, the following factors are present to influence the production of research knowledge.

In the first place, it tends to be produced because the research worker himself has not been socialized into the 'mores' of an independent profession. He typically attempts to combine two disparate functions — those of an 'educationalist' and those of a 'social scientist'. This may occur because the person concerned was originally trained as a teacher, subsequently worked in a school or college, and only at a later stage in his life acquired the type of further qualification enabling him to embark on his second career as an educational researcher. In short, he has been socialized at an early and formative stage in his life into the teaching profession and he may find it difficult to take the kind of independent stance which constantly questions the 'taken-for-granted-everyday references' of his former colleagues. In the second place, many research workers must, by the logic of their working situation, collaborate with a wide range of professional educationalists — administrators, teachers, inspectors, advisors, and so on. Consequently, they often find they are under great moral pressure, which may ultimately be reinforced by financial constraints, to look at those middle-range problems which are currently worrying our present-day managerial elites within the public's school system. Finally, many research workers, particularly if they have been working within the educational system for a long time, tend to have built up a series of strongly affective social relationships with a wide network of people concerned with education. In other words he is subject to the influences of a dynamic social conditioning field of friendship which can, unless he is strongly alerted to its influence, cause him to lose his sense of perspective and make him reluctant to raise radical or unpleasant issues, less he lose his source of funding, or put at risk his personal relationships. For all these good reasons, he largely tends to concern himself with what he, and other people, see as practical problems. The emphasis gradually becomes one of collaboration with practising 'educationalists' and the result is usually an attempt to expand the latter's technical knowledge, rather than to question the latter's activities or role within the social system.

The sociology of education

Largely as a result of this situation, little of what might be categorized as a fully articulated 'Sociology of Education' has been produced in England and Wales, in the sense that it is the product of work which has firstly been independently funded, secondly been produced in research agencies which are truly independent of the public educational service, and thirdly regards the present publicly funded schooling system as problematic and is concerned with taking a total view of what may be seen as a diffuse but nonetheless recognizable status interest. This work might well examine the latter's place within the present political, legal, and cultural structure of society; it might look in detail at the organization of educational knowledge, patterns of recruitment to the service, and its relationship to other social, cultural, and economic institutions. In all cases, it would work on the assumption that it was unwise to take current educational definitions as objective truths; rather these ought to be seen as problematical and treated as topics for investigation. Finally, it might well acknowledge that its sources of data did not only lay in a study of 'what men say' in assessments of attitudes and opinion, but might well extend to an analysis of 'what men do', both in the context of organized patterns of behaviour, specific interests, and the pattern of interaction between institutions.

Naturally, this attempt to practice a 'Sociology of Education' is fraught with a range of problems. In part, this is because the refusal to give due credence to conventional explanations, or due deference to the official rationale of a strongly entrenched organizational interest or status order, risks provoking the wrath of those we study. This is hardly surprising, for the attempt to view the claims of the administrator or professional as problematic, to give an equal amount of time and attention to the things their clients say and do, is always likely to generate suspicion and mistrust within the upper echelons of any social order the sociologist chooses to scrutinize. Perhaps, inevitably, the person who attempts a 'Sociology of Education' will be accused of bias. This is not surprising because the type of work he does is inevitably the product of an exploratory perspective which is concerned with viewing all social relationships as problematic. This practice invariably tends to upset those conventional hierarchies of credibility within which the highest members of an institutional or status order claim the right to 'define things as they really are'; and perhaps predictably, his subjects, be they teachers or administrators, will, as well-socialized members of their profession, tend to take up the interests of their leaders against him, if he persists in asking the kinds of questions they define as illegitimate.

Perhaps one very good reason for this reaction was elaborated by Howard Becker who suggested that, in one very real sense, the leaders of any publicly funded institution are the victims of their office.[3] These people are given formal and publicly acknowledge positions of responsibility within society, are expected to carry out certain designated objectives, and are held to be formally accountable for their actions. However, simply because people do not always behave, and institutions do not always perform, as they are expected to, then their leaders are forced to reconcile what is often the considerable gulf between the official view of what society expects of them, and what actually goes on within them. In this process of adjustment leaders are forced to cloak the fact that, for example, prisons do not always reform their inmates, doctors do not always heal their patients, and schools do not always educate their pupils.

Naturally, a critical 'Sociology of Education', or medicine, or public welfare, cannot only illustrate in some detail the consistent tendency for the expectations of society to become deflected or aborted within the context of those institutions which are expected to facilitate them, but can also spotlight the way in which the leaders of public institutions explain away these failures. However, precisely because it must do this task, the 'Sociology of Education' involves its practitioners in a personal dilemma, for they may provoke, often unwittingly, the distrust and even open anger of those they study. This problem may become particularly acute and personally stressful if, as in my case, as I pointed out in the introduction to this chapter, one has strong personal sympathies with the participatory democratic ideals of Sheffield's civic leaders and also enjoys close personal, if not professional, relationships with them.

Research into the Sheffield board system

It seems then that in the study of school boards, as in the study of any other element within the educational system, it is possible to work within two very different traditions. On the one hand, we may possibly, because of our too close identification with the values of the educational interest themselves, choose to adopt one of a series of research postures which may be categorized as falling within the general limit of a 'Sociology In Education'. This type of study might well take for granted current hierarchies of credibility, it might make a close study of 'what men say', but neglect to look at 'what they do', and it might produce a limited amount of technical information which was primarily of interest to those administrative and advisory groups responsible for organizing the present school system. Conversely, one might attempt a more radical approach and, working within the wider traditions of one's discipline, attempt a more far-reaching study which did not accept conventional hierarchies of credibility, which examined ideologies within the context of the groups they served, and which made a 'taken-for-granted' reference that something more than a pattern of belief will lie behind the espousal of a new set of ideas by an organizational leadership or status elite.

However, whatever choice is made, it must not be assumed that research is a static process; rather it involves the research worker in an ongoing process of social interactions, both with one's subject matter, ongoing developments in one's academic discipline, and events taking place in the everyday world.

Quite naturally, in the normal course of events, one's original ideas are questioned, old questions are reformulated or refined, and new ones posed and acted upon. Thus, although most research reporting tends to give a neatly distilled account of the project's initiation, development, and completion, in fact this culmulative wisdom is usually gained in what is both a lengthy and untidy series of working processes. Most reports tend, by their very nature, rarely to be true to themselves in the sense that they explicitly acknowledge the ambivalence of the research process itself and the intellectual growth of the people working upon it; rather in practice the completed report reflects one short, penultimate moment of reflection and assessment towards the end of the projects life span.

In my own case, when I started this work over four years ago, my 'take off' perspective was very largely due to my productive locale, one which might well be categorized as a 'Sociology in Education'. I was primarily concerned with finding answers to a series of middle-range questions such as the social antecedents, motivations, and opinions of school governors I tended to rely heavily upon attitudinal survey data and I produced a number of research reports and articles which have been favourably received by professional journals catering for the needs of administrators and educationalists.[4]

However, during the course of my work in Sheffield, I became aware, as I hope I have made clear in this chapter, that this perspective was inadequate and could not offer a satisfactory explanation of the role of school boards within the local school system. In view of this assessment, I want, in the following chapters, to present my readers with some fragments of what attempts to be the first tentative contribution towards the study of school boards, written from a research context which explicitly attempts to construct a 'Sociology of Education'. This study suffers from the constraints of a work which has been privately funded, both in the sense that it was financed from my own pocket and was largely written up in my spare time. However, these limitations offered me, at the same time, the obvious advantage that I was a 'free man' working both independently of any funding agency and responsible to no one but myself and my professional conscience. Unfortunately, I have not had time to attempt an exhaustive study of all aspects of the school board system and, because of this, my readers may feel that, in what follows, some areas, such as the role of auxiliary workers, local ward party politics, or the place of the coopted governor, are only fleetingly referred to. For the same reasons, I have only in the final chapter referred in the baldest of ways to the types of democratic structures which might replace the present system of decision making in education. This being said, what I have tried to do is to attempt a systematic and dispassionate appraisal of the role of those four specific interests most directly and obviously effected by recent school board reforms — the parents of children, the teachers of these children, the headteachers of the schools, and those officials and politicians directly concerned with the administration of education. Thus, while each of the subsequent chapters may also deal obliquely with a number of contingent issues, such as the role of the community representative, access to training opportunities, the conduct of meetings, and so on, the substantive focus of the study will remain spotlighted on the social actions of these four specific interests. This strategy will, I hope, achieve two objectives. Firstly, it will enable my readers to form a 'clearer appreciation' of the ways in which school boards work within the wider context of Sheffield's school system. Secondly, because this latter structure is so closely 'in line with' the Taylor Committee's major recommendations, it will perhaps give my readers some indications of the ways in which these proposals are likely to affect both people working within, and the clients of, the nation's school system in the latter half of the twentieth century. This being said, we may now return to the central theme of this work and perhaps because this interest was most directly affected by the decision to create individual and representative managing or governing bodies in each of the city's schools, first look at the influence of these reforms upon the role of headteachers in Sheffield.

Notes and references

1.   For the sake of brevity, I shall use the term governor, both to refer to school managers, who generally look after schools in the primary sector, and school governors who generally look after schools in the secondary sector.

2.   G. A. Hillary, 'Definition of Community: areas of agreement', *Rural Sociology*, Vol. 20, pp. 111-123.

3.   Howard Becker, 'Whose Side Are We On?', in *The Relevance of Sociology*, edited by Jack Douglas, Appleton-Century-Crofts, 1970.

4.   In particular see 'Adult Education for School Government', *Adult Education*, May 1974, Vol. 47, No. 1; 'School Governors in Adult Education', *Adult Education*, Vol. 47, No. 5, January 1975; 'A Seat on the School Board', *Education Guardian*, February 24, 1976, and 'School Governors in Sheffield', *Trends in Education*, June 1976.

CHAPTER 4

HEADTEACHERS AND SCHOOL GOVERNORS

Introduction

My readers will perhaps find it not surprising to learn that at first many
Sheffield headteachers were extremely worried about their authorities
proposals to break with their long centralized traditions of administration and establish individual and representative boards for each of its
schools. This disquiet was perhaps partly due to a natural
conservatism, and partly due to the uncertainty associated with
negotiating a new set of social relationships with an unknown and predominantly lay group of people. One Sheffield headteacher expressed
the views of many of his collegues when he told me:

> I was against it at first. The city had managed for many years with its
> primary schools being run by the schools sub-committee of the education
> committee, and I saw no need to change it. Indeed, I was anxious about
> the authority's proposals since I had heard so many nasty stories from
> colleagues in other parts of the country about governors trying to
> interfere with the curriculum and the proper professional concerns of
> teachers.

Potential loss of freedom

A number of headteachers took the view that the new board system
posed a serious threat to their traditional personal autonomy, while a

few simply saw the new participatory system as a public and formal confirmation of a subtle policy which sought to undermine their traditional 'leadership role', and transform it into that of a chief executive directly responsible to a powerful representative body. Some headteachers told me how much they had worried about the details included in the articles of the new boards and, in particular, the legal requirement that 'there shall be full consultation at all times between the headteacher and the Chairman of governors', and the direction that 'all major changes in the school shall be reported to the governors'.

This was mainly because they thought that these kind of legalistic stipulations might not only limit their general effectiveness as leaders, and stimulate a general 'looking-over-the-shoulder mentality', but would also increase their administrative burdens and make for indecisiveness in their day-to-day reactions to the crisis situations typically confronting a modern headteacher. One head made this very clear when he said,

> I was not terribly enthusiastic about the new boards. I saw them as a further bureaucratic assignment which my superiors had decided to load on me. I took the view that I had better accept the inevitable and that it was what my masters wanted, then it was my duty to do my best to make it work in the long term interests of the school.

However, perhaps the one feature of the new board system giving the greatest general concern to Sheffield's headteachers was the formal requirement that the managers were 'through the agency of the headteacher to have general direction of the conduct and curriculum of the school', and that they were to receive at their meetings 'the report of the headteacher on the organisation, curriculum, expenditure and activities of the school'.

Many headteachers were initially worried that well-meaning but misinformed lay managers might use these powers to interfere too closely in what they saw as their proper professional concerns. One headteacher made this explicit when he said,

> There was always a danger that governors or managers might tread over the delicate line, which separates their functions from those of the headteacher, who is responsible for the internal organisation of the school. There was always the danger that boards would tend to get at cross purposes with their heads, and try to interfere in the curriculum and other matters which were properly a professional concern.

This initial reaction was not simply a case of professional conservatism; rather many headteachers were worried that the new boards might tend to seriously limit the progress of some of the most innovatory curriculum developments taking place in their schools. They felt it might be difficult to convince a predominantly lay board, which was unfamiliar with the complexities of modern educational policy, of the merits in, or desirability of, introducing new developments into their schools. There were, of course, many good practical reasons for their disquiet, for some of the most radical innovations in English education in the last thirty years have been introduced in the primary sector, where in the main headteachers have not been fettered by the presence of effective lay managing bodies or a suffocatingly close supervision from their local authority inspectorate. Largely, as a result of this freedom, they have often been able to carry through some quite fundamental innovations in their schools' curricula and teaching methods. Consequently, it was hardly surprising that some Sheffield headteachers were worried that under the new participatory board system they might lose their effectiveness as the powerful, innovatory leaders of a professional team, and become little more than chief executive officers accountable to generally conservative lay boards, who were unfamiliar with the detailed day-to-day problems of their schools, or the latest trends in educational research and development. One headmaster of a large comprehensive school expressed this anxiety most cogently when he told me,

> There is very little the governors can do to help me as far as the internal organisation and curriculum of this school is concerned. They can't possibly know better than the professional who is working at the coal face. If some lay person tells me what to do without giving me the wherewithal to do it. I'll tell him to shut up. Lay boards don't tell doctors what to do, they respect his professional competence, the same is true of teachers. Of course I dont mind lay governors discussing educational issues, but they mustn't try and subvert the professional's judgement on these matters.

The strains of the headteacher's role

However, this initial response to the new board system was not simply a reflection of the headteachers' perhaps quite natural desire for the maximum amount of freedom and flexibility in their working situations; it also had deeper roots and must also be looked at in terms of their structural positions within Sheffield's school system. In spite of their official designation, I soon found out that most headteachers I met rarely had the time or opportunity to develop a substantial teaching programme; rather most of them performed an essentially managerial function and were concerned with the effective deployment of their school's human and physical resources. They were largely responsible for the overall organization of their school, the allocation of its financial resources, the appointment of staff, the admission and exclusion of its pupils, and the general nature of its educational provision. They were also, largely because of their dominant position, able to exert a considerable influence on the daily lives of their teachers and through them upon their pupils and the wider community. They were not only largely responsible for the initial selection and appointment of their staff, but were also in a key position to award, or to withhold, promotional opportunities from them. In the same way, they could direct them into congenial or uncongenial teaching situations, and ultimately, since they were invariably approached for references, were in an unrivalled position to influence their future career prospects.

However, I soon found that although headteachers enjoyed wide powers, their unique position as what at times appeared to be quasi-baronial figures in their own independent fiefdoms also generated its own peculiar set of problems. In the first place, simply because most schools are not organized as democratic institutions, but possess an essentially hierarchic line-management structure, then it was extremely difficult for a series of balanced social relationships to develop between the headteacher, who after all stands at the apex of an institutional power structure, and the remainder of the staff. Most headteachers occupied a strategic position where they were able to mobilize so many sanctions against people and policies they found undesirable, and so much patronage in support of those they found acceptable, that it became virtually impossible for their subordinate staff to engage in an open and free dialogue with them. The structural imperatives of these basically asymmetrical series of social relationships were perhaps unconsciously reflected in the everyday language of the staffroom. In Sheffield, as typically occurs in the rest of England, teachers customarily referred to their headteachers using such concepts as, 'the benevolent dictator', 'a liberal autocrat', the 'old man', or more simply the 'boss', or the 'gaffer'. These labels were not only used as slightly ironical terms of praise, but also reflected, perhaps unwittingly, the basic social if not geographic space separating the head from the ramainder of his staff.

In the second place, I also soon found that many headteachers in Sheffield also suffered from all of those traditional psychological discomforts and anxieties which are classically associated with people occupying what is perhaps best labelled as 'the man in the middle role' in society. They were not simply administrators primarily responsible for the effective deployment of their schools' staff and physical resources, but at the same time, and largely because of the centralized traditions of the Sheffield school system, they were also forced to assume a quasi-political role in the community. Thus they were typically 'caught between' and at times 'torn between' conflicting demands from local pressure groups, their teachers, pupils, parents, and local authority advisory staff. They not only had to balance all of these conflicting interests, but at the same time had to act as general advocates of their school, and seek to maintain good relationships with all allied institutions and interests in the surrounding community.

Finally, what is perhaps best seen as a series of interrelated structural and cultural developments has tended to increase the magnitude of all these problems in the last twenty years. In simple structural terms, the increasingly elaborate nature of the division of educational labour within schools, the increasing employment of graduates and subject specialists, and the growth in the size of all educative institutions has simply meant that the modern headteacher must develop new skills in, and spend most of his time performing, what may be seen as essentially managerial and coordinative tasks. At the same time, wider cultural changes have led both those who exercise power and those who are subject to it to question the legitimacy of many traditional structures of authority. Largely as a result of these complex developments, many of the headteachers I spoke to in Sheffield appeared to be suffering from a severe identity crisis in the sense that they were no longer the 'inner-directed', morally righteous, autocratic figures who were once so overtly conscious of their educative mission; rather they tended to be 'other-directed', mild-mannered, often diffident men, who were explicitly conscious of their power, but were at the same time uncertain as to how to use it wisely. These people often told me that they found their isolated, but peculiarly visible 'man in the middle' situation particularly distressing, since it subjected them to so many different, and often competing, interests and value systems. Some parents, teachers, and pupils expected them to display traditional qualities of leadership, and to uphold what were once seen as widely accepted community values; others were more critical of what they saw as the autocratic role of headteachers and their own marginal or subordinate position within the educational decision-making process.

Headteachers and elected representatives

In short then, largely as a result of all the pressures generated by this difficult working situation, it was not surprising to find that many Sheffield headteachers were worried about their authorities' proposals to introduce into the city what was at the time one of the most fully democratized school board systems in the country. Thus, although, as we have already seen, the proposal to include elected parents' representatives on school boards was receiving widespread political support by the late 1960s, many headteachers were not altogether convinced of the utility of this measure. They continued to worry that these elections would be dominated by the articulate 'pushing' middle-class parent who might support policies which were not in the long-term interests of all their children, and might also utilize their position to interfere in what they saw as matters of proper professional rather than lay concern, such as streaming, reading schemes, and examination strategies.

However, if some headteachers, particularly those who had traditionally followed a policy of discouraging a too active parental involvement in their schools, were worried about parental representation on governing bodies, they tended to feel even more threatened by the proposals for teacher representation. This was seen at the time to be a radical departure which might have considerable repercussions upon the existing power structure within schools. Under the new board system, teachers were not only to be given representation on the body which considered the appointment of the head and deputy headteacher but, perhaps more vital as far as the day-to-day life of the school was concerned, could examine and critically discuss, 'the headteacher's proposals for head of department and other above scale posts within the establishment approved by the authority' and recommend candidates for 'any posts carrying allowances above the basic scale which are to be filled by promotion inside the school'.

This general concern about the impact of the Sheffield reforms upon the internal power structure and status hierarchy of the school system was obviously highlighted by the decision to include representatives of the nonteaching staff — school secretaries, caretakers, dinner ladies, cooks, and cleaners — on their school's governing body. Their presence on the new Sheffield boards was of course in part an official recognition of the importance of the work of a group which has always done the least prestigious work in schools. However, it was also in some ways a gentle reminder to headteachers that, although these people have often been regarded as marginal to central educational tasks, they were in fact extremely important people who were not only very influential in the informal life of the school, but who, unlike most teaching staff, also lived locally and thus represented an excellent means of maintaining communication with the surrounding community. Nonetheless, whatever the merits of Sheffield's decision to include representatives from the nonteaching staff on school boards, their formal presence and potential involvement in discussion on such key issues as school policy, the curriculum, financial allocation, and staff appointments and promotions, made headteachers apprehensive. This was not only because their presence threatened to upset their school's traditional status hierarchy, but also because it might possibly lead nonteaching staff to ask fundamental questions about their present marginal role, or the utility of the social barriers separating them, and their work, from that of the professional teaching staff.

In short, I found that, although the Sheffield reforms were not introduced in the teeth of bitter opposition, local headteachers tended to take a generally cautious attitude to these changes. This concern sprang quite naturally from their own peculiarly isolated but pivotal position within the school system. They were worried that the new boards might not only diminish their authority, but also lead to a gradual weakening of their managerial role and their capacity to act both as educational innovators and leaders of an effectively integrated team of professional workers.

The headteacher's responses to the new board system

Although many headteachers had misgivings about the wisdom of the Sheffield reforms in general, and the inclusion of parents, staff, and nonteaching representatives on their school boards in particular, I soon found that their own experiences of the day-to-day workings of the new system over the last five years have gradually convinced most of them of the merits of their authority's initiative. They found that their new boards have tended to strengthen their managerial prerogative and have not only been a means of making contact with groups previously unfamiliar with the school, but have also acted as generally supportive bodies tending to protect them from some of the worst tensions associated with their peculiarly isolated 'man in the middle' position. An early official appraisal of the work of the new board system also reflected this changing mood; it reported that many headteachers were speaking enthusiastically about the ways in which their schools had benefited from the new boards as these bodies were drawing together groups of 'knowledgeable people' who really cared about education and were keen to serve their local schools. It also records that headteachers pointed out how valuable the new participatory system had been in 'tapping new sources of public service', and in attracting the 'splendid assortment of educational talent and zeal, local and city wide', which had been drawn in to help their schools.[1]

These initial and official impressions were reinforced by my own work in Sheffield. A number of heads, particularly those working in comprehensive schools in the middle-class suburban areas of the city, also told me how much they had come to value their governing bodies as insulating devices, protecting them from the buffets of local political controversy. This was mainly because as heads of large comprehensive schools they had, perhaps inevitably, found themselves much more closely involved in the local political process than was ever the case when pupils either went to grammar or secondary modern schools, and when most people pragmatically accepted the inevitability, if not the legitimacy, of a selective secondary educational system. In Sheffield in the mid-1970s many parents not only had strong views about the merits of comprehensive education in general, but also about streaming, examination policies, and discipline. One head made this quite clear when he said,

> I feel much more of a political figure as a head of a comprehensive school than I ever did when I was in charge of a grammar school. People in this locality of course did not all agree with the comprehensive idea, they assumed that this was going to be a 'rough school' since it was to be non selective, and they were determined to take a close interest in our activities and make certain that their children did not suffer. Moreover, I am a neighbourhood school now, my parents are no longer scattered all over the city, they live locally, and it is much easier for them to keep a 'close eye' on their children's progress in this school. I feel as a head that I am much more visible, and liable to be challenged about my policies than was ever the case in my old grammar school days.

It was perhaps quite natural that in this kind of volatile social situation that headteachers had learnt to attach more importance to their governing boards than was traditionally the case. From their point of view, these lay bodies could not only offer effective moral support for the policies of their schools, but were also able to act as effective filtering devices which could direct local criticism into the appropriate consultative channels. This process consequently lessened the probability of a situation of conflict developing between the headteacher and the leaders of factions within his school's local community or catchment area.

Many headteachers also told me how much they appreciated the ways in which the new board system had allowed them to establish new links with people and interest groups who were not encapsulated within the educational system for most of their working life, but who, perhaps because they were working in a variety of industrial and commercial situations, held points of view perhaps more typical of lay feeling generally. Consequently, they had soon found that their governing bodies provided them with an excellent sounding board through which they could judge the potential public support for, or opposition to, any policy they were planning to introduce into their school. The head of a small comprehensive school in the north of the city made this testing function quite explicit when he said, 'I find my governors a great help, they are a windtunnel I can use for experiments with my new designs. I think gosh!! if there are no reactions from them, then the idea must be fairly acceptable and I'll try it on in school.'

Nonetheless, while most headteachers saw their governors as basically helpful and supportive groups of people, a few of them still retained a predilection for Sheffield's older centralized system of administrative control. This was partly because they took the view that the assessment of priorities in education was purely a matter for the expert, partly because they thought a predominantly lay board could not serve any useful purpose in what they saw was a purely professional matter — the education of children — and partly because they were worried that the most vociferous and influential boards would secure the largest slices of the city's resources for their own schools.

Headteachers and new board members

However, apart from this critical minority of generally older people, most headteachers tended to value the new board system, and few continued to see the boards in terms of a real or potential threat to their authority. They had come to learn that their school boards were in the main generally supportive bodies, which not only helped them to maintain their own positions as managerial innovators, but which also made them less vulnerable to uninformed or radical criticism of their schools' policies.

Largely as a result of this situation, most newly appointed board members told me that they not only tended to look towards their head-teachers for advice, but also found their headteachers helpful in initiating them into the duties and responsibilities associated with their office. This impression was also clearly supported by the survey data. As we can see from the following table, the majority of people who replied to the following question,

Which people were most helpful when you first became a manager or governor?

reported that their headteacher had either solely, or in conjunction with the clerk or chairman, played a great part in helping them to settle into their new office.

Of course in the first stages of the introduction of the new system, some headteachers were inexperienced in the work of school boards and the chairman, clerk, or another person with previous experience of this

The people most helpful to new board members

	Primary Schools	Secondary Schools	Special Schools	Total
	N = 262 %	N = 54 %	N = 28 %	N = 344 %
The Chairman	11	11	4	10
The Headteacher	51	43	71	52
The Clerk	11	4	8	9
A Fellow Member	7	10	—	7
The Head and Clerk	3	—	—	2
The Chairman and Clerk	1	—	—	1
The Chairman and Head	4	6	4	4
Everybody	6	9	4	7
No Answer	6	17	9	8
	100%	100%	100%	100%

work might also take the initiative and help the newcomer. In some cases, all members were new to the school board system and all helped each other; in other places the clerk, or a local politician, had a fairly clear idea of the authorities' aims and took a leading role in initiating newcomers into the responsibilities of their office. However, as the system has gradually settled down and as people have gained experience of this type of work, then the influence of the headteacher has naturally grown, for they are usually one of the longest-serving members of the board and many new members, particularly the 'short service' parental representatives, tend to depend upon them for an introduction to the nature of their responsibilities and duties.

The growth of affective social relationships

This natural tendency for new board members to rely upon their head-teachers for guidance was reinforced by their own generally positive attitude towards the local educational service. These sentiments were articulated very clearly within the survey data and, in particular, in the pattern of replies I received to the question,

Why did you want to become a school governor/manager?

Apart from headteachers who were ex-officio members of boards and consequently had little choice in this matter, and teachers who generally said they wanted to represent their professional interests and be involved in their school's policy-making and administrative affairs, most people tended to give very general and sometimes exceptionally vague answers to this question. They obviously mentioned their interest in children and educational affairs, but apart from these fairly diffuse observations their main motivation was the desire to help, and serve, the teachers and children in their local school. Most of their replies tended to confirm many of the intuitive feelings of those who had fought to introduce a new system into Sheffield. A substantial reservoir of interest and latent goodwill for schools existed in the community at large, and the reforms had done much to mobilize these resources into the service of education. However, most people found it extremely difficult to articulate these sentiments in a precisely formulated series of statements; rather they characteristically gave such general and vague replies as, 'I wanted to serve the school and its community'; 'I wanted to take part in the life of the community and have some small say in matters.'

People had not sought this office because they had a personal axe to grind, or any definitive ideas about how their school or its teachers should conduct their affairs; rather most of them subscribed to what might best be called an ethic of community service and simply wanted to become involved with, and help in whatever way was possible, the work of their local school. This generally diffuse, if at the same time constructive and supportive, series of sentiments was expressed in a variety of different ways and included 13 percent who simply expressed some kind or form of general interest in education, 11 percent who reported an interest in community affairs, 16 percent who simply wanted to help their local school, 11 percent who felt an innate concern as parents for the education and future of their children, and 16 percent who simply said they were interested in the welfare and well-being of children. In contrast, only a few people gave passive replies and indicated they had originally been reluctant to take up this work, had simply become a manager or governor because someone had persuaded them to do so, or had been nominated without their knowledge. The greatest number of these 'reluctant draftees' were found amongst non-teaching staff and this may be because many of these people, after occupying a relatively subordinate position within the school system for most of their lives, needed a great deal of sympathetic encouragement by either a local councillor or their headteacher before they were willing to stand for this office.

In general, as one might reasonably expect, the balance of emphasis within this widely diffused concern for education and community service tended to vary between different types of board members. The majority of parental representatives reported seeking office because of their quite natural interest in the current welfare and future well-being of their children. One respondent, Mrs. Smith, was fairly typical when she said, 'I wanted to participate in the organisation and administration of the school in which my children are to be educated.'[2] Another parent, Mrs. Brown, recorded similar sentiments: 'I am very interested in the well-being of mine and other children and thought this the best way of showing my interest.'

In contrast, while many coopted board members also mentioned these parental concerns, a far higher proportion mentioned their interest in becoming more actively involved in local community affairs. The Reverend Bailey, an Anglican priest, made this distinction quite clear when he said, 'As the local vicar I wanted to act as a bridge between the school and the community.' Another coopted governor, police constable Clark, expressed a similar point of view: 'I am the local area constable and wanted to take a greater part in the activities of the community in which I live and work.'

Many of the people appointed to represent the education committee on school boards also had strong local interests and had often been involved in the 'rough and tumble' of local parish pump politics for many years. Mr. Green was a fairly typical member of this group. He told me, 'I was appointed by the local authority in recognition of my twenty years political work in this area, and because of my desire to help in some way the young element growing up in changing surroundings.'

Some of these political appointees were not only long experienced in local politics, but were also very sophisticated advocates of participatory forms of democracy, as the following statement by one Labour Party activist and school governor made quite clear:

> The community should accept part of the responsibility for the problems and trials of running a school, as well as simply enjoying the benefits. The teachers don't want to operate in isolation, they need to have positive feedback from people in non-educational streams of life in order to assess the viability and success of their work.

Nonetheless, although many of the governors appointed by the local authority had strong local interests, this was not always the case, and this group also contained many people who not only lived further afield, but who, because of their professional, business, or political activities, were able to bring to their school a different series of perspectives on educational affairs and a wide range of expert advice and cosmopolitan skills which often neatly complemented the interests of the local members. Mrs. Smith was fairly typical when she said, 'As a Principal Lecturer at the local College of Education I wished to be more closely involved in school work, and also to make available to my school such expertise as I have.' Mr. Jenkins brought his school a different but no less relevant type of experience: 'I was on the Education Committee until May 1973 and I wanted to maintain my contact with parents, staff, and children, and also give them the benefit of all my knowledge.'

Largely as a result of this generally positive attitude to education, most new governors tended to seek and, in the main, were successful in establishing strong effective relationships with their headteachers. This was not simply a personal impression but also emerged quite clearly from the survey data. Thus, as we can see from the following table, only

Relationships with headteachers

	Primary Schools	Secondary Schools	Special Schools	Total
	N = 244 %	N = 52 %	N = 27 %	N = 323 %
Exceedingly friendly	58	52	56	57
Friendly	36	40	37	37
Neither friendly nor unfriendly	3	8	7	4
Unfriendly	1	—	—	1
No Answer	2	—	—	1
Total	100%	100%	100%	100%

a very few governors indicated that any discordance or open conflict had developed between themselves and their headteachers, while in contrast most reported the development of strongly sympathetic and supportive bonds. No less than 57 percent of the sample reported they had 'exceedingly friendly relationships' with their headteachers; another 37 percent said they were just friendly; and only a minority, most of whom were recently appointed to their office, indicated that their relationships had not, as yet, passed beyond the formal stage.

The development of these generally harmonious relationships was also greatly facilitated by the attitude of most headteachers. Although, as we have already seen, some of them were initially wary of their authority's proposals for reform, they also made great efforts to generate good relationships with members of their school boards, and in many cases even before a member attended his first board meeting, he was invited to visit the head, discuss the problems facing the school, and receive a conducted tour of its buildings and surrounding playing fields.

However, these initial encounter sessions were not simply a means of cultivating goodwill, they also witnessed the beginnings of a subtle process which slowly incorporated the newcomer into the power structure of the local school system. Although this course of induction might take many forms, and vary with the needs of individual schools and social situations, it might typically have been achieved in the manner of the following scenario.

This account does not attempt to portray what happened to any specific governor in any specific Sheffield school; rather it is best thought of as an ideal construction which, drawing on the accounts I received from many governors, attempts to highlight some of the social processes which typically occur when a newcomer is first appointed to a school board.

A scenario of the incorporation process

The newly appointed board member is invited to the school and offered tea and biscuits in the headteacher's study. During the course of the meeting the headteacher remains sitting behind his large executive-type desk, but offers his guest a low but comfortable chair facing him. The discussion appears, at least on the surface, to proceed in a friendly and informal manner. The visitor probably talks about his own schooldays, his present work and leisure activities, and his interest in the welfare of children. The headteacher naturally tends to respond with his own anecdotal references, and also attempts to explain what he is trying to achieve in his school and the problems he is facing in pursuing these aims. At times the flow of conversation between them may be broken into, as the school secretary or a senior teacher finds it necessary to consult the head on some pressing administrative matter.

However, although this initial meeting is conducted in a friendly and informal manner, it is also a quite critical meeting for the future career of the newly appointed governor. This is because the first meeting with the 'freshman' gives the headteacher an excellent opportunity to sound out his interests and political views and to assess whether or not he is likely to offer any potential threat to his own long-term policies. If he suspects the latter is the case, then this apparently informal chat provides him with a good means of initiating his visitor into what he considers to be the appropriate role definitions for his new office.

This task of steering the new board member into what the headmaster may himself define as 'positive' or 'constructive' channels, may be accomplished in a number of different ways. In the first place, the process of conversion may be facilitated by the very structure of the inter-view situation itself. The dominating physical presence of the head-teacher, his strategic occupation of the desk of office, and the many urgent but nonetheless deferential requests for help which seem to put into his study, are all not only manifest indications of his power, but also tend to subtly convey the message that the new board member must be careful not to inadvertently place fresh burdens on the shoulders of this kindly but obviously overworked professional, who is unstintingly dedicating his life to the service of young children. In the second place, these initial meetings often tend to give the new board member the impression that the task of administering a school and directing its future development is a peculiarly complex matter which is best left to the appropriate professional manager, and in this way some of the most enthusiastic newcomers are effectively discouraged from taking too active an interest in the educational aims and objectives of their school. This is not of course to suggest that many headteachers don't encourage new board members to express their views; rather it is to note that these formal statements of intent are often followed by the subtle implicit, or explicit, rider that 'education is also a professional matter' and they would be wise to listen to the voice of experience.

Finally, the reeducation of the potentially dissident newcomer may be effectively accomplished by the ritual of the guided tour of the school. In the course of this perambulation his attention is constantly drawn to the pressing physical and financial needs of the school's fabric and equipment, its leaky roof, poor toilets, splintered floors, and crowded classrooms. The visitor is not only rapidly taught the lesson that education is a badly neglected service, and its teachers are devotedly labouring against impossible odds, but he also soon learns that he will be most useful in his new public role if he seeks to help and not criticize these worthy people.

Ironically, although the newcomer's attention is at all stages in this induction process drawn to the question of means, he is also reminded in many subtle ways that he is not expected, except in the most general terms, to ask questions about the ends of education. He soon learns that if he takes too close an interest in his school's curriculum, examination policy, or internal structure and administration, this approach is not only likely to be viewed with disapproval by the headteacher, but also by many of his fellow board members. This is mainly because most long-established governors, particularly those who are coopted or appointed by the local authority, have already developed strong affective links with their headteachers, and my dismiss the freshman's initiative as a

Should board meetings be open or closed?

	Primary	Secondary	Special
	N = 262 %	N = 54 %	N = 28 %
Yes (open)	16	8	10
No (closed)	82	92	90
No Answer	2	—	—

personally malicious and vindictive attack on the integrity of someone who is simply trying to do his best for children.

It is hardly surprising that most lay people experiencing this form of initiation are highly receptive to the role expectations of their head-teachers, and in most cases tend to accept without question the legitimacy of the part he wished them to play in the new board system.

This conversion of the hesitant but potentially critical outsider into the confident and helpful board member is of course greatly facilitated by the very secrecy of school board meetings. Partly because of the confidential nature of some of their work, partly because of their critical, if opaque, role in the school system, most governors' meetings are held in private and, as we can see from the following table, most people take the view that this is a natural and desirable state of affairs.

Thus, only a partial and, at best, highly stereotyped account of their activities is ever circulated to the school staff or general public. As a result of this secrecy, few people have the opportunity to familiarize themselves with the policy of school boards or the ways in which they conduct their business. Consequently, when the newly appointed or elected member attends his first meeting, he finds he is entering a strange new world. He is likely to be unfamiliar both with the issues which are under discussion, and, unless he is an experienced committee man, with the peculiar admin-politico style in which the new board conducts its business. He is also probably very dependent upon and, as we have already seen, usually looks towards his headteacher, clerk, or chairman for advice and information about the past experiences and present work of his board, the status and interests of fellow members, and the policies being pursued by the school. In short, he finds himself in a social situation where he is forced to 'learn on the job', and where most of the teaching is done by the headmaster, chairman, and clerk, with of course additional support from fellow governors and managers who, in their turn, have all been subjected to much the same kind of socialization process.

Role education and school boards

Although the above scenario is baldly sketched and capable of extensive refinement, it does help us to understand a little more fully why Sheffield governors tended to behave in the ways they did. At the same time, their general willingness to learn how they could best 'fit themselves neatly' into the established routine of their school board, their general acceptance of the commonplace assumption that 'I'll be able to pick it up as I go along', had a number of less obvious long-term implications for the local school system. In the first place, it meant that most people who serve on these important public bodies have accepted a form of education for themselves which is generally regarded as anachronisitic, and which is gradually being phased out of much of the remainder of the educational system. This is because learning on the job is essentially a craft form of activity, which may have a certain utility in a slowly changing world, but which is less appropriate to the dynamic technologically based society of the late twentieth century. It tends to be both time consuming and unsystematic, and, in the case of school boards, by the time most representative members such as parents have learnt enough knowledge to be effective, it is time for them to leave the board and be replaced by yet another freshman.

In the second place, learning on the job tends, like most other craft-orientated forms of education, to be a static form of learning. It only tends to familiarize the student with the status quo, and rarely encourages him to be imaginative and to seek alternatives to long-established practices and procedures. In the case of the school board, this usually means that the initiate simply learns the role definitions which the headteacher, clerk, or chairman think are appropriate for him to learn, and, unless he is a very unusual personality, or is politically sophisticated, he is unlikely to play a vigorous or independent role, but rather will generally support established conventions, policies, and their associated power elites.

This type of education is of course a cumulative process and is greatly facilitated by the strongly affective relationships which tend to develop between board members, and which may simply be the product of long

Relationships with fellow board members

	Primary	Secondary	Special	Total
	N = 262 %	N = 54 %	N = 28 %	N = 344 %
Close cooperation with all or most	72	46	60	65
Easy with some, difficult with others	9	15	5	10
Fairly formal	12	26	28	16
Discordant	1	—	—	2
No answer	6	13	7	7
	100%	100%	100%	100%

familiarity, a common interest in the school, a common allegiance to an ethic of service, or some collective experience of a challenging or critical situation. Consequently, as we can see from the following table, most respondents in the survey reported that they had developed 'close cooperative relationships' with all or most of their fellow board members and only 2 percent suggested that a discordant element had entered into their relationship.

The work of school boards

Largely as a result of the combined effect of all these very subtle social processes, most governors tended to generally accept their headteacher's view of what were their appropriate roles, and duties, within the school system. Moreover, on most boards, fresh arrivals generally tried to fit themselves into what they found was a pleasant and harmonious situation. One comprehensive headteacher described this intricate process of social negotiation and role definition very succinctly when he said,

> I was a bit worried about my new board at first, they were completely unknown to me, and they contained people who were very critical of non-selective schools. However, after the initial trial period, the system is shaking down well and there is a pretty clear understanding between us now about each others position in the general scheme of things.

Another headteacher said the same thing in a different way when he told me, 'I think our governors have settled down well now, they know what to do, and not to raise unpleasant issues of personality.'

Although this type of 'clear understanding' was not, as we have seen, usually negotiated between two sets of equal partners, but tended to be mediated very much on the head's own terms, it did also mean that the latter's initial worry that their new governors might concern themselves too closely with 'professional matters' had not occurred in practice. In general, most Sheffield boards have been reluctant to use their powers under the articles which direct them to 'receive the report of the head-teacher as the organisation, curriculum, expenditure and activities of the school, and through the agency of the headteacher have general directions of the conduct and curriculum of the school'; and they have been unwilling to discuss, except in the most general of terms when the headteacher gives his report, their school's curriculum, teaching methods, internal organization, or financial affairs. They have, in the main, accepted the legitimacy of the view that these issues are the appropriate professional concern of the headteacher and his staff, and that it is improper for them to interfere too closely in this area of their school's affairs. The primacy of this general assumption that the head-teacher should be left to get on with his job of leading and running his school largely explains why boards seemed to spend so little of their time examining or discussing what are after all not only some of the most important, but also some of the most fascinating aspects of the life of a school.

This general unwillingness to become too closely involved in what have traditionally been defined as professional matters was not simply a personal impression, but was also reflected quite sharply in the replies to a series of questions which examined the frequency with which governors discussed their school's curriculum, financial allocation, rules, teaching methods, or educational research in general. Consequently, as we can see from the following table, few board members reported discussing these quite critical matters on a regular basis; rather, most of them tended to spend the bulk of their time discussing routine administrative matters and maintenance and development problems.

This is not of course to imply that Sheffield's governors were un-concerned about education; indeed, as we have already seen, most of them were appointed to, or elected to, their school boards because of their manifest interest in the educational problems of young children.

Frequency of discussion of five key educational issues

	The Curri- culum	School Rules	Finance	Teaching Methods	Educa- tional Research
	N = 344 %	N = 344 %	N = 344 %	N = 344 %	N = 344 %
Regularly (three or more times a year)	11	3	34	6	9
Frequently (twice a year)	20	10	25	10	17
Infrequently (once a year)	37	37	30	25	30
Never	26	44	6	52	32
No Answer	6	6	5	7	12

Moreover, only a few people in the survey (16 percent) saw their main task as simply that of looking after the 'proper maintenance of the fabric of their school', and most of them (86 percent) said they thought they ought to discuss the educational aims and objectives their schools were pursuing. However, in spite of these general sentiments, in practice most governors were hesitant to raise these wider policy-related issues and spend much of their time discussing the aims, ends, and methods associated with the educational process taking place within their school. It seems probable that this reluctance was, in part, a reflection of their wish to avoid giving offence to their headteachers and thereby breaking the strongly affective bonds which have grown up between board members, and was in part due to their evident wish to avoid becoming involved too deeply in what they had been taught to believe were truly professional matters.

The headteacher's report

This diffidence was particularly evident in the way in which most school boards tended to deal with their headteacher's report. This item was of course in theory, if not always in practice, one of the most important points of their meeting, and was the occasion when the head-teacher gave a formal account of his stewardship and when governors fulfilled their overt function of taking responsibility for the 'general direction of the conduct and curriculum of the school'. However, it was not simply the formal occasion when they could familiarize themselves with the policies, problems, and achievements of their school, and in turn communicate them to the local community; it was also an excellent opportunity for them to ask critical questions and provide the professional teacher with the layman's often salutary, if sometimes illuminating, point of view.

Unfortunately, the evidence suggested that in practice most school boards did not always match up to this theoretical ideal; their head-teacher's report was often placed towards the end of the agenda and was often given and listened to in a somewhat perfunctory manner. This was hardly surprising, for a number of headteachers simply appeared to treat these occasions as a formality, and used the report record routine administrative matters and display the positive, if not the negative, side of their school's activities and achievements during the past term. Although, for the sake of confidentiality, the following composite example is based upon several different reports, it is not untypical of this type of eulogistic exercise.

Easton School

> Headmaster's report for the governors' meeting to be held on Friday, 11 October at 7.00 pm.
>
> 1 *Staff Changes* — The following staff have taken up their appointment at the beginning of this term:
>
>> Mr. Hunt (Rural Science)
>> Mrs. Smith (History)
>
> 2 The external examination results were very good. The percentage of G.C.E. passes was 85%. There were 76 Grade I passes in C.S.E.
>
> 3 Repairs have been completed to the school roof and work on the new bicycle sheds is near completion.
>
> 4 The school participated in a Sponsored Walk organized by the Variety Club of Great Britain, on Sunday, September 29, and raised nearly £200.00 for charity.
>
> 5 The school play *Hamlet* was well received by the audience on two nights. The involvement of Staff in the cast appeared to give added interest. Mr. Casey is to be congratulated on his first production for the school.

6 The following visits have been organized during the present term:

The Abbeydale Industrial Hamlet (1/11/77)

International Rugby Match, Twickenham (2/12/77)

The Sheffield Police Stables (10/11/77)

The Women's International Hockey Match, Wembley (31/10/77)

7 A Parents' Evening has been arranged for Tuesday 10/12/77 for pupils who entered school this term.

8 Canon Smith has kindly allowed us, as in previous years, to hold the Annual Carol Service in the local church.

9 I wish to ask the governors to confirm the allocation of the five occasional days for 1977/78 as follows:

Monday and Tuesday — 20/21 February 1978

Wednesday, Thursday, Friday — 25/26/27 October 1978

10 I enclose a brief account of school policy with regard to A-level choice.

Of course not all headteachers were content to simply give this type of bland and ritualistic account of their school's achievements in the last term. A number also recognized that this occasion could be usefully exploited as a means of galvanizing their governors into action on their school's behalf, and consequently their reports tended to concentrate on the more tangible and remedial aspects of the maintenance, building, or accommodation problems they were struggling with. However, although these initiations often sparked off a great deal of discussion and activity to solve these difficulties, it was only rarely that head-teachers extended their reports into the field of education proper, and made a determined effort to inform their boards about such items as books, equipment, examination policy, streaming, and so on. They were generally reluctant to introduce these topics and raise issues which would not only invariably stimulate a lengthy discussion about the long-term aims and interests of their school, but would also inevitably serve to educate their board members, and make them more sophisticated advocates of their school's educational policies in the surrounding community.

Paradoxically, even in those relatively rare social situations where head-teachers were manifestly attempting to initiate a general discussion on their school's educational aims and policies, most governors were reluctant to respond and become too closely involved in this debate. This was mainly because most of them tended to take the view that their headteacher was a friendly, but authoritative, person who was success-fully coping with a complex and extremely arduous job. Consequently, they were willing to discuss day-to-day administrative details but were generally reluctant to raise critical or fundamental questions of principle.

The reasons for what might at first glance seem this strangely deferential attitude are of course most complex, but might be explained in part in terms of the subtle incorporation processes I have already outlined in this chapter, partly because of a general reluctance, particu-larly by many working-class people, to become involved in a bitter and potentially divisive demarcation dispute, and partly in terms of the dominant social composition of so many managing or governing boards. As I shall illustrate in detail in the following chapter, a large proportion of board members were professional people who had, in the main, learnt to accept that one must fully respect the competence and professional integrity of one's fellow workers, lest they in turn question your own authority.

Largely, as a result of this situation, most school boards were not only reluctant to discuss their school's policies or aims, except of course in the most general terms, but also naturally tended to be ill informed about key areas of local educational policy. This was a generally un-fortunate situation and meant that, in many cases, governors had been remarkably ineffective either in representing the views, interests, and sentiments of local groups, or in making sure their school's policy did not become too isolated from the interests and values of its surrounding society. At the same time, their headteacher's reluctance to discuss the curriculum also meant that most governors were often quite ignorant about the details of their school's internal organization or long-term policy. Although this neglect may in the short term be quite a comfortable tactical situation for the headteacher, it also meant that in the long term his board was hampered from effectively playing its full 'advocacy role' in representing the interests of his school, either in the surrounding community or in the wider society.

Conclusions: new styles of democractic leadership

However, although most school boards were tactfully discouraged from taking too active an interest in the curriculum or internal affairs of their school, this is not to imply that they played a marginal role in the Sheffield school system. Their presence not only tended to strengthen the authority of the headteacher, but also encouraged him to develop a new, more flexible style of democratic leadership, and these factors helped him to cope quite successfully with many of the difficult problems which always emerge in times when the issue of 'who controls our schools?' is again troubling the public conscience.

Before the Sheffield reforms of 1971, the extremely centralized tradition of school government management left each headteacher in a peculiarly isolated and visible position, and he was extremely vulnerable to the criticism which inevitably starts to emerge when, as we saw in Chapter 1, a society raises fundamental questions about the justice of the system of social and political domination built into its present school system. Consequently, if a serious dispute broke out between a headteacher and his staff, parents or pupils, over such contentious issues as discipline, school uniforms, examination policy, or selection processes, then the headteacher was usually faced with the task of trying to resolve the conflict himself, or, if it became very serious, involving his local inspectorate and the city's education committee.

The new individual participatory board system not only tends to lessen the risk of this abrasive confrontation developing but, if it does occur, allows the headteacher to respond to the challenge on a local basis and in a more flexible manner. This is partly because the elected representatives of some of his potential critics — parents, teachers, auxiliary staff, and community groups — are all present on his school board and he is thus able to learn of and respond to their legitimate criticism at an early, and not at a later and potentially more explosive, stage of its development. It is also partly because the very presence of so many representatives of different and in theory potentially conflicting interest groups on his school board inevitably leads to their public identification with, if not acquiescence in, the policies of the school. It makes it more difficult for a critical group of students, teachers, or parents to challenge the headteacher on the emotive, if populist, grounds that he is an authoritarian leader and they, as groups of clients, workers, or inmates, are not consulted or even represented within the formal structure of the local school system.

Moreover, if in spite of all these insulating precautions, a serious local dispute does lead people to challenge their school's policies and the authority of its headteacher, then, under the new Sheffield system, the latter is able to respond in a much more flexible and adroit manner than was possible under the old centralized form of control. He is no longer faced with the personal tensions of his isolated 'man in the middle' position, but can initially discuss the matter with his chairman and other senior members of his school board and may then look towards a full meeting of his governors for advice and support in finding a specific and locally acceptable solution to the crisis. This approach not only has the advantage that the situation is a less personally stressful experience for the headteacher concerned, but also means that the final decisions resolving the dispute will be taken by a collective lay body and, as a result, the authority potentially damaging personal clashes with his local opponents.

It appears then that the new board system has enabled the headteacher to adopt a new, more flexible response to the problems of his school and community and at the same time has facilitated the development of a new, less brittle type of control, which in the long term promises to strengthen the present managerial prerogative within the school system. Despite some of their initial worries about the creation of individual school boards, most headteachers have found that in practice their governors have not attempted to challenge their authority or undermine their power, but have largely accepted the roles chosen for them. Consequently, most headmasters generally tend to see their governors as kindly, knowledgeable, and mainly professional people, who are invariably enthusiastic about the educational cause, are willing to lend their moral authority to the policies being developed by their school, but who don't usually wish to take too close an interest in its internal affairs or curriculum. One headmaster made this general attitude very explicit when he told me,

> I see my governors as advocates of this school. They are all terribly busy people and usually only come in on formal occasions. They don't simply have the time to spend visiting every week, but I don't think this matters since they know the school is running well and that I can rely upon their support in a crisis.

However, this being said and in order to gain a fuller and more rounded appreciation of the Sheffield reforms, it is now time for us to shift our focus away from those people who are essentially concerned with the management of schools and go on to look at the impact of the new participatory board system on those people who are mainly responsible for the effective daily functioning of the school system — the classroom teachers of the city.

Notes and references

1.   Report to Sheffield Schools Subcommittee, 11 January 1972.

2.   In order to respect the confidentiality of my respondents all names given in this and subsequent chapters are fictional.

3.   A content analysis of the minutes of 30 school boards is included in Appendix C.

CHAPTER 5

TEACHER PARTICIPATION ON SCHOOL BOARDS

Introduction

During the 1960s the case for introducing various kinds of schemes for workers' participation, both into the industrial and other related service sectors of the economy, was widely discussed and later became generally acceptable as a legitimate political objective. This development may perhaps in retrospect be seen by the historian as a belated attempt to 'catch up' with a wider European practice. Workers' representation on the boards of public and private enterprises has been obligatory in countries such as Norway, France, Federal Germany, and the Netherlands for many years and, in September, 1972, the draft Fifth Directive of the E.E.C. Commission called for the establishment of co-determination in all constituent countries. These initiatives were not only designed to secure a two-tier system of formal authority within an organization, but were also intended to guarantee the right of workers to formal representation on its managing board.

The case for extending workers' participation in all spheres of life is certainly a strong one and does not simply rest on a series of idealistic or Utopian premises; rather it can be strongly buttressed by many cogent moral, theoretical, and pragmatic arguments. Thus, it has been supported by the type of argument which makes an appeal to a general series of ethical principles and which would, therefore, tend to see this type of involvement as morally good in the sense that it is consistent with wider democratic ideals and the values of a society in which it is universally accepted that it is the inalienable right of each person to have sufficient freedom to have a voice in his own concerns.[1]

The case for extending workers' participation may also be supported by many cogent theoretical arguments about the nature of man and society. Thus, for example, a number of social psychologists, including Maslow, Likert, and McGregor, have suggested that human motivation can be readily explained in terms of a sequential hierarchy of needs culminating in the desire for self-actualization.[2] Thus it is argued that modern man, having satisfied his primary economic and social needs is currently seeking self-expression, actualization, and creativity in his working environment. Finally, the beneficial nature of a democratized working situation has also been strongly supported by many empirical studies, and, although these use different research methods, aims, and samples, the overwhelming drift of their conclusions is that participation leads to many beneficial consequences both for the workers themselves and for the overall efficiency of the institutions as a whole.[3]

The defence of the managerial prerogative

However, in spite of the strength of the case in favour of introducing workers' participation, both into the schools and other sectors of British society, there has always been a widespread resistance to this type of change. The reasons for this situation are complex but, in part, may be related to the continuing influence of classic models of representative democracy and, in part, to a perhaps natural desire to maintain clearly responsible systems of line management. Largely as a result of this situation in Sheffield, as elsewhere in England, quasi-oligarchical and extremely centralized styles of educational administration have been strongly defended and such school boards as did exist typically contained the following type of clause in their instruments of government specifically to exclude the participation of people working in schools:

'No master or other person employed for the purposes of the school shall be a Governor.'

Thus, it is only in recent years that the case for involving teachers on the managing bodies of their schools has either been widely pressed or accepted as a desirable innovation. As late as the 1960s, largely as a result of the continued dominance of traditional attitudes towards the place of the labour force within the educational system, the influential Plowden

Report was able to comment on the proposals to include representatives of the teachers on managing bodies in the following terms:

> It is laid down in the Instruments of Management produced by the Department of Education and Science for voluntary schools and by the local education authorities for county schools that a teacher may not be a member of the managing body of the school at which he teaches. This is reasonable as a headteacher could be placed in an intolerable situation if one of his assistant teachers was on the managing body of the school.[4]

Moreover, this was a widespread point of view and was largely substantiated by the many chief education officers interviewed by George Baron and D. A. Howell in the course of the pioneering research study of the constitution, membership, and functions of school managing and governing bodies in the mid-1960s. They commented that,

> In general chief education officers argued that teacher representations is unnecessary since the head is expected to act as spokesman for his staff. For him to have a member of staff, or even a teacher from another school or authority serving as a governor would be an embarrassment. Interviews with heads in the main supported these objections.[5]

In short then, although they worked in a radically different situation, until 1970 most teachers in Sheffield, as elsewhere in England and Wales, were in much the same structural situation as most other groups of industrial workers in the sense that they were effectively denied any significant degree of control over the aims or policies being pursued by the organization in which they worked.

The case for teacher governors

Perhaps quite naturally, the major teachers' organizations have been resistant to this attempt to define their members' sphere of activities unilaterally and in terms of what seemed for their perspective to be a very narrow definition of managerial authority. Thus, during the last decade, there has been a ready response amongst teachers to the wider workers' control movement and a growing support for the principle that teachers should play a greater part in all stages of the educational decision-making process, including representation on the education committee of the local education authority, school managing, and governing boards, and full consultation with the headteacher about all major items of school policy — the curriculum, staffing, and organization of the school.

Representation on school boards was a particularly important object. It was seen to be not only a means of increasing the status of teachers, but also as part of a wider process of change which, it was hoped, would facilitate the growth of a new, more open system of education within which teachers would be kept more fully informed about key decisions, and also given a voice in policy making. Thus, the 'Executive Report on Teacher Participation', presented to the 1973 Conference of the National Union of Teachers noted that,

> The greater difficulty is to ensure that once the machinery for consultation has been set up, it is used. To some extent this depends upon the preparedness of the staff to exercise vigilance over their rights. It is, however, probably better achieved by the appointment of elected representatives of the staff upon the governing or managing body, for by this means the staff can be kept fully informed as to the matters upon which consultation should have taken place, and the staff representatives can expand on and clarify the views of the staff council. Mandatory consultation and staff representation on governing and managing bodies thus go together and create an effective method of involving the staff in decision-making in the school. Staff representation on governors and managers is long overdue. At a time when it is more and more recognised that parents should be represented upon the managers or governors of a school, there is an even stronger case that the staff of the school should have a similar voice. Some LEAs have already recognised this.[6]

And in an appendix to this report the authors noted that,

> It is Union policy to secure representation of the Head Teacher and an elected representative of the staff on the governing body of each school, with full rights as governors, and such representation has already been secured in a number of areas. We believe that others will shortly follow suit. In our view, the achievement of teacher representation on the governing bodies of schools will have implications for teacher participation for in the event of such representation teachers will be unlikely to sit back in the staff room and have nothing to say about the matters which come before the governors; they will discuss these matters which will in turn lead to staff discussion of other matters connected with the general life and organisation of the school. Such discussions will reinforce the wish for participation, and give a new dimension to participation itself.[7]

Largely as a result of all of these developments in recent years, the tide of reform has run strongly in favour of facilitating teacher representation on school governing bodies. As we saw in Chapter 2, although Sheffield played a major and pioneering role in this development, these initiatives must also be seen as part of a wider movement to democratize the nation's educational system. Thus, a recent survey of educational

authorities in England and Wales indicated the speed of recent developments, in that in 74 percent of cases investigated elected teachers are
now full board members, while in many of the remaining cases they are
now allowed to attend meetings although not given full voting rights.[8]

However, in spite of all these recent developments, it is still far from
clear whether the types of reforms which have been introduced into
Sheffield and other school systems have achieved their objectives in the
sense that they have facilitated a more democratic and openly participa-
tive type of consultative structure. I soon found, in the course of my
investigations in Sheffield, that while the leaders of the major teachers'
organizations, education officers, and politicians were all broadly in
agreement that it was both desirable and necessary to allow the elected
representatives of the teaching staff to sit on governing bodies, that in
practice the 'rank-and-file' members of the teaching profession took a
generally cautious attitude to these developments. This response did
not appear to be a short-term reaction to a radical social change, for, at
the time of this study, teachers had been sitting on school boards for over
five years. Their diffidence rather seemed to be the product of a complex
series of social, structural, and cultural factors which all play a great
part both in underpinning the teachers daily life and influencing his
perception of the social world around him.

Teachers and school boards

In the first place, I soon found that, while many teachers valued their
classroom autonomy, at the same time they were usually indifferent to
those organizational affairs which did not impinge directly on their
teaching. They were typically concerned about the academic development of their pupils, specific student skills and learning difficulties, the
idiosyncrasies of daily school life, and the minutae of their inter-
personal relationships with other members of staff. Apart from a small
minority, many of whom ironically aspired to leave the classroom
situation and themselves assume a managerial prerogative, most
seemed unconcerned about the type of general administrative or policy-
related issues which were commonly discussed at board meetings,
unless of course, as happened in the case of a promotion or reorganization of the local school system, it had direct and obvious implications
for their own working situation. In other words, their level of critical
political consciousness was largely formed by their daily experiences in
the classroom situation, and this tended to generate an individualistic
view of the world which was primarily concerned with the technical
details of the job in hand.

In many cases I also found that this perspective was accompanied by, and rationalized in terms of, a value system which tended to think of the headteacher in forms of such classical managerial imagery as a 'leader', innovator, and 'director of men' and which saw their own role in terms of fulfilling a narrower, but highly specific, technical function within this overarching framework. While not all teachers I spoke to shared this highly functionalist view of their place in society, those who did were not only unhappy to assume a role which implicitly threatened their view of the world, but also tended to disparage their employers' experiments in the field of worker participation. They took the view that Sheffield had 'managed well enough' with its old centralized system of school administration and consistently suggested that the new boards were little more than 'time-wasting talking shops' with little real influence or substantial financial power.

Thus, general indifference to the world of school board politics tended to be reinforced by the contraints of the teacher's daily working commitments. Many people I spoke to told me they simply did not have the time to take up what many saw as a further onerous series of commitments. Apart from the alternative constraints of their social, familial, and recreational activities, many teachers said their normal class work was so demanding that they were unwilling to assume fresh burdens. Moreover, in many schools, recent organizational and curriculum developments had created such a multitude of subject-based, task-directed, or child-centred liaison and coordinating committees that service as a teacher governor simply appeared to be yet another task threatening. to further divorce them from their primary duty — the education of children.

Finally, many Sheffield teachers eschewed the new board system because of their personal assessments of the very real powers remaining in the hands of their headteachers. Partly because of the structure of their working situations, partly because of the ways in which they are selected for and socialized into their profession, it was clear that many teachers had become motivated by what may be labelled an 'individual level of consciousness' and the 'pursuit of a career'. Thus, although they have a strong loyalty to fellow members of their work group, at the same time many personal tensions arise when they are faced with making a choice between what they see as a quite legitimate personal concern and the alternative claims of an often quite diffuse collective interest.

Teachers and headteachers

All of these tensions were substantially exacerbated by the classroom teacher's relationships with his headteacher. As we saw in the last chapter, despite his official title, the latter occupies an essentially managerial role within the school system. He is not only largely responsible for the initial selection and appointment of teaching staff but is also in an excellent strategic situation to award or withhold promotional opportunities from them. He can also direct teachers into congenial or uncongenial working situations and ultimately, since he is invariably approached for references, is in an unrivalled position to influence their future career prospects. Largely, as a result of this situation, many teachers who, in theory, approved of teacher representations on school boards were also reluctant to stand for this office once they had made an intuitive assessment of the distribution of power within their school. Many people I spoke to were worried that this type of public service might inadvertently lead them into a 'para-shop steward' role, in which they might be forced to represent their colleagues' views on such critical and delicate issues as staff promotions, differentials, or internal school organization at managers' or governors' meetings. In this way they might be unexpectedly, but nonetheless effectively, thrust into a conflict situation with the headteacher and this might have a deleterious impact upon their subsequent career opportunities.

Although I found little evidence to substantiate the correctness, or other-wise, of this viewpoint, and indeed from an alternative perspective one might equally assume that a close familiarity with the kind of general policy and administrative issues which are discussed at board meetings might have well facilitated a teacher's occupational advancement, it was nonetheless a common type of response amongst many teachers I spoke to. Mr. Taylor summarized the attitude of many of his colleagues when he said to me: 'I was probably elected because I made it clear in my staff room that I wanted no further promotion and I would be able to speak freely. Some of my colleagues felt this desire to speak freely could make future advancement difficult for them.'

The candidates

Largely as a result of this complex situation, many teachers saw school boards as relatively distant and marginal bodies which had little immediate relevance to their own daily concerns. Thus, even in those schools where the teachers' representatives gave reports about their work to staff meetings, this occasion was often seen as one small, and often boring, interlude which seemed very distant from the immediate world of their classrooms and the daily routine of school life. Indeed, in some schools it was not always easy to find teachers eager and willing to assume this responsibility; this post was typically seen as yet another onerous administrative burden which was best filled by someone who did not feel too threatened by the incipient role conflicts which might be generated by holding this office. Thus, it was rare to find a school where the choice of candidates was a hotly contested issue, where people were offered a choice from a slate of interested parties, and where candidates were chosen because they advocated a specific interest or proposed a specific programme of action. Rather, in most cases, people were chosen because of their personal qualities. In some cases, the 'blocked spiralist' was a suitable choice since it was felt that his overt rejection of any future career advancement more readily facilitated the adoption of an 'advocacy role'; Mr. Taylor, as we have already seen, was a fairly typical case in that he had made it clear that he was prepared to be independent and 'speak out in the staff interest'. However, perhaps more typically, teachers tended to choose their representatives from well-established members of their profession who already occupied a fairly senior place in their school's hierarchy. Mrs. Keen was a fairly typical case in point. She said, 'as the longest serving member of my school's staff, I was judged by my colleagues to have the required knowledge and experience of schools.'

Finally, in a number of schools, the teachers were so reluctant to engage in the school board politics that their headteacher was forced to assume an overt 'sponsorship role' and actively encourage people to stand for this office. Since they were not, for reasons we have already analysed, successful in recruiting the services of their younger or mid-career staff, then they were often forced to call upon the services of their deputies or senior colleagues.

Teachers' representatives in action

However, whatever their antecedents, I soon found that, in most schools in Sheffield, the teachers' representatives were extremely reluctant to exploit their new offices and adopt a radical role which might serve to challenge the authority of their headteachers, or lead to any fundamental diminution of the managerial prerogative. This was primarily because, while most teachers' representatives genuinely wished to represent their colleagues interests, at the same time they found this an extremely difficult task to perform, simply because they were not guided by a specific mandate for action. It was rare to find a case where candidates were elected on the basis of a specific programme, and where teachers continued to maintain an active interest in their candidate's behaviour once he was in office. In contrast, most representatives simply paid a nominal allegiance to a series of emotive and diffuse statements. They typically reported they had been elected to:

'Put forward the staff point of view.'

'Be a watchdog for the staff.'

'Look after the teachers' interests.'

However, in practice, these statements were so general that they were also meaningless and once the representative came to the board meeting he enjoyed what virtually amounted to an open-ended brief.

This situation was in one very real sense a reflection of the inherently fragmented occupational structure within which all teachers spend their working lives. Their schools are typically divided into a series of lateral and vertical organizations based on subject, classroom, year, house, pastoral care, interest groups, and so on. All of these divisions tend to generate interests which are specific unto themselves and effectively discourage the emergence of a strong collective viewpoint on such common issues as organizational, promotional, or curriculum structures. Indeed, in the course of this study, I consistently gained the impression that current trends are leading to an ever-increasing complex division of academic labour and a consequent greater fragmentation of the workplace itself. This may not only serve to make it more difficult for a teaching staff to agree on a common programme of action, but also perhaps ironically tends to facilitate a process in which people attempt to find individual and private solutions to what well may be common problems.

Thus, in practice, I soon found that most representatives were unwilling to assume a radical role and attempt in any overt way to challenge the 'managerial prerogative' exercised by their headteachers. In most cases they were prepared to 'go along with the system', and accommodate themselves to the role expectations of the most experienced and senior members of their boards. In practice this usuallly meant that the newly elected teachers' representatives attempted to fit themselves into the already well-established power structure we examined in the last chapter and which typically consisted of the school's headteacher, the chairman of the board, the clerk, and perhaps one or two senior local authority appointees. This group tended, in many subtle but nonetheless effective ways, to discourage them from raising the kinds of difficult issues which might call into question established conventions and the authority of the headteacher, or the long-term aims and policies being pursued by the school.

This process of what may be termed, from a purely technical point of view, incorporation into an existing 'power structure' was in part aided by the newly elected staff representative's unfamiliarity with this kind of work. As we saw in the last chapter most governors' meetings are held in private and only a restricted account of their deliberations is disseminated publicly. Thus, most newly elected teachers' representatives were, perhaps inevitably, entering a 'freshman' situation in which they must learn about the extent and limitations of their new powers and duties. In most cases they tended to look towards the more experienced members of the board for informal guidance and typically the headteacher or the clerk assumed an informal tutorial role, which tended to further reinforce the power of their own positions, since they usually guided the 'new boys' into what they defined as appropriate and legitimate avenues of activity. They, perhaps quite naturally, effectively discouraged most teachers from raising the kinds of searching questions which might not only challenge the managerial prerogative in general but might also lead other members of the board to question the legitimacy of the established internal structural or long-term policy objectives which were being pursued nominally in their name, but effectively by the headteacher of the school they were appointed to serve.

Role tensions

This process of accommodation to the expectations of a sometimes opaque, but nonetheless effective, power structure often tended to place the workers' representatives in an extremely stressful personal situation; consequently, there perhaps inevitably tended to be a high rate of 'turnover' in this office and, for example, no less than 40 percent of the respondents in my sample reported that they were new boys in the sense that they had only recently been elected to their school's managing board and had only held their office for less than one year.

The roots of these difficulties lay in the role tensions which are typically created by the very serious conflicts of loyalties which tend to be invoked when schemes for workers' participation are introduced into any hierarchically structured organization, be it an industrial, educative, or public welfare institution. In the case of schools, the headteacher, perhaps quite naturally, expects that the democratically elected member of his staff will remain publicly loyal to him, the policies he is pursuing, and ultimately 'his' conception of the nature of the school they work in. They perhaps quite naturally feel extremely threatened if their teachers' representatives raise potentially difficult, delicate, or embarrassing issues in an arena where the school's policies may come under close scrutiny from a wide variety of interested parties, including the representatives of parents, students, auxiliary staff, local community groups, and political parties. If this critical situation were to arise, then it might not only lead to a serious loss of support for the policies being pursued within the local school, but might ultimately undermine the headteacher's confidence, both in his own role as an educationalist and as a professional leader of a team.

However, as we have already seen, the leaders of many teachers' unions have been pressing for representation on school boards, not only because they want to raise their status as a profession, but also because they want to safeguard their members' interests. Many local teachers' leaders and also school board representatives, if not all of their colleagues, strongly supported this point of view and they made it clear to me that they thought their main job was:

'To represent members of staff; to have a choice if there is anything which concerns them.'

'To be a watchdog for the staff and to keep an eye on what goes on.'

'To represent the teaching staff and look after their interests and to see that nothing "goes through which is detrimental to them".'

However, if the teachers' representatives simply took the view that their prime role was to articulate their colleagues' points of view and represent their legitimate interests, this concern might well pitch them into an unanticipated conflict with their headteacher. The latter might, simply because of the logic of his essentially managerial position, have a different point of view about such key issues in his school as teacher promotion, internal organization, the division and direction of his labour force, and so on. Some teachers' representatives in Sheffield were obviously alerted to these difficulties and told me that, although they were elected to look after their colleagues interests, at the same time they felt:

'One must be careful.'

'It is a role which requires prudence and discretion.'

'I should back the headteacher, but there may be difficulties.'

In most cases where disagreement occurred between a headteacher and a teachers' representative, then it seemed, at least publicly, that this situation was resolved in favour of the headteacher and the representatives were extremely reluctant to represent their colleagues' interests in such a way that it would undermine the authority or self-confidence of the headteacher, or seriously diminish the standing of the teaching profession in the eyes of leading members of the general public.

Asymmetrical conflict resolution

The reason for this typically asymmetrical resolution of most conflict situations in favour of the person exercising the managerial prerogative is complex. However, for the purposes of this analysis it is probably best understood in terms of the dynamic interplay of the following key factors.

In the first place, although within most educational establishments serious differences of opinion may often occur between members of the workforce and representatives of the higher management, at the same time both sides are also united by a series of common interests, prime amongst which is their need to maintain an effective and ongoing dominance over the internal clientele of students or pupils and their schools reputation in the wider society. In short, in any latent crisis, the headteacher is always able to appeal to and invoke an ethic of 'institutional loyalty' whose central tenants are, firstly, that whatever contentions or diversive internal difficulties break out within the institutions, these are essentially private matters and must not be raised publicly, particularly in a predominantly lay managing or governing body, one of whose prime rationales is to act as an interface between the school and its surrounding community. One must try to mute one's personal and private disagreements in public and thus, at school board meetings, management and workers must unite in a common endeavour and aim to create a favourable and constructive image of their establishment. Mrs. Yates, a recently elected teachers' representative, gave a clear illustration of the effectiveness of this ethic when she said, 'I feel I can't always bring up all the business I want to do. There was something I didn't agree with, but couldn't say. I don't feel I can go against the headteacher. I feel we should be united but I also feel we are boxing with our hands tied.'

Secondly, the tactical position of the headteacher is substantially reinforced by the fact that, although many serious disagreements may erupt between people working at the managerial and technical levels of a school system, at the same time these conflicts rarely blaze into open warfare since both interests also share so many common bonds and experiences. Both have been socialized into the teaching profession at an early and formative stage in their lives, both may belong to the same union, both place a great value on the role of education in our society and would not like to see this interest, or their careers, threatened by an acrimonious dispute which might seriously diminish their profession's standing in the eyes of the wider society. Thus, although teachers may often be most critical of the managerial strategies used within their schools, at the same time these incipient disagreements rarely break out into the bitter conflicts which typically occur when managers and workers are recruited from different social stratas, have different educational, occupational, and career expectations, and, typically, radically different views about the nature of the social world they both must live within. Mrs. Jones, a teachers' representative on one large governing body, made this point most explicit when she said, 'Our hands are tied on burning issues; well!! the headteacher has an aura to keep up. One feels restricted and the other governors would think I was at the headteacher's throat. One has to be careful for the profession's sake.'

Thirdly, the general diffidence of most teachers' representatives was further reinforced by two more obvious, if nonetheless critical, structural factors. Firstly, since most teachers spend most of their time either preparing themselves for or actually teaching their students, they tended, by the logic of their occupational situation, to be less familiar with the type of general administrative/policy issues which are typically discussed at the managerial/executive levels of the school boards. Moreover, as we have already seen, since governors' meetings are usually held in private, they had little opportunity to prepare themselves for their new responsibilities, and thus usually looked towards their headteacher, who was usually one of the most experienced and leading members of the board, for help and advice about their new duties. In turn, their headteacher was able to capitalize on the 'new boy' situation and assume an informal, but nonetheless effective tutorial role, in which he guided the newly elected teachers' representatives into what he defined as appropriate and legitimate fields of activity. Secondly, many teachers were also deeply concerned about their own career prospects and conditions of service. As we have already seen, many teachers were reluctant to stand as candidates for school board elections, since they did not want to be labelled as 'troublemakers'. They worried that, if their colleagues asked them to raise an issue which might be seen as difficult or threatening to the headteacher, then this might result in serious, if long-term, consequences for their own careers. Although I found no evidence to support this contention, it was nonetheless a widely held view and did mean that, even in those cases where teachers' representatives had overtly rejected a conventional career trajectory and identified themselves completely with a worker/advocacy role, nonetheless they were still reluctant to raise issues which might question the managerial prerogative, or which might be seen as 'unconstructive' or 'damaging' to their school in the eyes of the general public. Mr. Rigby made their diffidence very explicit when he said, 'It was not easy to introduce new points; it was unpleasant for me, I wanted to say such a lot, but I wasn't free to speak.'

In short then, the evidence tended to consistently suggest that, certainly in public if not in private, the role tensions which break out between management and labour within schools are typically resolved in favour of the interests of the headteacher. Most teachers' representatives were extremely diffident about raising contentious issues in public and judiciously refrained from playing the kind of 'shop steward' role which overtly challenges the managerial prerogative. They tended to be generally appreciative of the work of their headteacher and were reluctant to exploit their new position within the higher levels of the formal structure of the school system in order to undermine his authority or power within their school. Thus, in practice, whatever type of relationship developed between a headteacher and his staff representatives on the governing body, whether it was close, friendly, and cooperative, as was so often the case, or cold, formal, and largely impersonal, as was rarely the case, the representatives tended, because of the logic of their situation, to become closely identified, at least in public, with the work of their school. They would invariably 'jump to the defence' of their headteacher if they felt his policies were under attack, or if they felt the layman was treading over the 'delicate line' which customarily prevented him from interfering with the academic work of the school. Indeed, one deputy headteacher made this supportive role very evident when she told me that one of the main reasons she wanted to become a governor was because she, 'felt I should be there at all meetings about the school to support the headmistress.'

Another teacher made it quite clear that his support would include what many people might see as a peculiarly narrow interpretation of the legitimate role of a lay governor. He said,

I feel convinced that the headteacher is the one person who should judge what is best for our children in terms of curriculum, internal policy and so on within that particular school, with those particular children. Some of our managers, who are clamouring for control over these matters, would be the first to object to the Vicar or the Grocer being on their union committee, on the grounds that such people, however good in other ways, couldn't be expected to understand the particular problems of their workers or industry.

Another teachers' representative put the same point of view in a slightly different way when he said,

May I say I am an ardent supporter of the new school board system and I am sure that with goodwill from all concerned, the educational system can only benefit by it. However, I'm concerned that some of my colleagues, that is lay managers, are over-reaching themselves in the quest for power. Although the diversity of interests on a board will give a more general and also more objective view of problems, so perhaps helping to get them in perspective, I feel convinced that the headteacher is the one person who should judge what is best for our children in terms of curriculum and internal policy.

Conclusions

It seems then that although the elected representatives of teachers are no longer excluded from school boards in Sheffield, at the same time this kind of involvement has not led to any fundamental changes in the power structure of the local school system. Indeed, the evidence consistently suggests that one of the major, if at the same time, unexpected consequences of these reforms, has been a substantial increase in the latent, if not always manifest, authority of management.

The reasons for this development are perhaps explicable if one acknowledges that, in the case of schools, as in any other large organization, workers' participation and control are not independent variables but are rather, as Poole has recently suggested, 'functions of the latent power of particular industrial classes, parties or groups and the value "climate" which may or may not be favourable to participation experiments.'[9]

Thus while, as we have seen earlier in this chapter, the case for teacher participation and control is buttressed by an impressive theory and an emotive rhetoric, its ideals remain largely aborted in terms of social action, since its successful implementation is contingent upon the need to change many other structural and cultural factors. In practice, most teachers in Sheffield, as elsewhere in England and Wales, continue to work within an organizational framework which is fragmented vertically and laterally and are usually compliant with the immediate day-to-day directives of the management, since all of their relationships are contingent upon a deeply asymmetrical distribution of power. Paradoxically, the consciousness of most teachers further legitimates this situation in the sense that it typically favours the adoption of private and personal solutions to what may well be public or collective interests.

Thus, while this type of experiment in school board reform is overtly consistent with the values of a democratic society, I gradually came to realize that it tended in practice to facilitate a new kind of less brittle managerial control. As we saw in the last chapter, it encourages head-teachers to develop a more flexible style of leadership, allowing them to cope more effectively with the difficulties which typically occur in periods of rapid social change when people, including teachers, are no longer prepared to accept traditional or consensual definitions of education but are raising fundamental questions, both about the nature and functions of the educative system in contemporary society. Thus, particularly in a tightly centralized school system, headteachers occupy what can at times become an isolated, stressful, and peculiarly visible position. They are especially vulnerable to the type of social criticism which occurs when once dominant unitary assumptions break down and people raise fundamental questions about the policies being pursued within the schools in which they work. Thus, if a serious dispute breaks out and the head's policies are seriously challenged by a group of teachers, then the headteacher is either faced with the task of trying to resolve the conflict himself, or directly involving the officers of the local education committee and, of course, the teachers' unions.

The new participatory board system tends to effectively reduce the risk of this abrasive confrontation developing and, if it does occur, allows the headteacher to respond to it in a flexible manner. This is because the elected representatives of his workforce are now included within the school board system and, although, as we have seen, they are usually excluded from an effective degree of control, nonetheless they are publicly identified with the headteacher's policies. Thus, it is now extremely difficult for the leaders of the teachers within a school to criticize or overtly challenge their headteacher on the emotive, if populist, grounds that he is an autocrat and they are not represented within their school's governing body or consulted about the policies being pursued in their school. In short, this type of innovation may be seen as one further example of what Mandel has termed the ideology of comanagement, in which the workers become a party to the functioning of a system over which they have little control.[10] At worst, as we have seen, teachers who become enmeshed in the work of these bodies experience profound 'role conflict' and, at best, acquire and disseminate to their constituents a set of managerial concepts about the proper functioning of their enterprise.[11] However, this being the case, it is now perhaps time for us to shift our perspective away from an examination of the place teachers occupy within the new board system and move on to an examination of the impact of the Sheffield reforms upon the school's most important group of clients — the parents of the children currently passing through the educative facilities provided by the state.

Notes and references

1.   For an extended discussion of this point see M. Poole, *Workers Participation in Industry*, Routledge & Kegan Paul, 1975

2.   A. H. Maslow, *Motivation and Personality*, Harper and Row, 1970; R. Likert, *New Patterns in Management*, McGraw-Hill, New York, 1961; D. McGregor, *The Human Side of Enterprise*, McGraw-Hill, New York, 1960

3.   P. Blumberg, *Industrial Democracy*, London, 1968; C. Pateman, *Participation and Democratic Theory*, Cambridge, 1970.

4.   *Children and their Primary Schools*. A Report of the Central Advisory Council for Education (England), Vol. 1: p. 416.

5.   G. Baron and D. A. Howell, *The Government and Management of Schools*, Athlone Press, 1974, pp. 89-90.

6.   *Teacher Participation, A Statement and Recommendation on Teacher Participation*. Presented to the Annual Conference, 1973, of the National Union of Teachers, p. 5.

7.   Ibid. p. 19.

8.   *National Association of Governors and Managers: some facts and figures*, NAGM, May 1975. (A survey of 104 authorities in which 91 replies were received).

9.   M. Poole, op. cit., p. 37.

10.   E. Mandel, 'Workers' Control and Workers' Councils', *International*, 2.

11.   For an extended discussion of this point of view, see H. A. Clegg, *A New Approach to Industrial Democracy*, Blackwell, Oxford, 1960.

CHAPTER 6

PARENTAL POWER AND STATE EDUCATION

Introduction

Although, as we saw in the first chapter, the case for involving elected representatives of the parents on the managing or governing bodies of schools was widely discussed in Victorian England,[1] and agreed in principal as a desirable development during the parliamentary debate on the 1944 Education Act,[2] it is only in the last five years that this proposal has been widely implemented. Thus in the postwar years many councillors and education officials in such large urban authorities as Sheffield, Manchester, and Birmingham seemed generally reluctant to implement the spirit, if not the letter of, the 1944 Act. They worried that this initiative might not only lead to a diminution of their own authority and ability to control the school system, but might also legitimate the 'power' of their clients and in this way make the work of the headteachers more complex and personally stressful. Moreover this pessimistic assessment was not simply a phenomenon of the larger urban education authorities. In many suburban or rural areas, where schools often tended to be provided with individual governing bodies, the parental interest was also viewed with suspicion and excluded from formal representation. Moreover, even in those places which did allow some form of 'parental involvement' on school boards, this type of participation was often purely nominal in character. This was because the parental interest was not expressed through the normal democratic procedures of nomination and the ballot box. Thus in some authorities a headteacher would simply nominate a parent of his own choosing, while in others the governors would nominate a parent, or even a new parent, to look after the client's interest. Obviously none of these 'quasi-sponsored' procedures was democratic, nor was the governor so appointed a true representative in any conventional sense of the word.

However, in recent years the tide of reform has moved strongly against what many people see as this traditional 'hands off' policy to parental involvement in all aspects of school life. This movement is partly a result of the work of the influential Plowden Report,[3] which specifically recommended the appointment to governing bodies of parents having children at the school concerned. Partly as a result of the work of a number of pressure groups, including the Campaign for State Education (CASE) and the National Association of Governors and Managers (NAGM), which have consistently pressed for the democratization of school boards, many authorities have made a long and thorough assessment of their traditionally negative attitude to parents as representatives. Largely as a result of this situation, the tide of reform, both in Sheffield and in many other former bastions of the 'hands off' policy, has moved strongly in favour of facilitating a more truly democratic parental representation on school boards. A recent survey of local educational authorities in England and Wales indicated that in over 85 percent of cases they now allow elected parents representatives as full board members, while in most of the remainder parents now attend as observers, but without full voting rights.[4]

Moreover, largely as a result of the success of these initiatives, the proposals to further extend the scale of parental representation on school boards is also receiving widespread support. At a local level in Sheffield the original scheme introduced in 1970 was judged to be so useful that a new scheme providing for a third parental member was introduced into the city in 1975. At a national level there is also a widespread support for this type of initiative, for these newly democratized bodies are not only seen as a means of effectively democratizing the nation's educational service, but also of making schools more accountable and responsible to local society. Indeed, in the case of the Conservative Party their educational spokesman has recently promised that his party would, once it regained office, introduce a 'parents' charter' which would, amongst other things,

> give parents the right to be represented on all school boards of managers and governors. The proportion of parents should be substantial; it could be between a third and a half of the governing body.

And he went on to suggest that this reform would lead to,

> a Copernican turn, away from the power of officials and pressure groups, and back to the influence of parents. This is a development which the great majority of parents desire.[5]

Research into parental managers

At the time I started looking at the role of parental governors in Sheffield the new board system had been in operation for over five years. It had been given wide publicity both in the national educational and local press, and in turn had been judged such a successful innovation that it had been copied in part, or in full, by a number of other educational authorities. In turn, and perhaps quite naturally from their point of view, most of the leading councillors and senior educational administrators spoke enthusiastically about the merits of the new system. It had not only added to their own and the cities prestige, but given Sheffield a new image as a radical and pioneering educational authority.

In view of all these developments I was at first extremely surprised to find that a wide gulf existed between what I recognized in retrospect was 'officially claimed' for the new system and the everyday perceptions of the school system held by most parents or the 'ordinary man in the street'. I found in the course of my fieldwork that most people I spoke to did not know what school managing or governing bodies were, did not know who sat on their own local board, and had only the vaguest of ideas as to what these bodies were supposed to do. In short, such was their general ignorance of these matters that I found, as did my students, the actual process of asking such questions a disconcerting experience since people reacted as if they thought it was obviously novel, if polite, conversational gambit, and that I really wanted to talk to them about other, more personal matters. In this way I was characteristically led on to talk about their children, their marital problems, their housing difficulties and so on, and thus my respondents studiously avoided talking about that which they knew so little about, Sheffield's new governing bodies.

It was obviously a relief for me to find respondents who could be slightly more specific, and who told me, after an appropriate pause for reflection, that they thought school boards were:

Intended to act as a watchdog.

That they were something to do with the policy of the school.

That they look after things like broken windows.

However, only a small minority of informants, most of whom were professional people and working in occupations directly or indirectly connected with the local educational industry, were really able to give me a really accurate assessment of either a school board's powers and functions, or to name the elected parents' representative serving their interests. People in this group typically told me that governors were:

A lay committee deciding school policy.

There to ensure the school met desired educational requirements.

Required to comment on the headteacher's report and look into school problems.

School board elections

This general impression that apart from a minority of articulate and educationally conscious professional people, most parents in Sheffield were simply not aware of or, if they were, were indifferent to the idea of having their general interests represented through the formal institutional mechanism of a local school board system, was not I believe simply an operation of a research methodology which largely depended on talking to the man in the street, pub, bus, or park. These initial assessments were largely reinforced when I attempted a more critical test of the strength of 'grassroot' interests in school board politics. In this second exercise I decided to look at the level of public involvement in the elections for the three governors who were intended to represent the parental interest in the further democratized system of school government introduced into Sheffield in September 1975.

In these elections all parents with children in Sheffield schools were naturally eligible to vote or to stand as candidates. All parents were also notified by their child's school of the date and place of the public meeting at which prospective candidates could introduce themselves, explain their reasons for seeking office, and where in turn the parents could decide who they wanted to choose to represent their interests. This type of active and open meeting was seen as a preferable alternative to the postal ballot system in which parents simply choose from a list of nominees, most of whom are unknown to them, and then simply return their ballot forms back to school via their children. In the Sheffield elections the parental candidates were required to display themselves, publicly justify their policies, and in turn all parents were required to make a conscious effort to leave the comforts of their hearth and home, and spend for one day in the year, roughly one-eighth of the time their children, and their teachers, typically spend at school in one normal day. In short the Sheffield school board elections promised to offer an interesting and critical test of the strength of 'grassroot' interest in this type of community activity.

Results of the elections

I was, largely because of my initial findings, not surprised to find that the results of these elections did little to substain the enthusiasm of those participatory democrats pressing for more local involvement on school governing bodies. Thus, most election meetings were not well attended, and in most cases involved less than twenty parents, or roughly 4 percent or less of the total electorate. Even in Sheffield's more affluent suburban areas, which contained a larger proportion of 'educationally conscious' professional workers, and where parents were often more overtly critical of schools and anxious to be closely involved in all stages of their child's education, the turnout was generally low. Thus in one large comprehensive school, serving a predominantly middle, and upper middle-class district in the exclusive 'west end' of Sheffield, 26 parents attended the meeting out of a possible electorate of over 2200. In a neighbouring feeder middle school, 7 parents turned up out of a possible 1000, and in an adjacent first school 8 people met to elect 3 representatives. In many other areas of the city the response was worse than this, and in one new primary school serving a generally 'deprived area', no one could be found to serve at all.

This kind of response was not of course unique to Sheffield. Recent elections for parental governors in Liverpool also resulted in a generally dismal turnout.[6] However, in Merseyside the situation was complicated by an electoral system which not only sent the parents three informatory letters, one of them long and complicated and containing 750 densely printed words dealing with the duties and functions of this public office, but also required the candidates to pick up their nomination forms from the education offices in the city centre and return completed nomination forms by a personal visit. In contrast, in

Sheffield few of these obviously inhibiting devices were used; a simple message was sent to parents and all they were required to do was to turn out once in the year for a short public meeting at their child's school.

Results of a minority ballot

Most of the successful candidates I spoke to were, perhaps quite naturally, dismayed by the generally dismal response to these elections. They not only clearly worried about what they defined as a widespread 'public apathy', but also told me that their self-confidence had also been shaken by their experiences. One candidate, Mrs. Ryder, summed up these sentiments very well when she said, 'I feel only partly elected,' while another parent simply told me, 'It was all terribly disappointing.'

Some people complained to me about the way in which their election meetings had been held, and others suggested it would have been much better to have held a postal ballot. Indeed, in some of Sheffield's schools the headteachers ignored their authorities' instructions to hold election meetings, and went ahead and organized a postal ballot. This strategy certainly brought a much higher response, and also increased the confidence of the person who was subsequently elected, and from this point of view might be seen as a preferable alternative to a public election meeting. Nonetheless, if as seems likely, most local educational authorities are forced to resort to this type of essentially passive and depersonalized means of achieving a nominally respectable level of parental involvement in school board elections, then it is also in a sense a tacit public recognition of the fact that most parents are unwilling to actively involve themselves in school board politics, and are also generally reluctant to attend their child's school for even one short annual election meeting.

As I reflected further on this situation, it seemed to me not only to raise a number of general questions about the effectiveness of school boards as vehicles for facilitating a greater degree of public accountability within the school system, but to lead one to ask how far the elected parental representative genuinely represents the interests of the total parent body.

Certainly I found in the case of Sheffield, and I suspect in most other parts of England and Wales, that the successful candidates did not, except in the most general terms, represent viable and distinctive constituencies of parents with a common interest and agreed programme of political action; rather they were chosen because they were well-known local personalities, members of local action groups, or simply people whose name came at the top of a list. Their election addresses or appeals rarely referred to specific policies, but typically made a generalized and highly personalized appeal for support, and characteristically contained such statements as

'I am employed as an architect and am interested in serving the school to the best of my ability.'

'I am interested in the children at school.'

'I am interested in music and want to help the children.'

However, candidates rarely went beyond stressing aspects of what might be called this vague ethic of community service and public involvement, and were generally reluctant to make a direct appeal to specific parental interest groups such as the handicapped, the immigrants, the working classes, or to develop specific programmes advocating such contentious actions as, a move towards the 'abolition of streaming', better reading standards', or 'stricter discipline'.

The candidates' perhaps unconscious rejection of an overtly politicized appeal to the parental electorate was also reflected in their replies to the question, 'Why did you stand for election to a school board?'

As we saw in a previous chapter, parents, like most other governors, indicated they had a general interest in the present welfare and future well being of children. However, beyond these conventional observations, most indicated a personalized and individual, rather than a group-centred or policy-related interest in their local school. Mrs. Smith was fairly typical when she said, 'I wanted to participate in the organisation and administration of the school in which my children are to be educated.' Another parent, Mrs. Brown, recorded a similar point of view: 'I wanted to find out more about the comprehensive complex. I am very concerned for my children's education and I wanted to know what to do if the system was not okay.' And Mrs. Keen told me, 'I am keenly interested in the well being of mine and other children and thought this the best way of showing my interest.'

However, perhaps the most striking indication of this characteristic individualization of these elections emerged when I asked governors why they thought they had been elected as parents' representatives. Most of their replies made it clear that they had been chosen for their personal qualities, because they were seen as good people, not because they were associated with a particular interest group or policy. Thus Mrs. Redmond told me she thought she had been elected, 'because I am a familiar face at the local playgroup.' Mrs. Baylis thought she was successful, 'because I am well known as the local lollypop woman.' While Mrs. Black simply replied, 'because of my outgoing personality.'

Absence of constituencies

This remarkable degree of personalization in these elections, and the absence of any but the vaguest type of parental constituency, inevitably leads one to question whether this type of structural innovation, which essentially aims to widen the composition of governing bodies and involve client groups such as parents in the government of schools, is likely to lead to any greater level of public accountability within the education service in general, or make schools any more responsive to local needs and interests in particular. Indeed, if one examines the situation further, then one also finds many related cultural and structural factors consistently operating to frustrate even the most ambitious attempts to democratize the school system and effect a decisive transfer of power away from the hands of administrators and headteachers and into lay control.

In the first place, while most people in Britain perceive education to be a public service provided by the state, few of them certainly in Sheffield, and I suspect in most other parts of the country, see it as an overtly political activity. Rather, most people I talked to subscribed to the view that education was an ethically neutral public service, and hence there was a fundamental reluctance to politicize school board elections. Thus, although various groups are represented on school governing bodies — parents, teachers, community leaders, political activists, and so on — most people take the view that it is inappropriate to introduce contentious and divisive issues into what is essentially defined as an act of public service. Rather one must strive to 'keep politics out of schools' and remain united in a common endeavour to 'do one's best to serve the children'. This prevailing consensual definition of the essentially non-political function of a school governor was well summarized by one prominent member of the National Association of Governors and Managers, when she wrote in a recent Home and School Council Publication — the New Governor's Guide — that the role of a manager was best thought of as a, 'voluntary task undertaken to serve a school and the community, an opportunity to help the young people of today to benefit fully from their education, so that young people may in the future wish to make their contribution to the community.'[7]

Secondly, the popularity of this prevailing ethic of 'depoliticized service', was greatly reinforced by the structural composition of the parent body. Partly as a result of recent advances in educational technology, partly as a product of the present nature of the division of academic labour, children are typically placed in a variety of age bands, subject settings, houses, year groups, and even buildings, in each school. All of these very manifest differences tend to effectively divide the parental body into a heterogeneous series of interests concerned with quite small groups of children, for example, the backward 8s, the forward 8s, the 8s in Mrs. Smith's class, the musical 8s, and so on. This situation tends to effectively block the emergence of any common issues concerning the total school programme, which might lead to the emergence of an identifiable, politicized, parental interest. Rather, the very fragmentation of modern school life tends to encourage parents to seek private and personal solutions to what may well be common public issues, but which are defined by nature of the present school system as private wrongs.

Finally, in Sheffield, as in the rest of Britain, since the passing of Balfour's Education Act of 1902, school boards are not rate-levying bodies and governors have very limited financial powers. Consequently, we don't find, as often occurs in America, that school board elections are contested by well-organized 'rate-paying' groups wishing to restrict educational expenditure, and whose presence often generates a parental-dominated counter lobby, who are at least united in their wish to secure their children the best possible educational resources available.

The parents' representative

Largely as a result of these facts, one rarely finds in British school board elections a large coherent body of parents who have united to elect a candidate on a specific policy-orientated programme, and who maintain an active interest in their representative's behaviour once he is in office. Rather, in most schools, parental representatives enjoy a considerable amount of freedom to act as they wish to, since they are not restricted by an election manifesto, or are directly responsible for their decisions in office to a definitive and recognizable group of electors. This fluid open-ended situation usually means that when an elected parental representative attends his first governors' meeting his behaviour is not guided by a clearly articulated policy; rather, since most are elected on a personal basis and subscribe to what might be called an ethic of community service, then he usually tries to 'fit in' and accommodate himself to the role expectations of the most experienced members of the board.

In practice, this usually means that the newly elected parental governor attempts to fit himself into an already well-established power structure, characteristically composed of the headteacher, chairman of the board, vice-chairman, and the administrative official acting as clerk. This group tends to discourage the parental governor from raising issues which might call into question established conventions or the long-term aims and policies of the school. As we have already seen, lay governors are often encouraged to spend their time discussing details of administration, and in the case of parents are often diverted into marginal fund-raising or ceremonial, but nonetheless symbolically important, activities.

This process of incorporation into an existing 'power structure' was in part aided by the newly elected governors' unfamiliarity with this kind of work. Most parents I spoke to found themselves in precisely the kind of 'freshman' situation experienced by the teachers' representatives. They had to learn about the extent of their new powers and duties, find out about the complexities of educational administration and finance, and familiarize themselves with the peculiar administrative-political style in which public bodies normally conduct their business. Perhaps, inevitably, most newly elected parents entering this type of unfamiliar situation for the first time tended to make the 'commonsense assumption' that 'wisdom will gradually settle upon their shoulders' as they settle more firmly into their office. In most cases, this usually meant that, in practice, parents looked towards the more experienced members of the board for informal advice and guidance. Typically, and simply because they were, in many cases, the longest serving and most knowledgeable members, the headteacher or the clerk assumed this informal tutorial role and, in this way, they tended, perhaps unconsciously, to further reinforce the power of their own position, for they usually guided the newcomers into what they saw as appropriate and legitimate avenues of activity. These rarely included asking searching questions about the long-term aims, curriculum, or general accountability of their schools.

This reluctance to discuss the 'aims and ends' of education was further reinforced by the complicated technological nature of the modern educative process. Most parents in Sheffield were evidently aware that their children were receiving an education which was different both in terms of content and variety from their own experiences. Moreover, when they visited their child's school they found that education was a complex, highly sophisticated activity, characterized by an elaborate organizational system and a highly specialized division of labour. Largely as a result of this situation, I found that, although most parental representatives in Sheffield had some fairly general knowledge of education, typically based upon a combination of their own experiences as school children and a smattering of the popular educational culture found in magazines, television programmes, and Sunday colour supplements, they were in the main unfamiliar with the policies, techniques, philosophies, or even linguistic codes used in their child's particular school. Consequently, most parents were forced by the logic of this situation to look towards the headteacher for guidance on the policy of the school, and to the chairman or clerk for guidance on the policy of the local authority. Thus, in order to be active within their own local school system, the parental representative was forced by the logic of his structural situation to enter into a de facto pupil relationship with the headteacher representing the dominant professional interest concerned, the clerk representing the administrative perspective, and the chairman articulating the views of the local authority. Naturally, people entering this type of dependent social relationship were generally unlikely to want to raise general questions of aims and ends which might facilitate a greater degree of responsiveness or accountability to the client interests, and were usually more willing to take the prudent approach, 'that I had better shut up, and learn as much as I can, as I go along, and leave education to the professionals'. Consequently they mainly concerned themselves with those more tangible, if mundane matters, concerned with fund raising, maintaining the school's fabric, and taking part in annual ceremonial events.

This tendency to concern oneself with the more marginal, if tangible, aspects of their office was subtly reinforced in many different ways. When parents visited schools and talked to teachers or administrators they were often tactfully reminded that present-day education was an involved, complex, highly specialized series of processes and, in view of the manifest physical needs of their school, they would be best advised to spend their time and energies getting their school extra resources, and not raising more general issues about the present nature of long-term aims of the educational process itself. In the rare cases in Sheffield where parents refused to accommodate themselves to this series of professional expectations, but raised general questions imputing criticism of the competence of teachers or the aims of the school, then it was evident that the headteacher had many sanctions at his disposal to quell these 'dissident newcomers'. They might be reminded quite publicly that they were 'new boys' and had a lot to learn about education, they might be provided with a reading list and told to start talking once they had read some new books on education, they might be effectively excluded from certain key subcommittee meetings or appointment committees, and their 'outsider' status might be publicly acknowledged by relegating them to a 'scapegoat placement' at the board's deliberations.

Finally, the general willingness of most parental representatives to accommodate themselves to this existing structure of power was naturally influenced by their own personal concerns for their children. Many people in Sheffield told me they were hesitant to stand as candidates in parental elections since they didn't want, as must inevitably occur if they become involved within the formal administration of education, their children to be labelled as 'different' or treated as special cases. In the same way, some parental governors also worried that if they raised difficult issues at board meetings, then their behaviour might be construed as threatening to the headteacher, and their child might be singled out for unfavourable attention and inadvertently punished for his parent's misdemeanour. Although this was a quite natural parental concern, there was of course little evidence to substantiate this general worry, and if anything the reverse situation might operate. Nonetheless, these prevailing sentiments did mean that most parents were extremely reluctant to raise issues which might be seen by the headteacher to be unconstructive, and which might brand them from an official perspective as a troublemaker. This diffidence generally meant, in practice, that most parental governors judiciously avoided concerning themselves with issues which teachers defined as an illegitimate incursion into their professional territory — the curriculum in general and teaching skills and competence in particular. In short, they were frightened of 'triggering off' a hostile reaction or of reinforcing their own imaginary, if for them the very real, worry that their child might suffer from their parents' indiscretion. In all of these ways then most parental representatives were happy to maintain a fairly low profile and concern themselves with low-key and marginal concerns.

Parents and their children

This generally marginal role of the parental representatives within the Sheffield school governing system was further exacerbated by the day-to-day behaviour of most parents in the city. They tended to share the same conventional wisdoms held by their representatives, and thus they did not tend to think in group terms and identify with a general parental interest which might think in terms of 'our school', 'our children', and 'our teachers'. Rather they possessed a conventionally individual level of consciousness, and characteristically spoke in terms of 'my child', 'his school', 'his teacher', and 'his friends'. Naturally, their social actions tended to be guided by these general attitudes, and they rarely considered an alternative method of relating to the school system. This very person-centered frame of action reference emerged very distincitively when I asked parents the following question:

> 'If your child is having problems at his/her school, who would you go and see about it first?
> And who next?

Most people I spoke to characteristically replied that they would first approach their child's class, form or year tutor and, failing a satisfactory response in this quarter, might, if the issue were deemed serious enough, approach the school's headteacher. However, I found it interesting to note that very few people mentioned approaching a parental governor, and in those cases where this course of action was mentioned, a general interest such as a local traffic problem affecting all children in the area was involved, and not the particular interests of a child within the local school system.

This conventional response was also quite spontaneously reinforced by the day-to-day working assumptions of the child's class and head-teacher. They quite naturally took the view that, 'we like to think that our parents will come and see us if they have a little grumble', and they were unhappy if parents approached an 'outsider' who might quite legitimately, from their point of view, be seen as having little detailed knowledge of the relevant educational issues involved in each particular situation. In this way, the already isolated and marginal role of the parental governor was further negated in the sense that in most key issues his nominal constituents consistently ignored him, and simply found it more expedient to make a direct approach to their child's class teacher or headmaster. Thus the already considerable professional authority of the teaching interest on governing bodies was further reinforced in the sense that they were not only experts within the educational field but, largely as the cumulative result of the parents individuated activities, were generally better informed of the totality of parental concerns, expectations, and criticisms than the elected public representatives nominally representing this client interest.

Social class and school boards

For all of these reasons, while the attempt to facilitate a greater amount of parental involvement in the government of schools may be seen from one point of view as a brave attempt to introduce some degree of participatory democracy into the educational decision-making process, the sociological reality differs greatly from the utopian expectation. Certainly in Sheffield, and I suspect in most other parts of the country, these participatory innovations had not generated an active response amongst parents at the 'grassroots' level. Most people I spoke to appeared to have little interest in what appeared to them to be the extremely formal and socially alien world of school administration, and preferred a direct personalized level of involvement with their child's teachers and school.

In this way, although Sheffield remains a predominantly proletarian city in the sense that the bulk of its population is employed in manual occupations, these workers were often less willing to serve on school boards.

This reluctance was less characteristic of the skilled manual worker than it was of those who were semiskilled or unskilled. In general this apathy was most noticeable in some of the schools serving large council estates and inner-city areas; but this trend was uneven and, in some of the longer established communities, working people were extremely involved in the affairs of their local school. Nonetheless, in general most school boards contained only a minority of 'blue-collar' workers and it was rare to find a semiskilled or unskilled workman taking part in this kind of public service.

This picture was not simply a personal impression, but was also largely substantiated by the subsample of people filling in the extended questionnaire. They were presented with the following statement and then given the task of finding out the social composition of their own board.

> School Boards are often perceived as middle-class institutions, sometimes they are seen as simply puppet bodies with no real power. Obviously these assertions can only be adequately countered if we have detailed information about the political affiliation and social class of managing and governing bodies. In order that we may investigate this in more detail, I would like you to fill in the following schedule.

In general people found this both a daunting and a difficult exercise. The main problem was that it probed what, for many people, was a taboo subject. Mrs. Pike summed up this disquiet well when she said, 'Let's keep politics out of education and get on with the job. If we want to produce a classless society let's stop labelling people. Do the sociologists wish to perpetuate a class system by constantly classifying and grading people?'

Largely as a result of this attitude, fifteen people out of the subsample failed to participate in this exercise, and I only gained information about the social composition of some fifty boards. In spite of this quite high (23 percent) refusal rate, there was no reason to suspect that the remaining answers were in any way inaccurate since the question was intentionally designed to encourage people to think critically about the social composition of their boards. Thus, as we can see from the following table, in nearly one-third of all boards professional workers held between 20 percent and 40 percent of places, and in 38 percent, half the available places or more.

Occupational compositions of Sheffield school boards[8]

	Professional Workers Number of Boards = 50 %	Blue-Collar Workers Number of Boards = 50 %	Housewives Number of Boards = 50 %
None present	2	34	18
Under 20% present	6	55	40
Over 20% and under 40%	30	8	40
Over 40% and under 50%	24	–	2
Over 50%	38	2	–
	100	100	100

In contrast, there were no blue-collar workers on over a third of the boards in the sample, and on most of the remainder they were badly underrepresented. Mrs. Smith summed up the feelings of many people who took part in this exploratory investigation when she said, 'I am a bit taken aback to find out how middle class we are though largely socialist.'

The reasons for this differential pattern of engagement are complex and in part may be due to the fact that professional people tend to be more familiar with the relatively abstract patterns of thought and formal administrative procedures inevitably required in this type of work, partly to their allegiance to a diffuse but nonetheless recognizable ethic of public service, and partly to their relatively privileged structural position in Sheffield society. In contrast, as we can also see from the table on the preceding page, most people in Sheffield took far less interest in this type of formal public involvement and, while from the point of view of the city's educational elites, this behaviour was a cause of much regret and was typically labelled as 'mass apathy', 'indifference', or 'opting out of one's social responsibilities', from another, essentially subordinate perspective it may be seen as an intuitively rational assessment of, and reaction to, the distribution of power in the city.

This is not, of course, to deny that the formal involvement of parents, or other lay people, within the school administrative structure is unimportant. As we have already seen, their presence is especially valued by those who are responsible for the day-to-day management of the local

Type of appointment and length of service

	Long Service		
	Heads N = 21	L.E.A. (Politicals) N = 131	Auxiliary N = 22
	%	%	%
Under 1 year	14	10	5
1 — 3 years	10	20	18
3 — 4 years	5	14	18
4 or more years	71	56	59

	Short Service		
	Parents N = 83	Teachers N = 38	Coopted N = 48
	%	%	%
Under 1 year	10	21	11
1 — 3 years	60	21	33
3 — 4 years	8	18	28
4 or more years	22	40	28

school system. However, in the main, the evidence consistently suggests that their presence is essentially symbolic and, as we have already seen, out of all proportion to their real capacity to represent the parental interest in general, or to influence the decision-making process.

Length of service

At the time of this study the parents representatives had to seek annual reelection. This procedure has been subsequently modified so that they may now serve for up to three years. However, they must still retire from their office when their children leave the school concerned. Largely as a result of this situation, most parental governors tend, for one of a number of reasons, to lose their office when they have finally 'learned the ropes', and might, because of their knowledge and experience, start to play a more active role on the board. Thus, as we can see from the preceding table, in most school boards the parents join a fluid outer 'peripheral group' of relatively inexperienced short-service members, while effective control typically rests in the hands of an 'inner cabinet' made up of long-serving professional or political appointees.

Conclusion

In short, the evidence suggests that certainly in Sheffield, and one suspects in most other authorities which have sought to facilitate parental representation on school boards, this innovation simply gives an illusion of local participation in the decision-making processes. This may well have the manifest effect of strengthening the public's confidence in the legitimacy of the policies being pursued within the schooling system. However, its latent, if unintended, function may well be to strengthen the position of those administrative-political elites ultimately responsible for the public's education. This being said, it may well be time for us to move on from our study of the clients of the school system, and go on in the next chapter to look in some detail at the ways in which the new board system facilitates the work of those dominant groups ultimately responsible for the efficient day-to-day running of the educational service.

Notes and references

1. P. Gordon, *The Victorian School Manager*, Woburn Press, 1974, pp. 173-181.

2. G. Baron & D. A. Howell, *The Government and Management of Schools*, Athlone Press, 1974, p. 31.

3. *Children and Their Primary Schools*, Vol. 1, London HMSO, 1967.

4.   *School Governors and Managers: some facts and figures*, NAGM Publications, May 1975.

5.   Norman St. John Stevas, quoted in *The Times Educational Supplement*, 16 August 1974.

6.   Poll Defaulters, reported in *The Guardian*, 7 October 1975.

7.   Barbara Bullivant, *The New Governors Guide*, Home and School Council Publication, 1974.

8.   This table is based upon the 50 answers I received to a section of the extended questionnaire examining the occupational compositions of school boards.

ADMINISTRATORS, POLITICIANS, AND SCHOOL BOARD DEMOCRACY

Introduction

We have seen that although the introduction of a democratized and participatory school government structure does very little to reallocate the balance of power, either in favour of the clients or employees of the educational system, nonetheless it does tend to substantially reinforce the strength of the managerial prerogative within each school. However, this being said, I must at the same time point out to my readers that my perspective within the foregoing analysis has been a relatively 'middle range' one, in the sense that it has been mainly concerned with the everyday actions of people located within the managerial and lower echelons of the school system. In other words, I have of necessity been concerned with the everyday social actions and experiences of teachers, auxilliary staff, parents and children, and I have not as yet looked in any great detail at the behaviour of, nor problems facing, the local 'educational establishment'; that is, the relatively small group of politicians and administrators who are responsible for, within the wider constraints of the guidelines laid down by the state, the overall leadership and direction of the local educational system in Sheffield.

Largely as a result of this gap in our perspective, what I want to do in this chapter will be slightly different from what has been presented to date, in the sense that I shall now proceed to a more critical and wide-ranging analysis. I shall no longer be concerned with the minutae of school board meetings, the everyday problems facing parents, or the routine of daily school life; rather I shall take a radical, and at times of necessity slightly speculative, perspective and try to look at the ways in which the new participatory style of school board politics may be related to some of the very real political and social difficulties typically confronting the leadership of a school system in the mid-1970s.

In the course of this analysis I shall endeavour, as I have in the past, to consistently address the question of who benefits and who loses out by the adoption of participatory styles of school government. I shall moreover for the sake of brevity and clarity simply refer to, and consequently label, this small and at times self-effacing group of politicians and administrators who carry out the task of leadership as an administrative-political elite or 'educational establishment'. This is because I consider the refusal to make any hard and fast distinctions between full-time senior officials and politicians in this context to be a useful one to adopt. It seems to me that in day-to-day practice it is always difficult, and sometimes impossible, to distinguish between the interests, philosophies, and activities of educational politicians, be they elected representatives or leaders of interest groups, including teacher trade unions, and the senior officials they nominally control through the formal agencies of the local government structure.

Of course a number of concrete sociological factors have contributed towards the development of this rather opaque situation. In the first place, many senior education officials and politicians have at one time or another in their lives, and usually in their younger and more formative years, been trained as teachers preparing for a subsequent career in the state schooling system. In other words, they have undergone, and by definition successfully completed a common process of socialization, which has not only inducted them into the mores of the teaching profession, but which has also facilitated the growth of a common allegience to the aims and ideals of the educational interest in general. In the second place, simply because senior administrators and politicians occupy elite positions within the local schooling system, then they must by definition, at least publicly, display a passionate interest in and concern for education and in many cases be seen to base their daily actions firmly upon the working assumption that further investment in and expansion of the state schooling service will lead towards the creation of a more just and egalitarian society. Thirdly, since both full-time senior officers and educational politicians typically work together in a variety of ways, including visiting schools, going to conferences, sitting on working parties, and of course attending the various committee and subcommittee meetings of the education committee, then they are not only constantly exchanging ideas and opinions with each other, but at the same time tend to become identified with, and consequently lend their support to, any new policies which are jointly developed. Finally, the social logic of this working situation tends to underwrite what may be seen as the creation of an continuing consensus within the ranks of the local educational establishment in the sense that the politicians who after all appointed their officials in the first place, and who work with them in the course of daily life, must also assume responsibility for their servants' actions. They tend, at least publicly, to be wary of acting in such a way that their officers' confidence, or indeed their capacity to undertake their professional duties, will be seriously impaired by any untoward public criticism or substantial withdrawal of political support for their activities.

The problems faced by the educational establishment in the mid-1970s

Naturally the leaders of any large public welfare organization, be it an educational service or one dealing with the peoples' social, recreative, or housing needs, must seek to confront and successfully cope with a number of traditional, if endemic, problems. These might typically include such concerns as the recruitment and training of a labour force, the maintenance of an effective level of labour discipline, the development of various quality control procedures, and the constant review of and updating of one's policies and products. In these and in various other ways, state agencies constantly respond both to what they perceive to be the changing patterns of consumer demand and the needs of the wider society.

However, this being said, in the political situation which is developing in Britain in the early 1970s the leaders of the educational interest are facing a number of different problems which are quite new to them, and which in turn may be related to a number of more general structural and cultural changes taking place within the wider society. These multi-faceted developments have had many repercussions, both within the various sectors of the educational service itself and also in the way its activities are now viewed and evaluated by the wider public. However, for the sake of this analysis, my readers may find it useful to examine them as a series of three different, if contingent, problems which may be categorized as follows.

Problems faced by local educational establishments in the 1970s

1   The problem of maintaining authority, or the legitimate acceptance of one's right to rule in a historical period when there is no longer a basic consensus about the aims of public education, and large numbers of groups including teachers, school students, parents, businessmen, trade unionists, and politicians are becoming more critical of the nature of the existing school system.

2   The problem of maintaining an effective degree of executive control over an organization which is not only large in size and costly to operate, but which many people feel is becoming increasingly remote from the everyday world of the school and the community.

3   The problem of gaining a sufficient degree of public support for often contentious new policies, including the introduction of comprehensive education, destreaming, contested catchment areas and so on.

Obviously all of the above problems are closely interrelated. Thus, for example, it will be more difficult for a leadership to successfully initiate change if its rule is seen as illegitimate. In the same way it will find it more difficult to maintain its authority if its policies are based upon information which is distorted because its channels of communication with the 'shopfloor' or 'grassroots' levels of its organization are ineffective. Equally, it will find it difficult to initiate effective programmes of action to deal with a rapidly changing world if it lacks the time to think clearly because it is burdened by the minutae of administrative detail.

Although the new participatory system of school government introduced into Sheffield and other large educational authorities in the 1970s was not intended to be a universal panacea which solved all of the above problems, nonetheless the evidence does suggest that it substantially reinforced the tactical position of the local educational establishment and helped it to respond more effectively to those wider changes taking place in society. However, in order that my readers may understand the mechanics of what are often a subtle series of social processes, it will now be necessary to look at each of the problems we have so far identified in a little more detail.

Authority and the school system

The changing social and cultural structure of Britain in the mid-1970s has caused many fresh difficulties for those small groups of politicians and administrators who are responsible, within the framework of the democratic system, for the efficient maintenance and effective development of the nation's schools. The roots of these new problems are complex and it is obviously not possible to enumerate them all within the parameters of this study. However they may all be related to one dimension in the sense that a once dominant moral order has broken down into what is commonly referred to as a plural society, and in which there is no longer any common or widely accepted agreement about the objectives which a public educational system should seek to pursue.

Moreover, the problem is compounded because the public at large is becoming increasingly aware of the key role formal schooling and certification plays in life. This is not to suggest that they necessarily value scholasticism for its own sake, but rather to emphasize that the formal educative process has become the major vehicle for selecting and then allocating people to the labour market. In short, schooling, as distinct from education, has become a common concern and the various technical processes, activities, and philosophies of the nation's school system have become part of a far wider conventional wisdom.

These cultural developments, perhaps inevitably, tend to generate a number of severe political problems for the leaders of any school system in the sense that their actions are subject to the closest public scrutiny and are likely to be challenged both by groups within and outside the organization. Moreover, this process is also a reciprocal one in the sense that since so many politicians and administrators are also liberal 'other-directed' men, then they in turn will question in private, if not publicly, their own right and capacity to introduce the kind of changes which will inevitably, for better or for worse, effect the life chances of many thousands of people — to introduce comprehensive education, to abolish streaming, to change a school catchment area, to abandon corporal punishment, and so on.

This situation, which from a technical point of view may be seen as a crisis of authority, is somewhat alleviated, though obviously not resolved, by the type of limited administrative innovations we have been reviewing in the last five chapters. Although, as we have seen, the new board system does not in practice lead to any substantive devolution of power to parents, teachers, students, or community groups, the evidence does nonetheless suggest that it helps to increase the public's confidence in and support for the policies being pursued by the leaders of the school system. At the same time, since it also tends to make opaque the loci of decision making, it tends to leave the latter group less exposed to harsh and sometimes personally stressful criticism. The new system works precisely because it capitalizes on the widespread public interest and concern for formal schooling and effectively recruits large numbers of local notables, representatives of teachers, parents, auxilliary workers, and so on. However, largely because of the social processes we analysed in the last four chapters, most, if not all of these recruits tend to become closely identified with and concerned with the problems of their own school, passionate advocates of the educational cause in general, and stout defenders of the policies and interests of the headteacher and his staff. However, although these new lay recruits are closely identified with the school system, at the same time they enjoy little effective power within it and their influence tends to be marginal and confined to largely minor concerns. The majority of the major decisions and thus the balance of power remains largely, as it has for most of this century, in the hands of a leading group of politicians and administrators and with their local professional managers — the head-teachers. Nonetheless, the presence of so many prominent local people within the formal administration of the school system tends to obscure this decision-making process, and in turn effectively shields policy makers from criticism or a hostile opposition. This protective and insulating function operates in a variety of ways; thus boards of managers and governors are often involved in cases where difficulties may arise between the school and a pupil and his parents, and where the headteacher wishes to emphasize that his decision has been a collective, not a personal, one. The following letter to one parent is not untypical of this type of procedure.

Dear Mrs. Smith,

I regret that after a long discussion with senior members of my staff, and the Chairman of my Board of Governors, it has been decided that your son is suspended from this school until the beginning of next term. We are all prepared to consider his readmission to school if you can guarantee his reasonable behaviour. At present his refusal to attend various lessons and spending much time in toilets, creates a situation which could spread to other pupils if not corrected. As you know, many members of staff have done their utmost over a long period to help your son. In spite of this, the position has got steadily worse.

The date for starting the new term is Tuesday, 12th January 1976. By that time I hope you will be able to bring your son to the school to discuss the question of his future education. We will leave his entry for G.C.E. open until this date.

Yours sincerely,

Headmaster

Similarly, school managing and governing bodies are often involved by the local educational establishment in questions where there is a widespread public concern about issues such as discipline, reading standards, or school uniforms. However, this process is perhaps best seen at work within the context of those grand 'set piece dramas' occurring throughout the school year — speech day, sports day, open day, parents evenings, drama festivals, Christmas concerts, and so on. These occasions are important not only because they manifestly assert the dominant values of a power structure, but also because they allow us to observe, clearly and explicitly, the key legitimizing and protective role which school managing and governing bodies play within the political structure of the local school system.[1] Thus, while the following analysis of a speech day in a Sheffield school is not unique, it is valuable in that it illustrates, in the clear and precise fashion that no amount of theory could, the key affirmatory role school boards play in expressing local societies' support for the values and policy being pursued by their school.

Speech Day, A Content Analysis

A. *The Governors and Other Participants*

1. The headmaster (exofficio member)
2. A local councillor (deputy chairman of the board)
3. A local councillor's wife
4. Chairman of the board (an ex-councillor, who is a manager in a large local industry)
5. Chairman's wife
6. Visiting speaker (a prominent county councillor)
7. Parents' representative (a local businessman)
8. Parents' representative's wife
9. Local primary school headteacher (a coopted member)
10. Primary headteacher's wife
11. Local authority nominee (ex-councillor, now retired)
12. Local authority nominee's wife
13. Representative of the local university (a lecturer)
14. Parents' representative (college lecturer)

15. Coopted member (active in the local community association)
16. Coopted member's wife
17. Nonteaching staff representative (school secretary)
18. Teachers' representative (senior tutor in the school)
19. Teachers' representative (deputy head in the school)

B. *The Main Events* — a commentary

1. *Chairman's Opening Remarks*

After the conventional pleasantries, the chairman takes up the issue of the present decline in disciplinary standards. He points out that the school is, as yet, mercilessly unaffected; nonetheless, he tells the parents that this question is essentially their responsibility and not the school's or the teachers'. He stresses that we must do all we can to support the authorities in their battle against this problem.

The chairman then goes on to congratulate the school on its excellent academic record and suggests that the school is consistently demonstrating its success and quality by gaining consistently high numbers of qualifications. He makes it clear that certification is going to become even more important in the future; however, he concedes that the emphasis must be on the 'right type of qualification' and laments the fact that he spends so much time interviewing 'people who have studied sociology and find no use for that qualification'. He concludes by making a plea for more technologists.

2. *The Choir*

The choir, which is composed of girls all dressed uniformly and all wearing ties, then sings 'Little Jack Horner'.

3. *Headmaster's Report*

The headmaster then gives his report. He starts with a few general remarks about the recent changes taking place within the school as it has become comprehensive. He points out that this development has caused a great deal of work and effort and he goes on to say that the recent proposals to cut real educational expenditure will undoubtedly lead to a serious setback in all the splendid advances the school has made in the past five years.

He goes on to give details of current academic developments, the G.C.E. 'O'-level results have been good with an 81% pass level, the decision to build a sixth form, and the staffing needs which this will undoubtedly create. He gives details of the school's success in sport — Brown and Smith are both regular members of the city rugby team, Hargreaves and

Jennings have distinguished themselves in cross-country running, the hockey and badminton teams have all had a 'fair measure of success', and the school has won the city tennis trophy for the first time in many years. He goes on to give details of school visits to neighbouring European countries, local industrial and historical centres, and the work of pupils in caring for local old people, visiting the sick in hospitals, and children in nurseries.

Comments   Everyone in the hall is most impressed by this account. All the governors look very proud and satisfied with their school.

The headteacher goes on to talk about some new academic developments, including the construction of a new Mode 3, CSE exam in physics for those who find this subject a 'bit strenuous', the development of computer-marking schemes for biology, history, and mathematics examinations, the successful production of *Iolanthe*, the choir's work with local community associations, and so on.

He concludes by thanking all of the staff for their efforts in maintaining the 'high academic standards we have come to expect in this school', and he thanks the chairman and the governors for their loyal support and help over the past year. Finally, he thanks the parents and stresses that the great majority are 'obviously supportive and helpful of our efforts'. However, 'unfortunately a few pupils won't, or can't make a reasonable response to the school'. This is unfortunate, but in the end ill discipline is a parental responsibility and 'the parents can't divorce themselves from responsibility for their uncooperative attitude'.

Comments   All of the school governors, by their stern looks, nods and grunts, obviously agree with the head's comments.

4. *Prizegiving*

The wife of the visiting speaker then presents the prizes. This is a long ceremony and lasts over half an hour. Generally, it is a very formal affair; the whole proceeding is ranked in terms of age; the youngest children come first and the oldest children receive their prizes last. All of their prizes are books, most of them are for academic or sporting excellence or general endeavour in the service of the school. The clapping is extremely formal and takes place after each year or group has been processed.

5. *Chairman*

The chairman thanks the wife of the visiting speaker for presenting the prizes, and says it does great credit to the school that so many people are achieving these distinctions.

6. Orchestra

The orchestra then plays a military march and follows this with a piece from a comic opera.

7. The Chairman

The chairman introduces the visiting speaker and says it is a great privilege to have him with us tonight; indeed if there were more people with his sincerity and common sense then this country would be a better place. He goes on to say, 'the speaker is not only a powerful and eminent public figure, but he is also unaffected by his responsibilities and understands the common man, so we can all be proud he is looking after us. This school should be privileged to have such a man addressing our speech day.'

8. Speaker

He opens by remarking how delighted he is to visit the school on this particularly important occasion. He stresses that speech day is a 'fundamentally important day' in the life of the school, and it is 'vitally important that politicians attend these occasions' since they are splendid opportunities for them to get the 'feel' of the success of their policies.

He goes on to make some generally humorous remarks about his misunderstanding of modern teaching methods and then gets on to the main theme of the evening. He was born sixty years ago and in that time, although we have made great material progress and largely abolished poverty, we have not solved our human relations problems. There is a 'general lack of respect today', a 'strange selfishness and a general moaning amongst us'. Something is wrong somewhere, and it is up to the young people to cure this malaise and change the world. Any economic measures which damage our educational system are wrong and misguided. They will damage our future. We must see education as an investment in the future. 'I never object to paying my rightful share of the rates to achieve this goal.' Education will give us the kind of Britain we want to build in this country. The speaker then finishes by congratulating the school on its tremendous development in the past ten years and wishes it the 'best of luck in the future'.

9. Vote of thanks

This is respectfully given by the local councillor, who also has a 'surprise in store' for the distinguished guest; he has arranged for a present, an afromosia table, to be made in the school workshops and this is now presented by the craftmaster and two boys.

The headgirl thanks the chairman of the board of governors for the interest he has shown in the school over the last seven years. She asks for the grant of a one-day holiday and the chairman graciously acceeds.

10. *Finale*

Everyone sings the national anthem, which is accompanied by the school orchestra; everyone in the hall — pupils and parents — stands as the platform party leave.

Maintaining an effective level of executive control

However, apart from helping the local educational leadership gain a widespread communal support for its policies, the new participatory system of school government also enables it to cope more successfully with a number of purely administrative difficulties.

The roots of this problem are two fold. In the first place, Sheffield, like most other large industrial cities, is gradually losing its monolithically proletarian character, and is slowly growing into a more complex society in which it is no longer possible to recognize easily a distinctive series of social groupings, classes, or communities, in the sense that each of these possesses its own tribal territories, values, interests, and social hierarchies. Rather, as the economic base of the city slowly changes and the division of labour becomes more elaborate, then at the same time the social structure of this society becomes more differentiated and gradually evolves into a more pluralistic social order composed of a kaleidoscope of formal and informal multi-bonded groups.

The consequences of these deeper social changes for the local and national leaders of all our state institutions, whether they be concerned with the social services, law and order, or, as in the case we are examining, education, are of course quite profound, for in a very real sense, they can no longer assume that they or their policies reflect widely held communal or class values, or that they will necessarily gain a wide-spread public support or tacit acquiescence. In short, in the kind of society which is emerging in contemporary Britain, a local political leadership operating within those structures normally associated with traditional representative models of democracy is often badly informed about the opinions of, as well as being socially and geographically distant from, the hetrogeneous clientele they are elected or appointed to serve. They can no longer rely upon the kind of informal support and flow of information which was once supplied to them by a galaxy of local tribal leaders; rather they find they are often 'working in the blind' and are largely ignorant of the likely reactions of teachers, parents, students, or community leaders to their policies.

This problem, which is essentially one of maintaining an effective communications system with a variety of local groups and interests, is exacerbated by the sheer growth in size of all statal and parastatal units, including the education service. Partly because of the needs of all advanced industrial societies for a more highly trained and adaptable labour force, partly as a result of the successful work of groups which have been pressing governments to spend more money and extend the provision provided by the state, the publicly funded sector of the educational system has grown rapidly in size in the 1960s and 1970s. As a result of this situation, in the case of Sheffield, as is common elsewhere in the country, the leaders of the local educational service are responsible for the effective day-to-day maintenance of a machine which is by far the largest spender of money in the local authority sector, but which employs some 5500 teachers, serves the needs of over 100,000 students, and encompasses nearly 300 different institutions.

Perhaps inevitably a leadership confronted with this kind of logistic situation and working within the confines of the new kind of social order which is gradually developing in Britain finds it difficult not only to maintain effective links with grassroots opinion in the city, but also to maintain an effective degree of control over the work of their own employees, whether they are located within the central bureaucracy itself or are employed as managers or teachers with the various subunits of the system. In short then, in this new situation, a local political-administrative leadership, whether it is responsible for education or any other state service, must attempt to solve two contingent administrative problems. Firstly, how can it ensure that it gains a reliable and continuous flow of information about the views and problems of its clientele, and in this way judge the likely degree of opposition its policies might generate amongst the people it is serving? Secondly, how can it ensure that its officers remain well informed about and alert to the diverse needs of the communities they serve and, at the same time, operate the service in a way in which is flexible and responsive to a variety of client-centred needs and interests?

A cybernetic model of administration

The new system of school government may be seen as a first tentative and still highly experimental attempt to solve these problems. It effectively replaces an older centralized system of control with a new structure which bears many resemblances to cybernetic modes of operation. Thus, it seeks to involve a cross-section of workers, clients, and other groups in the process of administration, and at the same time give them the opportunity to effectively articulate their concerns about the effectiveness of this operation to the local educational establishment which is responsible for the organization of the entire structure.

Thus, under the old highly centralized system of control, the only effective monitoring agents was the corps of full-time school inspectors whose task it was to ensure that the aims and objectives of their employees were being effectively carried out in each school. These officers typically relied upon the method of listening, examining, and finally reporting to the political masters on whether or not a school had achieved its objectives. However, although this system might appear from a superficial examination to be an effective one, it proved in practice to be a remarkably ineffective form of administrative control. Moreover, there were a number of good reasons for this development. In the first place, as we saw in Chapter 1, the adoption of the payments by results system in nineteenth-century elementary schools had, perhaps inevitably, generated the development of a peculiar kind of occupational culture amongst teachers in the twentieth century. This was generally characterized by a very real suspicion of, and at time open hostility to, any form of external assessment or inspection, whether it be carried out by the agents of the state or the local authority, and which jealously guarded what it saw as its professional prerogative to decide what, and how, subjects were taught both within schools and in their classrooms.

Largely as a result of this situation, the local or national inspector's visit to a state-supported school was often an extremely formal and sometimes surprisingly tense occasion. The teachers were naturally wary of the inspectorate, but at the same time were concerned to give their visitors a thoroughly favourable impression of their work. As a result, during the course of 'the inspection', they naturally paid particular attention to their own dress, behaviour and teaching routines, the decoration of their classroom, the sponsorship of special pupil works, and all other aspects of the common rituals of institutional display. Because of this type of traditionally closed and defensive response to their visits, the inspectorate in the main tended to see what the teachers wanted them to see, and thus gained a very distorted impression of what really went on within the daily life of the school when its routine was not so radically altered to accommodate this type of extremely formal external assessment.

At the same time, the school inspectors, by their very nature, could only look at and assess the work of the institution itself, and could thus only relate to their political masters what was going on within the particularly narrow world of the school. They could not, since they had neither the power or the means to, report on the mood or feeling of the community served by the school, nor could they, since they typically related to the teaching force in an extremely tense and formal situation, accurately judge the 'mood of the staffroom', or the current private view of 'rank-and-file' teachers on educational affairs.

A state of creative tension

Most of the evidence I have examined seems to suggest that the new participatory system certainly helps to alleviate some of the rigidities of this old centralized inspectorial system, and helps to provide Sheffield's educational establishment with a steady and more comprehensive flow of grassroot opinion, both from within their schools and from the surrounding community. This development was largely achieved through the creation of a new tier of educational administration, the school board, which was legally seen as a subcommittee of the education committee and which included representatives from a variety of concerned and interested groups. Simply by means of establishing these new bodies, and thus formally acknowledging that it wished to bring such a variety of concerned people together, the local authority not only generated a process of discussion, but also created a new series of interests whose views needed to be taken into account both by the local schools and the central bureaucracy.

This quite radical change to what may be seen from a sociological point of view as a more client-centred and conflict-oriented style of educational administration was made very clear in the directions the new managers received. As we saw in Chapter 2, these reforms not only brought directly into the business of school administration nearly 4000 influential local people who were previously largely unconnected with or unfamiliar with this kind of work, but at the same time encouraged them to be active and critical members of their boards. Thus, the new governors were specifically requested to visit their school regularly in order to find out as much as possible about its policies, what it was trying to achieve, and how it was setting about effecting its aims. The new governors were also encouraged to act as advocates of their school, and they were reminded that if they found any deficiencies hampering its work, they were to

> draw the Committee's attention to the deficiencies or needs of the school. You will appreciate, however, that the Committee would find it difficult to respond to requests from individual governors. Your requests will have much more force as the collective view of the governing body.

However, the governors not only intended to fulfil an advocacy role; rather they were also reminded that it was part of their new job to express legitimate criticism and concern if it was so merited. Thus, their booklet of instruction also included the following suggestions:

> If you wish to pursue any complaint you hear about the school refer it first to the headteacher. If you still feel uneasy get in touch with the Chairman of Governors, who may suggest that that question should be raised with the Chief Education Officer.

School boards and school administration

In general, although as we have seen in the last three chapters, the new school governors are in the main reluctant to discuss matters of general policy and the locii of power, in the sense that decisions about which issues are discussed and which are largely neglected are effectively taken by the head-teacher, chairman, or clerk to the board. Nonetheless, the evidence does suggest that many people have taken their general duty both to discuss and to report to the authority on a whole variety of matters reflecting both the immediate concerns of the school and wider local community most seriously. Largely as a result of this process of discussion and communication, the local educational elite is both better informed about what is happening within its schools and their local communities and is also, largely because of this, better able to assess the efficiency of its officers' work and the strength of any potential long-term opposition to its policies.

The clerk

Typically, the interests and concerns of school boards are expressed to the local educational elite in a variety of ways. If the matter in question is a minor one, such as the failure of a department to repair a leaking roof, provide adequate cleaning and caretaking services, or to arrange adequate transport facilities for the children, then the clerk to the board may simply promise to initiate actions personally, or to investigate the matter in an informal manner with his senior colleagues. Indeed, simply because the person who clerks the meeting of all school boards in the city is an employee of the authority who typically spends most of his working life working within, or relating to, the central educational bureaucracy, then he is in an excellent strategic position to convey both to his senior administrative masters, and through them to the councillors all of the moods and feelings of board members on a variety of delicate issues which may not be recorded in the minutes of the formal proceedings of the board.

The clerk of course, as we have already noted, occupies a key role on any board. He typically occupies a high status role since he is formally representing the chief education officer of the authority, and his opinion and advice is normally treated with great respect. Largely because of this, many lay governors tend to defer to the person who is not only officially identified with the loci of power within the local educational hierarchy, but who is also, because of the nature of his daily work, able to demonstrate a unique knowledge of the schooling system. Moreover, the clerk is able to mobilize many tactical devices to reinforce his overall power. He can, for example, choose to withhold or dispense key items of information, he may wish to place bureaucratic obstacles in the paths of people whose views he finds distasteful, he can, since he keeps the official minutes of the board, decide which items of opinion he wished to record and which he chooses to omit, and finally, since he plays a key role in drawing up the board's agenda, he can decide the vital question of how, and in what order, items are discussed at each meeting.

However, this being said, the process of interaction is not entirely one-dimensional, for the new participatory system has also had a notable influence upon the clerks themselves in the sense that whereas once, as officers working within a centralized system, they spent their daily lives within the social context of the educational bureaucracy itself, they have now, since they must go out and clerk board meetings, been forced into assuming a new role which involves them in a complex routine of visiting schools, talking to professional and lay people, and explaining as simply as possible the aims and policies being pursued by their administrative or political masters. In order to carry out these new tasks, the clerk must not only make himself familiar with a whole new range of affairs, but also, since he represents the chief education officer at school board meetings, must make himself familiar with his authorities' overall policies. In short, simply because he has become a school board clerk, the official can no longer continue to function as a narrow specialist who spends all his life in the central bureaucracy and simply relates to schools through the abstract and impersonal means of the administrative letter, report, or memoranda. Rather, he has been forced, to some extent, to assume the role of a generalist who, simply because he clerks school board meetings, comes to possess a deeper understanding of the problems facing teachers and children, and a more realistic perception of what schools are really like.

The formal resolution

Of course, if a school board feels a matter is sufficiently serious and merits something more positive than its clerk initiating an action on a personal basis, then it may typically discuss the matter in question at some length and them move to compose and pass a resolution which will serve to formally communicate its sentiments to the education authority. In the course of my analysis of the minutes of school boards, I found that most managers decided to pass at least one formal resolution at each of their meetings. These covered a variety of topics and, as we can see from the following examples, ranged from such concerns as matters of fabric maintenance through to staffing matters and sometimes included quite sharp implicit criticisms of the educational authorities' policy.

Some typical school board resolutions

1. *Decorating of the school*

    'Resolved: The Managers support the Head Teacher's request for the redecoration of the interior of the school. Attention is drawn to the state of those rooms used for multifunctional community purposes.'

2. *Community access*

    'Resolved: The Head Teacher's request for a bollard to be so placed at the entrance to the school path to prevent its use by motor vehicles be endorsed.'

    'Resolved: That the Chairman and Headteacher of Black School meet the Chairman and Headteacher of White School to discuss the matter of their common use of footpaths, and to consider the provision of other means of access to the schools.'[2]

3. *Caretaking*

    'Resolved: That the Governors express their grave concern about the caretaking situation and ask the Authority for some action to provide adequate cover as soon as possible.'

4. *Transport*

    'Resolved: That in view of the serious shortage of buses for transporting Pink and Yellow Schools' children to the Warwick area, that stronger representations be made by the Education Committee to the Transport Executive to implement the transport inspectors recommendation that 4 buses be provided not 3, and to replace the 1 man by 2 men double decker buses.'

5. *Staffing*

'*Resolved*: That the Governors express to the Education Committee their serious concern that Black as a Group 10 School has not been given approval to the appointment of a Third Assistant Head. The Governors feel strongly that the expansion of the school and of its activities fully justify such an appointment in the best interests of the pupils and staff.'

6. *Examination policy*

Dual entry for external examinations

'*Resolved*: That the Governors deplore the Authority's decision to meet the cost of only one entry when candidates chose dual entry for external examinations as this policy is detrimental to the financially poorer pupils.'

Naturally, all of this activity means that in the normal course of the educational year the Sheffield authority may be literally 'bombarded' by hundreds of resolutions. I gained the impression that all these developments help to establish a situation of more creative tension, in the sense that the local admin-political elite is now provided with a constant flow of information concerning what representative and influential groups of local people are thinking and feeling, both about their own schools and the educational service as a whole. In short then, these resolutions provide them with a ready means of assessing not only the day-to-day effectiveness of the work of their officers in, for example, providing effective cleaning, transport, or staffing facilities in each of their schools, but also of judging the reactions of influential local notables to those policies they are presently executing, as well as those they may wish to introduce in the future. Largely because this flow of information keeps them better informed both about the work of the education machine itself and the mood of 'grassroots' opinion, most members of the local educational establishment made it clear that they took the new participatory style of administration very seriously, and few were content to dismiss the whole exercise cynically in terms of a therapeutic safety valve for local feelings. This judgement was made very explicit by one senior officer of the authority, when he reminded a group of governors attending a training course that,

    ... the education committee takes the views of school managers and governors very seriously indeed, and expects informed comments on their resolutions from its officials. The committee will be very cross if they find that what is being complained about is being neglected by its officers.

Of course it is not possible, in the course of this quite short analysis, to illustrate in detail how the new board system facilitates the process of keeping the local decision makers fully informed about the state of local feeling in each community. However, my readers may find the following case of particular interest since it illustrates in some detail how school boards, by their very presence, can serve to make the local educational bureaucracy more flexible and sensitive to local needs and interests.

The case of the Blackshire Community Association

Background   The Blackshire Community Association is a flourishing organization which has many branches including a large sporting section. However, it faces a major problem in that there is a chronic lack of sporting facilities in the Blackshire part of the city. In view of this its members were naturally delighted to learn that the local Blackshire Comprehensive School planned to build a large, well-equipped sports hall on its campus. Since the local authority had formally adopted a policy which encouraged the community use of school buildings outside of school hours, the community association made an early request to the school lettings department responsible for organizing all school lettings in the city, requesting the use of the sports hall facilities when they became available for the use of its badminton and gymnastics section.

Stage I   The lettings department approaches the headmaster of Blackshire school, and then sends a letter to the community association thanking them for their inquiry concerning the use of the school sports hall, and which goes on to say, 'We have been in touch with the head-teacher who is unable to offer you accommodation at present. However, when the new sports hall is completed in January he will probably be able to offer you the use of a hall or a gymnasium.' Naturally, the community association is delighted with this positive reply and its members look forward to using the newly built premises.

Stage II   However, once the sports hall is completed and in general use, the community association is surprised to receive a further communication from the lettings department pointing out that 'the sports hall is booked every night of the week for various school activities and in addition the staff and pupils of the school use the sports hall. I regret, therefore, that I am unable to offer you accommodation.'

Naturally, the community association was concerned about this unexpected development and its officers approached their local councillor requesting his aid in gaining them access to the local school's facilities. In a letter to him they point out that their members have noticed that the facilities at the school are seldom fully in use and 'that invariably the users leave by 9.00 p.m., whereas our group continues until 10.00 p.m. Even that extra hour would be appreciated. As we have so far been unsuccessful, please could you help?'

The councillor, who is a busy man and who does not live in this part of the city, tries to help. He approaches the letting office, but again receives the same kind of negative response the community association has already received, pointing out that the school is fully booked and no further accommodation is available.

Stage III   In view of this situation the association decides to take up on what it sees as its 'last resort', the offer of facilities in another school some five miles away. They write to their councillor thanking him for his help, and they go on to say that, '... they have not abandoned their hopes concerning the use of the (local) school sports hall.' Consequently, they continue to press the local educational authority for the use of accommodation at their local school, and continue to receive from the lettings office a succession of bland but evasive replies, which are typically couched in the following terms: 'I have arranged for your community association's request to be placed on our records, and should any accommodation become available at Blackshire School Sports Hall I will advise you.'

Stage IV   The surprising thing about all the developments was that the governing body of Blackshire School was not informed either by the headteacher or the clerk to the board of this affair. While this omission should in the light of the evidence we have already reviewed hardly surprise my readers, in this case it was particularly illuminating for two reasons. Firstly, the local authority had specifically requested its managers and governors to 'Try to strengthen the links between your school and the local community,' and, to this end, the formal powers of the board included the following specific mandate:

School Premises

The governors shall, subject to any decision of the Authority regarding the letting of school accommodation or offical evening, weekend or holiday use, determine in consultation with the headteacher the use to which the school premises or any part thereof, may be put additional to its use for the purposes of the school.

Secondly, the general policy both of the local authority and of successive governments has been to encourage the efficient multi-consumer use of public buildings, including school premises, for communal purposes in the evenings and at weekends. Certainly in this case the evidence seemed to suggest that the school buildings, which represented one of the most expensive public investments in the local community, was being seriously underused.

Stage V   After making another series of fruitless pleas to the officials of the lettings department of the local authority, and receiving a further series of bland and evasive replies, the community association, in desparation, wrote to their local M.P. and finally the Minister for Sport. In both letters they pointed out that:

1. Many people want to participate in sport in the city, but can't do so because of a chronic lack of facilities.

2. Their local sports hall is used by senior pupils and teachers, other people are using it who have no connection with the school, and at times it is not used at all.

3. Their local councillor has tried to help them, however; she had in turn advised them that our hands were tied, and that the headmaster's word was 'law as regards the use of facilities outside school hours'.

Obviously, by this stage in the proceedings, the officials of the community association were thoroughly estranged from their local educational authority. They saw it as a large, inpersonal institution, which was constantly evading its responsibilities and refusing to respond in a positive manner to what they saw as their very reasonable case. In short, vital decisions effecting their members' lives and the local community were being taken in a seemingly arbitrary manner, with little opportunity for consultation or discussion. The local headmaster was perceived in an equally negative light; he was seen to be a powerful authoritarian figure who effectively dominated all of the decision-making process and who was most insensitive to local needs and interests.

This was obviously a potentially volatile situation which might well be damaging to the authorities' reputation if it became public knowledge, and in particular might well cause considerable personal embarrassment for the senior members of the local educational establishment. However, purely by chance, the community association made contact with, and mentioned the issue to, a governor of the local school who was also a member of a political party. Although this person was quite active in local politics, he was unaware of the community associations difficulties, and was at first suspicious of their motives in approaching him. However, on talking to their officers, and reading what by now had become an extremely voluminous correspondence on the matter, he realized that the community association had a strong case and because of this took the view that if something was not done rapidly then the affair would reflect badly upon his school and ultimately upon the local educational establishment.

Stage VI   The school governor raised this issue under the item of 'any other business', at the next meeting of his board. He pointed out that the governors had a duty to perform vis-à-vis the use of school premises, and he asked for the matter to be put on the agenda of the next meeting. The rest of the board were extremely interested in this matter; however, the clerk and the headteacher were initially hostile. The headteacher pointed out that the policy of his school had always been to support the community in every way possible, and he went on to say that the community association had never approached him personally on this matter and so on. The clerk strongly supported the headteacher and pointed out that the school was indeed fully booked in the evenings. However, the governor who raised the issue pressed his initial point and illustrated it in some detail by quoting the community association's correspondence on the matter, both with the letting office, the councillor, the local M.P., and the Minister for Sport. Largely as a result of the strength of this supportive evidence the following resolution was passed by the board:

> *Resolved*: To discuss the matter of school lettings at the next meeting.

In other words, the issue had now been raised formally and at the next meeting of the board the school's letting policy was not only explained but justified in detail to the governing body of the school. After the meeting had finished, the governor who raised the issue also discussed the matter with the clerk to the board and made it clear to him that he considered this to be a potentially explosive issue which could, it it became public knowledge, lead to the considerable embarrassment of the local education establishment.

Stage VII   Shortly after this matter was raised for the first time in the governors' meeting, the community association received a letter confirming that 'it will be in order for you to use' the new sports hall, and requesting them to start using the premises as from the 7th April 1975. Naturally the community association was delighted with this positive outcome, and wrote to the governor who had originally raised the matter expressing thanks for his efforts on their behalf.

Obviously it is impossible to judge how far this end result was a result, as was officially claimed, of another organization suddenly finding it no longer wanted to use the sports hall and consequently leaving a vacancy for the community association. Certainly the evidence seemed to suggest that the discussion and formal resolution of the school board had been a most effective means of not only informing the local educational establishment of the strength of community feeling in an area but also of helping it to 'head off' a potentially damaging public confrontation with an important local grassroots organization. At the same time, this activity had also enabled it to maintain a more effective control on the actions of the local headteacher, in the sense that largely as a result of this discussion his actions were likely in the future to be slightly more responsive both to local needs and interests and the general policy laid down by his political masters.

Informal communication

Of course the formal system of communication through the means of the clerk or the committee resolution was not the only means the local educational establishment had of maintaining contact with, and receiving an informal flow of information about, local opinion and interest. As we have already seen, precisely because the new participatory system has recruited into the services of the educational interest so many people, including local party political activists not previously connected with or formally involved in the work or problems of the local school, then it can also call upon this new force to keep it informed about what is happening within each community. In turn, these new recruits to the educational interests will often communicate either verbally at local ward meetings or more formally through correspondence with senior party members on those aspects of the educational service which are currently worrying them, but which for the sake of prudence they would not wish to introduce directly into the formal arena of a school board meeting.

Thus, in the case of one school in the city, a local labour party member and political activist was surprised to find that when he examined the staffing provision of his local school that no graded post allocation had been made to facilitate the employment of specialist teachers of English or mathematics, although he knew that this was the normal practice amongst most schools in the area. She did not wish to raise this issue formally at a board meeting without first sounding out the views of the local educational establishment, and as a first step sent a local councillor and chairman of the committee looking after primary education in the city, the following letter:

Dear Councillor Smith,

Just an informal note to let you know I attended Yellow School Managers' meeting on Monday night. I was surprised to find that in this middle school of some 400 pupils there was no teacher with responsibility for either the teaching of Maths or English.

The headteacher claimed that he was responsible for the organisation and direction of these subjects throughout the school and he told us that he assumed these other duties in addition to performing all his other tasks as a headteacher. There were, of course, scale posts in the school for Music, Art, Crafts and so on, but none for the core subjects. I find this situation, particularly in the light of the Bullock Report, the present debate on the core curriculum, and the fact that teachers are given scale posts of responsibility for Maths and English in the feeder first school, a most disquieting one. Moreover, I would add that many parents have expressed to me privately their concern vis. a. vis. the mathematical and reading standards, as well as the general organisation of Yellow Middle School.

I would be grateful if you could let me know, in confidence, whether my worries on the Maths and English issue are justified ones and, if they are, advise me, as a local authority appointed manager, what I can do about it.

Looking forward to hearing from you,

Yours sincerely,

Similarly, in the case of another school, a local party activist became concerned when he received reports from parents about the evangelical activities of one local church, who not only took over the morning assemblies of schools in the area, but also used this occasion to invite children to a Christian crusade which was being held at the church in the evening. Some people had already criticized this particular crusade since, in the words of one local minister, it 'Represented evangelical militant Protestantism which was obnoxious to Roman Catholics, to other religions, to humanists, and to people who take more liberal attitudes towards the religious message.'

The point of concern was not, of course, the nature of the crusade, but the fact that it had taken place within schools and that parents had not been informed in advance that this particular group was not only to attend their child's school, organize the morning assembly, but was also able to use this occasion to distribute an invitation and tickets for a series of evening meetings at a local church.

In view of the fact that she thought that this was too delicate a matter to raise at a board meeting, since it might be construed as a personal attack on the headteacher who had officially sanctioned the 'crusader's' visit to the school, the local political activist sent a private communication to a senior member of the education committee pointing out that he had received many complaints from parents in the area concerning the Children's Christian Crusade, and going on to say that

> ... Many parents are reluctant to complain in person on this matter either to the school's headteacher, or the officers of the authority. This is because in part they are worried about the status of the Crusade, some feel I hope incorrectly, that this was an official event and was sanctioned or tacitly supported by the local educational authority. However, it is also in part because parents are naturally concerned about the educational career of their own children in school, and are unwilling to cause 'a fuss' lest their child is singled out, and perhaps because of this treated differently from the others. Obviously there is no evidence to support the latter contentions nevertheless this is not to say it is a very real worry for many parents, and effectively stops them from complaining as vigorously as they might on these matters.

> I hope your officers will investigate this matter in the schools concerned, and if, as I suspect, the main points in my letter are substantiated by more detailed evidence, then perhaps the local managers may be able to see a report at a later juncture. ...

In short, the evidence I have examined in Sheffield suggests that, although the system is far from perfect, nonetheless the creation of the new school government structure has contributed significantly to the solution of the many administrative problems which were facing the local educational establishment in the late 1960s. Today they are better informed about what is going on in each school, in each community, and in each pressure group, and this general awareness has generally lead to a substantial increase in their overall effectiveness and power. This is because, under the new participatory systems, they usually learn about the various difficulties, problems, or criticisms of people at an early and not late and critical stage in their development, and can consequently act quickly to prevent an explosive 'head of steam' building up. At the same time, the system has encouraged the officers and advisers employed within the central bureaucracy to play a more active and community-oriented role, and as a result they are not only better informed about what is going on in each school but able to keep their political masters better informed about what is going on in the city. However, this being said the administration, and the execution of policy, cannot be studied in isolation from the formulation of, and introduction of, new policies themselves. Thus, in the next section of this chapter, I want to move on from this examination of the ways in which the new boards tend to facilitate the maintenance of an effective degree of executive control, and examine in turn their impact upon the decision-making processes itself.

Introducing new policies

I found, in the course of my work in Sheffield, that the new participatory school board system also tends to help the local educational leadership cope more successfully with the often delicate task of introducing new and often contentious policies into the city. Thus, in those parts of Britain which still continue to maintain a totally centralized system of school administration, or indeed within those authorities which lack an effective participatory school board structure, the process of facilitating radical change and innovation is often more politically dangerous for a local educational leadership than it would be in a participatory system. This is simply because it has little alternative but to take direct and publicly acknowledged responsibility for its actions; in so doing it inevitably risks exposing itself to the kind of highly damaging criticism and attack which typically occurs when long-established practices or conventions are called into question and new policies are being initiated.

The new participatory system offers a local political leadership a new and more subtle, if more time-consuming, means of initiating change. This is because the creation of a network of representative school boards does, as we have already seen, effectively incorporate a wide cross-section of local people into the service of the educational interest. In turn, these forces can be rapidly mobilized if support is needed for any radical innovation or potentially contentious change in policy. Thus a leadership can, once it has decided to embark on a new course of action, be it concerned with a school's catchment area, the curriculum, discipline, examination policy, sixth form education, and so on, first discuss its ideas with its junior officers and headteachers, and then, through the agency of the clerk, informally disseminate these new ideas to school board meetings. It may choose to 'sound out' the governors' views in a variety of ways, it may decide to distribute an elaborate document on, for example, the place of French in the primary school, the teaching of reading, a proposed catchment area change, and ask the board to place this item on its next agenda and discuss the report on the matter. It may alternatively simply ask the clerk to 'sound out' the governors' view in an informal way on a specific item, or it may, as I shall illustrate in detail later in the section, ask the headteacher, chairman, or clerk to raise an important issue independently. However, whatever channel of communication is used, these 'probing discussions' are typically used by a leadership to introduce school boards to, and to convince them of, the practicality and reasonableness of often quite radical new policy proposals.

Of course, in some exceptional cases, these initiatives may, particularly if they are badly thought out, spark off a hostile or critical reaction. However, if as usually happens, the initiative is well planned and executed and thus is successful in convincing a representative cross-section of local board members of the wisdom of the new policy in question, then the overall strategic position of the local educational establishment is usually considerably strengthened.

Thus, for example, in one part of the city, an increase in the local population, together with the excellent academic reputation of one comprehensive school, led this institution to become oversubscribed and thus heavily overcrowded. The education authority in these difficult circumstances had little alternative but to introduce a new policy which effectively diverted pupils to two neighbouring small and low-status schools, offering children a restricted range of facilities and a particularly limited curriculum. However, before these proposals became widely known to parents, they were first explained in detail in a number of governors' meetings in the area concerned, and in the course of this initial 'sounding out exercise', the local educational leadership managed to obtain a substantial amount of support for its change of policy. Thus, when the decision to modify the high status school's catchment area was finally made public, although these proposals generated a fierce local opposition, the force of this reaction was less explosive than it well might have been in a centralized administrative system. This was mainly because the local educational establishment was able to point out that it had not acted precipitously, but had already consulted with, and gained the agreement of, a number of representative school boards in the area concerned. In turn, these bodies had become convinced of the inevitability, if not necessarily the wisdom, of this development. Consequently the authority was able to develop this bridgehead into the community concerned and after a further series of public meetings its plans gained a general local acceptance and went ahead.

In the same way, in another leafy suburban part of the city, the authority decided to change the boundaries of the catchment areas of a prestigious comprehensive school. These proposals meant that a number of middle-class parents, some of whom had bought houses in the area at a premium in order to send their children to the school concerned, would now be required to send them to an institution which they considered unsuitable and of extremely low status since it's catchment area included inner-city and multi-racial areas. Again, as in the last case, this process of initiating change was greatly eased by the presence of participatory school boards. The new proposals were patiently explained to the governing bodies concerned, and the strengths and advantages of the low-status school in question were also carefully considered. Largely as a result of this preparatory 'educative' work, many governors in the area became convinced of the eminent practicality, wisdom, and justice of the new policies, and once the authorities' proposals became public, the parents who opposed this development found they were in a relatively weak tactical situation. Thus, although they set up an action committee to fight their educational authority, they found it extremely difficult to mobilize a substantial amount of support for their case, since so many key people in the community already, and in advance of the event, had been not only convinced of the merits of, but had also become advocates of, the very process of egalitarian change the local authority wished to initiate in this part of the city.

However, since we have only looked so far at how this process of initiating and engineering a widespread support for one's policies works at a fairly general level, and not in the detailed context of one particular school board meeting, my readers may find it useful and informative if I conclude this section with a detailed case study of the ways in which one school board gradually came to accept and support a particularly radical policy initiative.

The governors discuss school discipline and the school refuser — a case study in the legitimation of a new policy iniative

Background   Blackshire is a large comprehensive school situated in a leafy, surburban district of the city. It has a predominantly middle-class intake and, until recently, its staff have had little difficulty in maintaining what they see as a reasonable standard of discipline. However, in the course of the last three years the catchment area of the school has been slightly changed in order to incorporate a rundown innercity area containing pupils from poor white, as well as immigrant, families. Some of these new pupils have found it most difficult to accommodate themselves to the prevailing expectations of the school and, as a result, have caused a number of quite severe discipline problems for senior members of staff. Events have slowly moved onwards towards a crisis and Blackshire's headteacher, Mr. Smith, is finally convinced after a long discussion with his chairman of governors that perhaps the wisest course of action for him to take in the short term would be to suspend some of the most disruptive pupils from the school. However, the chairman of the governors remains unhappy about this general deterioration in the behavioural standards of pupils in his school and, as a result, he decides to send, firstly, a letter to the chief education officer requesting information as to the authorities' policy for coping with disruptive pupils and, secondly, having received this information to discuss the matter fully with his fellow governors at their next board meeting.

The chairman's letter to the chief education officer   The chairman's letter to the chief education officer is perhaps worth quoting in full, both because it gives some important background details to this case and because it also reflects the type of quite strong local concern which was felt by most parents in the Blackshire School catchment area, about the interrelated problems of school indiscipline and the school refuser.

Dear Mr. Taylor,

Suspension of pupils from school
As you probably know, Mr Smith was forced, at the end of last term, to suspend four girls from attending Blackshire School for the last

two weeks of term. This is the first time in the school's history such drastic action has been necessary. The issue of uncooperative children is clearly not peculiar to Blackshire, and as far as I can tell, is on the increase both in Sheffield and other big cities.

I am very disturbed that the final sanction left to a headmaster, for the sake of the rest of the pupils, involves an action which, far from being punishment of the offenders, must increasingly be seen as an extra holiday. Once this action has been taken in a school, the knowledge that uncooperative children can get this extra free time if they cause enough disruption can well be storing up even more serious problems for the future.

Before I attempt to discuss this very difficult problem at the next Governors' meeting, can you please give me some information as to how the Education Committee is attempting to cope with this problem on a city-wide basis.

One hesitates to suggest the creation of 'treatment' centres purely for this kind of offender but I would not like Blackshire Governors to waste time and emotion discussing this issue without a clear understanding of what the Committee feels should be done to prevent further escalation of this type of behaviour.

Our next meeting is in the third week of March and I look forward to hearing as much about the city's programme as possible before that date.

Yours sincerely,

B. Baker

Chairman, Blackshire School Governors

The education authorities' proposals for dealing with disruptive children and school refusers   The chief education officer replies to the chairman's letter and, in turn, arranges for him to be briefed thoroughly about the authorities proposals for coping with this problem. In essence this new policy involves the establishment of a number of purpose-built centres, popularly to become known as 'sin bins', which are specially designed to cope with disruptive young people in an informal manner and in the social context of the locality they have grown up in. No further attempt is to be made to require immediate attendance in the formal schooling structure, and similarly traditional and formal pedagogic approaches to these children are also to be abandoned. In the case of Blackshire Comprehensive School, this new policy involves the development of a new centre, the Swallownest Project, located within the area of inner deprivation served by the school. Swallownest is seen by the local educational establishment to be both an exciting and an experimental departure; it is to be staffed both by community workers and teachers who are specially experienced in working with 'difficult' children. Moreover it will also receive special 'back-up' assistance from the city's educational welfare officer's and the school's psychological service. The pupil-teacher ratio at Swallownest is to be extremely favourable, 7 to 1, and it is envisaged that the customers will include 'school refusers' of various types, as well as ultimately being extended to disruptive pupils and those with severe behavioural and learning problems. Pupils who can't or won't fit into the formal routine and structure of Blackshire School will be expected to attend Swallownest on a regular fulltime basis, but will stay on the nominal roll of the parent school, since ultimately it is envisaged that after a period of 'rehabilitative community-centred informal education' they will be more ready for, and receptive to, the more formal expectations of the secondary schooling structure.

Comment   Quite obviously these proposals reflect quite a shift in the authorities' policy in the sense that it is formally developing and thus officially sanctioning a programme of quite radical alternative education which quite specifically and publicly rejects the claims of the traditional, teacher-centred, school-based, approach to difficult or problem children. Naturally this new development is likely to generate a fierce opposition from a number of quarters, including those people who take the view that disruptive children should be 'coped with' within the context of the institution they disrupt, and should not, in any sense, be rewarded for their bad behaviour by being removed to a new centre which is seen as a 'soft option' from the rigorous demands of the formal schooling system. In turn, since so many of their members are sympathetic to such new developments as the Swallownest Project, the local educational establishment is anxious to gain the general support of the governors of Blackshire School for this development. If it can achieve the support of this representative and prestigious body, then it will gain a badly needed strategic advantage which will enable it to cope more easily with those criticisms which may be made by more traditionally minded parents, teachers, or community leaders.

The Blackshire governors discuss school discipline

The chairman   At the next meeting of the governors following his letter to the chief education officer, the chairman raises the issue of 'the discipline problem' within Blackshire School. He says how much he regrets the fact that the headteacher was forced to suspend pupils from the school last term, for 'this is the first time in the school's history that this drastic action has been necessary'. He goes on to refer to his letter to the chief education officer, which has previously been circulated to all governors, and he makes it very clear that he is very disturbed that 'the final sanction left to our headteacher, for the sake of the rest of the pupils, simply involves an action which, far from being a punishment, must increasingly be seen as the granting of a holiday'. He voices his fears that 'once this very serious step, that is, the suspension of a pupil, has been taken in this school, then the knowledge that uncooperative children can get this extra free time if they cause enough disruption, will only stir up more serious problems for the future.' He concludes by reminding the board that this situation is not unique to this school; 'it is rather a more general situation which raises a fundamental question of morality in that the interests of most children in the school conflict with the interests of particularly disruptive and uncooperative pupils.'

The clerk   The clerk then describes the authorities proposals to deal with these disturbances. He says that several experimental schemes are being developed in the city, one of them, the Swallownest Project involves tackling the problem of the school refuser within the context of the community within which the young person has been brought up, and where he or she, in fact, spends most of his time. He goes on to describe the Swallownest scheme in some detail and he points out that 'one of the specific aims of this project is to provide an alternative educational provision for this difficult type of child which will meet both their special needs and will also secure their eventual return when appropriate to the school and the wider society.' He makes it very clear that the decision to refer a 'difficult child' to the project will be taken by a management committee consisting of educational welfare officers, psychologists, social workers, teachers and so on, while the curriculum at Swallownest is likely to resemble that of a primary rather that a secondary school. There will be no subject periods and a skilled social/community worker, who is to supervise the project, will attempt to stimulate an educational interest in children through various art, craft, dramatic, and outside activities.

The headteacher   The headteacher then gives the governors a graphic account of the particular difficulties which a few disruptive pupils are causing in his school. He describes the attitudes of the pupils concerned, which is in general 'one of accepting they have a legal obligation to attend the school building, but which does not extend to a parallel obligation to attend lessons. As a result these children spend most of their time in the toilets, outbuildings, and other nooks and crannies of the school and valuable teaching time is lost in "rounding them up", and ensuing that they attend at least physically, if not in any other kind of way, their lessons.' The headteacher goes on to say that 'these children's parents are equally at a loss as to what to do with their offspring; they admit they can no longer control their own children and appeal constantly to us for help. One mother rings us up everyday to check on the behaviour of her daughter who is beyond control.' He concludes by saying that in the last few months the 'situation has gone from bad to worse, and these children's behaviour has become intolerable. In the end and after a tremendous waste of teachers' time, a vast dissipation of our energies and a constant flow of disruption and damage, we felt that we had no alternative but to suspend them.'

A general discussion then develops on the reasons why children misbehave in school. The chairman bring this to an end by reminding the board that in his opinion 'it is extremely naïve to think that the school won't have more problems like this in the future. The normal school mechanism is obviously breaking down in this case and we, as governors, have a general duty to debate, discuss and ultimately decide on the merits of alternative educational solutions to this problem.' This being said, the chairman asks the clerk to spell out to the board the authorities' proposed solution to this problem.

The clerk   The clerk, who officially represents the chief education officer at the board meeting, then outlines the authorities' proposals for dealing with 'school refusers' and other behavioural problems. He makes the point that this is 'really part of a general national problem. No one knows all the answers, indeed no one really knows what questions to ask. All we can do in the short term is set up a number of pilot project schemes such as the Swallownest Centre. Indeed, we see this development as an essential one, for we can't learn more about these children without conducting such experiments. Moreover, we want to monitor the work of this and other projects in the city as we go along. However, since this does involve such a major change in our policy, we hope to have the backing of the governors of this school for this development.'

Comment   A general discussion then breaks out among the governors following the clerk's statement. Some people are evidently unhappy about this proposal since it is not only a major policy change but will also need explaining to both their constituents and neighbours in the local community. Moreover, since it is such a radical initiative, it may be particularly difficult to provide a convincing account of the need for this kind of change. One governor speaks for a minority, when she says the 'problem of ill-discipline reflects the way this school is organized; it is streamed and very examination conscious, and simply has no place for children it has labelled as social and academic failures from the day they set foot in the place.' Another governor makes the point that his political party has spent years 'struggling to build up a series of fine, large, lavishly equipped schools in the best parts of the city and now, after all that effort, working-class kids from the most deprived areas simply don't want to know these places but simply prefer to opt out and spend their days in the place they were brought up in.'

The discussion develops into a wide-ranging argument on the pros and cons of comprehensive education, but is gradually brought back to the main theme by the clerk who points out, 'We don't know why children behave in this disorderly and disruptive manner, indeed we don't even know how much the school will be involved in the Swallownest Project. All we do know is that a dedicated community worker has started to develop an alternative type of community-centred education in this area, and that this experience does seem useful and meaningful to some of the pupils who are currently disrupting this school's routine. In the authorities' view, the idea of building upon this experience does seem an acceptable one and, in any event, whatever we do will be far better for the children than letting them continue to be suspended from school so that they spend their time hanging around dubious coffee shops, shop lifting, assaulting people, and committing sexual offences.'

Most of the governors respond favourably to the clerk's plea for their support and they are in the main convinced of the short-term prudence, if not the wider theoretical implications of, giving their support to the Swallownest Project. This being said, the discussion then moves on to consider some of the technical problems involved if the school is to liaise effectively with this new development. The main problem which now emerges is one of a potential role conflict developing between teachers working at Blackshire and those at Swallownest. At Blackshire each teacher plays a particular and specific role in an examination-oriented, hierarchical structure. Social relationships with one's pupils are formal and subject-based and the teachers are naturally worried about the kind of diffuse social relationships which may be expected of them in the Swallownest Project. This issue is discussed at some length. In general the governors hope that several of Blackshire's teachers would also assume a part-time teaching commitment at Swallownest; however, the teachers' representatives are obviously very unhappy with this and press for the appointment of a specialist teacher working full-time at the experimental centre.

The chairman   Following this essentially technical discussion, the chairman again moves the business forward and takes up the clerk's earlier suggestion that the governors should, in principle, support the development of the Swallownest Project. This suggestion now receives the general support of the board, although a minority remain unhappy. One local councillor makes it clear that he considers 'the scheme to be a diabolical liberty which will disrupt the whole work of the school and the teachers' timetable'. He goes on to say, 'We are just giving an excuse to kids who aren't academically inclined; it is an invitation to pupils to be disruptive.' This critical theme is taken up by a fellow party member who raises the issue, 'Why isn't this type of rehabilitation taking place in the school?', and this point is in turn elaborated by the councillor who charges that 'this development is simply a retreat into barbary'. He goes on to ask, 'Can you honestly say that these kids will be doing anything remotely academic at Swallownest?' However, by this stage in the debate the majority of governors are evidently out of sympathy with this traditional approach and in general respond more favourably to the clerk who chooses this moment to make two very effective points. Firstly, 'these children are in fact opting out of school anyway.' Secondly, (The alternative school is not in fact a soft option and the community worker at Swallownest has already established the type of positive relationship with these children that the school has failed to do, or lost.'

The chairman then guides the discussion along and says, 'In principle then, do we have a majority of governors present who will support this initiative; which of the governors feels that our school should not support this exciting innovation?'

The headteacher then moves to support the chairman; he says, 'Many of these difficult children obviously resent being moved out of their home area and sent to this school. For these difficult types of children it will be better if they perhaps don't have to travel from their homes but can receive an alternative type of relevant education in their own community.' Most governors agree with this assessment; however the local councillor is still unhappy about this innovation. He argues strongly that 'The school is admitting defeat in accepting this proposal; the kids who have opted out have won.'

Some governors seem impressed by the strength of this argument and the chairman, sensing the mood of the meeting, seeks to reassure the board by reminding the board that 'We are in fact only proposing our support for an experimental venture. Does anyone think that it would be wrong, in principle, to give this limited commitment?' None of the governors continue to press their opposition to the Swallownest scheme and the clerk minutes their decision to 'Support in principal this development with the provision that this experiment be reviewed further after one year's work.' The chairman is delighted with this decision and comments that he 'anticipates that this a very wise move, which will delay further trouble breaking out in the school for a long time to come.' He moves on to take the next business, the headteacher's report.

Concluding comments   Quite obviously in this meeting the role of the clerk, chairman, and headteacher in persuading the other governors to lend their support to this quite radical decision was critical. In turn, the very fact that the governors of a large and prestigious comprehensive school have given their formal backing to the Swallownest Project does make it much easier for the local educational establishment to engineer a wider degree of support in the city for their policies. But some more 'traditionally minded' members of the education committee continued to press the charge that Swallownest was merely 'encouraging other youngsters to play truant' and some local parents blamed the centre for 'their children's refusal to go to school'. These quite serious and legitimate criticisms offered less serious challenge to the local educational leadership than they might have done under a totally centralized system of school administration, for they can always be met with the counter-assertion that very serious attempts have been made to consult a wide and representative cross-section of interested parties and in the event the governors of many schools directly concerned with Swallownest have, in a variety of ways, indicated that they wish to support these exciting developments.

Conclusion

As I said in the introduction to this chapter, in the course of this examination of the relationship between a local educational leadership and a participatory form of school government, my perspective has of necessity been a wide-ranging and at times a slightly speculative one. Moreover, the evidence I have produced to illustrate the major thrust of my argument has simply, because of the exigencies of time and the nature of the subject matter in hand, not been as tidy nor as exhaustive as I would have liked to produce. However, this being said, the evidence I have examined to date does nevertheless tend to lend a substantial degree of support to the general thesis I outlined in the introduction to this chapter, namely, that the development of a representative and openly democratized school board structure does tend to play a major part in solving the many complex difficulties typically facing an educational leadership in the new kind of society which is gradually evolving in Britain in the late 1970s.

However, although school boards can thus play a key role in defending and ultimately legitimizing the policies and practices developed by the leaders of a school system, at the same time they operate in such a way that they do not, nor are they usually expected to, offer any substantial challenge to the existing structure of power. Indeed, the very term manager or governor is in many ways a misnomer, for they cannot by their very nature play a major part in such specialized professional tasks as the drawing up of budgets, the maintenance of buildings, the direction of labour, or the admission of pupils. These tasks are all done more quickly and efficiently by full-time officers and advisors and, if lay managers or governors do choose to involve themselves in what are usually quite routine and time-consuming tasks, then as we have seen in practice their role remains an extremely nominal one, and the real loci of power continue to reside with the full-time official or professional manager. Similarly governors are not usually invited to concern themselves too closely with major issues of policy, involving such concerns as the educational character of schools, catchment areas, staffing policies, core elements in the school's curriculum, and so on, for in the main many items in this field are quite properly the prerogative of the local educational leadership. This group is after all charged with the responsibility, within the guidelines laid down by the state, for ensuring that the local educational service is reasonably uniform in character and offers each child within its remit a roughly equal kind of access to educational opportunities. Indeed, if school boards were to effectively and not merely nominally concern themselves with such key fields as the curriculum, financial matters, admission policies, and so on, then it is extremely likely that this would lead to the development of significant differences between schools in different parts of a locality. In turn this could well lead to the institutional perpetuation of inquality in the sense that different classes and groups of children living in different social, geographic, and ethnically dominated areas of a locality would receive access to different types of educational opportunity. In short, this would lead to a situation where existing social divisions were even more closely reproduced than they are at present by the nation's school system.

Thus, in spite of the rhetoric which currently surrounds the proposed role of a reformed and participatory school board system, the social reality is that these new structures must coexist in a world in which long-established centres of administrative, professional, and political power are firmly entrenched. Simply because of this, the main role of these new bodies is, as the Sheffield experience suggests, likely to remain a marginal and largely symbolic one. They represent a cross-section of local interests and concerns and their primary role is to identify themselves with and, if necessary, defend the policies of the local educational establishment. This is not of course to deny that this tactical role is an unimportant one, particularly for a leadership in the social climate of the 1970s. However, in turn, this critical perspective does help us to understand why the rationale for the board systems both in Sheffield and in the Taylor Committee Report remains so diffuse and open ended. It is in a very real sense reminiscent of a 'sociological surprise ball' in that every few unwindings of the covers serve to expose a new thesis which seems to change the character of the whole product. In short, the whole package is so tricky that teachers, administrators, politicians, and parental leaders all tend to stop at the thesis which best suits their particular interest. Thus, typically in Sheffield, the new boards were seen as 'a vehicle to make the school more accountable to the general community served by the school,' and as 'a local forum where the different views of teachers, headteachers, and other interested groups, can be expressed, debated and reconciled.' At other times they were seen as 'a local cooperative activity, a place where professionals and amateurs can cooperate to make the education service really sensitive to the needs of the community.' More radically it was suggested that they were 'a voice for local people who feel alienated and deprived of any say in the decisions of a large and remote organization.'

Similarly in the Taylor Committee Report we find the same type of quite generalized language. Thus, in the preface, the committee outlines a series of principles underlying its work which are not only remarkably loosely worded, but also offer many surprising parallels to the types of open-ended statements which have been used as a rationale for the Sheffield system. These statements of belief include the following:

> one body should have delegated responsibility for running the school, and in forming that body no one interest should be dominant — it should be an equal partnership of all those with a legitimate concern, local education authority, staff, parents, where appropriate pupils, and the community;

> the governing body thus formed should be responsible for the life and work of the school as a whole: we did not consider that a school's activity could be divided, and neither could accountability for its success;

> the decision-making role of the governing body is only part of its functions: equally important is its responsibility for promoting and protecting good relationships both within the school and between the school and its parents and the wider community: where we recommend particular measures to achieve effective communication and harmonious relationships, we therefore charge the governors with the task of ensuring their satisfactory operation;

Again, in the various chapters of the Taylor Report, the same kind of language patterns constantly occur, thus, in the case of section 8.12, Appointment of Other Teachers, it states:

> However, on balance we recommend that the selection of deputy heads and other teachers should rest with the governing body, who should give due weight to the professional advice made available through the local educational authority and in particular to the responsibility of the local educational authority to find suitable posts for teachers whose schools are closed or reorganised.

Similarly, in section 3.17, the report recommends:

> that there should be as much delegation by the local education authority to the governing body as is compatible with the LEAs ultimate responsibility for running the schools in its area, and as much discretion in turn granted to the headteacher by the governing body as is compatible with the latter's responsibility for the success of the school in all its activities.

Again, on the issue of the curriculum, section 6.19, the report states:

> We have concluded that there is no aspect of the school's activities from

which the governing body should be excluded nor any aspect for which the headteacher and his colleagues should be accountable only to themselves or the local education authority. It follows that the responsibility for deciding the school's curriculum, in every sense of the word, must be shared between all levels and all those concerned at every level.

However, while it is still far too early to make any effective assessment of the long-term impact of the Taylor Report upon the balance of power within the nation's schooling system, certainly in the case of Sheffield one gained the impression that, while the rationale for the whole participatory governing scheme was tricky enough to appease local interest groups, at the same time it was quite clear that the functions which were constantly being officially emphasized were the consultative and representative ones. Thus, school boards are typically requested to:

'Undertake wide ranging discussions.'

'Take part in clarifying educational objectives.'

'Deliberate and weigh-up issues.

'Draw the heads out and relate their views to the local community.'

'Criticise and support the headteacher.'

'Act as an ambassador for your school.'

The very generalized and diffuse nature of this rationale makes it extremely difficult for an observer to effectively access whether school board members have attained many of these objectives. However, in balance, the evidence I have examined to date does tend to suggest that managers and governors tend to discuss the kinds of issues troubling Sheffield's educational elite, and not those which necessarily trouble the clients of the school system. In short, a process of controlled or sponsored dialogue takes place, in which the new board members are effectively incorporated into a power structure, and which in turn their presence makes more powerful. One senior official made this quite clear when he said: 'it would help the Education Committee to get the views of a representative body of people in a community. We want to find a way of helping school managers and governors to help the Authority.' This process of initiating a closely circumscribed dialogue is perhaps seen most clearly in the way the local educational leadership went about the task of introducing further reforms into the school board system during the period 1974-1975.

These modifications led to additional parental, teacher, student, and community representatives on the boards, and thus from one point of view might be seen as one further brave attempt to further democratize the whole board system. However, the significant point was that when the educational establishment decided to introduce these changes, they did not effectively mobilize the consultative machinary they had already established and ask for the collective views of the very bodies which constitutions were to be further modified by these initiatives. Rather, key decisions on such vital matters as the number of teacher or parental representatives, the method of appointing the chairman, and cross-representation between neighbouring school boards, all probably took place privately in informal discussions between leading politicians and senior officers, and in caucus meetings of the majority party in the city.

In short, the whole process, including the surprising decision to restrict the chairmanship of the boards to a limited number of people appointed by and approved by the local authority, was veiled in secrecy. Some well-informed people, such as myself, who were aware that change was in the wind, raised the matter for discussion at school board meetings only to receive the following type of bland reply from the clerk, acting in his capacity as representative of the chief educational administrator: 'this matter is being discussed by the Education Committee, and the board will be informed of the outcome at a later date.'

Naturally, it was difficult to assess the amount of disquiet this official evasiveness generated; however, the minutes of one board in the city recorded that the managers had reacted to the document outlining the authorities' proposals to further modify their constitutions in the following way: 'The Managers noted the document, and whilst applauding the decision to aim for greater participation, deplored the lack of participation in reaching this decision.'

Indeed, many people I spoke to, largely as a result of this particular development, began to express strong reservations about this exercise in 'consultative democracy'. One said to me:

> This is a good system, but it was not used as it should be. We all felt left in the dark, and there was only courtesy consultation in reforming the articles and instruments of government. We felt we were not consulted, or given enough information.

Another said:

> The Education Committee spent a long time gathering peoples views about the changes which should be made following the first four years of the new system, but they didn't consult existing managing or governing bodies, they had made up their minds anyway.

In short, towards the end of my field work in Sheffield, I found that a process of political conscious raising was taking place, in the sense that some managers and governors were becoming more critical both of the nature of participatory politics in general, and, despite the rhetoric of good intentions surrounding democratized school boards, their own quite marginal role within the educational system. However, in order to place these local experiences within a wider context, and to consider the likely future national evolution of democratized school board structures, it is now time for me to move on from this particular concern with Sheffield. Thus, in the next and final chapter, I shall consider some more general and theoretical issues, and I hope that this analysis will in turn help my readers towards a deeper understanding of the wider social and political factors which are of necessity involved in the Sheffield experiment in school board democracy and which are of national concern within the context of the Taylor Committee Report on school management and government in England and Wales.

Notes and references

1.   It may be that precisely because so many people are aware of this situation, many schools have decided to abandon or extensively modify their more traditional public ceremonial routines.

2.   In this, as in previous chapters, I have used nominal school names so that the institution in question cannot be readily identified.

3.   *A New Partnership for our Schools*, HMSO, 1977.

CHAPTER 8

PROFESSIONAL CONTROL AND THE ENGINEERING OF CLIENT CONSENT

Introduction

Having in the last four chapters examined some of the scripts of the major social actors taking part within one of the most radically democratized school-governing systems in the country to date, and one which clearly anticipates most of the main recommendations of, if not all the details contained within, the Taylor Report, we are now in a better position to return to the central focus of this study and ask ourselves two questions. Firstly, how far does this type of reform facilitate the development of a more democratic school system? Secondly, how far does it serve to make our schools more responsive to local needs and accountable to a general public interest?

However, before I attempt to answer these two questions, it may be necessary to remind my readers once again of the cautionary notes I made in Chapter 3. In this work I am of necessity concerned with making a contribution towards a sociology of education and largely because of this naturally approach the schooling system as problematic in itself. Thus, I hope I have not, certainly in my professional capacity as a sociologist, identified myself too closely with issues which are currently defined as problems within the educational world. Rather I have consciously chosen to look at issues which some people may see as contentious and others as personally threatening. While this exercise may, of necessity, risk one's personal relationships and arouse fierce passions in the hearts of those whose actions are being scrutinized, nonetheless this task is an extremely necessary one to perform. For, if we are to take such concepts as 'participatory politics', 'community involvement', or 'the democratization of education' seriously, and after all these ideas underpin both the Sheffield system we have examined to date, and also the work of the Taylor Committee, then we should also be concerned about the ways in which these ideals work out in practice. Largely because of this, it is not only necessary to constantly maintain scrutiny of, for example, new structures of participatory school government which promise to disseminate these values more widely, but also to address ourselves consistently to the following two questions. Firstly, how far do these innovations work to extend the common good? Secondly, how far do they function to maintain existing centres of privilege and balances of power?

Education and the state

If we adopt this critical perspective, then it seems that the evidence we have examined in the last four chapters leads us tentatively towards the conclusion that there is often a surprisingly wide gap between our publicly expressed democratic sentiments and the realities involved in the citizen's daily interaction with the various social organizations of the welfare state. The reasons for this development are complex, but in part may be understood if we recognize that all modern industrial societies, whether they pay a nominal lip service to liberal-democratic or collectivist utopian ideologies, attempt to solve their problems by the adoption of centralized planning strategies and the creation of large public organizations which are charged with the pursuit of specific objectives in such fields as welfare, industrial development, recreation, the environment and, of course, education.

However, the evidence tends to suggest that in all industrial societies these relatively new and often large departments of state suffer from an inherent, if continuing, paradox. On the one hand they exist to provide a series of services designed to make life more comfortable or richer for the bulk of the population. At the same time their personnel are, in the course of their daily work, forced to make moral judgements about how people ought, and ought not, to lead their lives. Largely as a result of this situation, many of their clients come to feel a sense that they feel they are gradually losing control over some of the more important and intimate aspects of their lives — their ability to care for their own health; the freedom to educate their own children, plan their own leisure life-styles, and so on. This feeling of 'powerlessness' is not only a subjective articulation of a series of individualistic cultural values, it may also be substantiated empirically in the sense that modern industrial man's remaining spheres of autonomy are largely confined to his home, garden, and family life, and by contrast he enjoys relatively little influence over most of the major decisions taken by the officials of those state bureaucracies providing for his educational or social needs, or indeed, those who provide for his immediate employment or related life-support services.

This pervasive feeling of estrangement is perhaps intensified because of the refractory tendencies inherent in any large organization. Although these institutions are set up to attain a specific series of general and public goals or objectives, they also tend to develop their own private ethos and momentum. In the case of the state welfare institutions, it is not always easy to distinguish between these two areas of formal and informal activity. Indeed, from a critical vantage point some of these services seem to share many of the characteristics of 'rambling medieval fiefdoms', rather than rationally ordered public services. Thus, most of them recruit their key personnel in their late teens or early twenties, and these people then tend to spend the remainder of their working lives within the institution they have chosen to serve. Moreover, since all recruits tend to take part in a common series of training programmes and induction processes, then they also share a common series of loyalties, not only to the general official doctrines justifying their work, but also in the sense that they have a specific occupational interest in maintaining and, if possible, extending their estate's claims over the resources of society. In turn, their leaders play an active role, both at local and national levels, of decision making, and are naturally, if not always, overtly concerned to maintain the stability of the prevailing socio-economic system within which their status flourishes.

Largely as a result of this complex social situation the leaders of all welfare bureaucracies are forced to adopt a quasi-political role, in the sense that they don't operate within a social vacuum but must constantly pay heed to the consequences of their actions upon other competing groups and forces in society. Thus, whatever specific interest they serve, be it education, welfare, planning, or recreation, they must consistently address themselves to three key and universal issues. Firstly, the need to maintain their authority. Secondly, the need to maintain the stability and security of their organization. And thirdly, the need to justify their continued claims upon the wider sources of society.

In the course of this work a successful leadership employs a number of social devices to achieve its aims. These practices may be usefully conceived of as tools in the sense that they are social instruments designed to do a specific task. They are not, of course, immediately and readily visible in the sense that they share the physical attributes of those technical devices used in industrial production — machine tools, spanners, hammers, assembly lines, or pickup trucks. Nonetheless, they are just as usefully conceived of as a technology, since like their very tangible physical counterparts they can, as we shall see, be just as effective in achieving the objectives of the people who employ them.

Cooptation

One of the key tools in the armoury of the leaders of all large organizations is a social device sometimes known as cooptation. This concept has been extensively described and analysed by Phillip Selznick in his pioneering study *T.V.A. and the Grassroots: A Study in the Sociology of Formal Organisation*,[1] and refers to the process of '. . . absorbing new elements into the leadership or policy determining structure of an organisation as a means of averting threats to it's stability or existence.'

This concept is a very helpful one, in the sense that it helps us to delineate more systematically some of the social processes which often take place in the kind of institutional innovations we have been examining in the last four chapters. Cooptation may take many forms; however, for the purposes of this analysis, it will only be necessary to consider two basic types, namely formal and informal cooptation.

Informal cooptation   The concept of informal cooptation is used to refer to the kind of response which typically takes place when an organizational leadership decides to share effective power with a group which it had previously ignored, but which can no longer be avoided, since it has gained a position where it can make specific and concrete demands for a claim upon the organization's wider resources. This process usually typically occurs when a leadership finds that its authority, or ability to dominate, is in a state of imbalance with the true state of power within the community it serves. However, it is not always a readily identifiable state of affairs since this exercise is typically conducted in an informal manner and no explicit public statement describing and no recognition of this changing balance of power takes place.

Formal cooptation   In contrast formal cooptation refers to the kind of social processes which often take place when the leadership of an organization formally seeks to develop new and publicly acknowledged relationships with previously disenfranchised, or excluded, groups of workers, clients, or dependents. It generally involves the establishment of a series of new, formally ordered and publicly recognized relationships. Thus, appointments are made to newly created official posts, constitutions are drawn up, and new and sometimes extremely elaborate organizational structures are developed. The whole of this social process tends to convey, both through the creation of new symbolic interactive devices — committees, community councils, and local assemblies and joint meetings — and through the development of a new ideology stressing the value of interaction, consultation, participation and dialogue, that the organizational leadership now intends to adopt a new and more democratic style of government.

In general Selznick suggests that the leaders of an organization tend to adopt formal cooptive strategies when they face either one or both of two classical, if recurrent, problems. In the first place, these tactics are often used when an organization lacks a sense of historical legitimacy. This may happen simply because its leaders no longer feel they possess an unquestioning belief in their own right to rule, or in the 'correctness' of their policies and actions. However, as is more usually the case, cooptation also tends to occur simply because the organization's right to rule is called into question by those it has traditionally dominated.

Cooptation and social control

The reasons for these responses are in theory quite simple, though in practice often complex and difficult to describe in detail. The leaders of any organizational system, be it an army, a prison, a hospital, or even a local educational authority, depend for the effective day-to-day maintenance of their rule upon the tacit consent and cooperation of those they govern. Although they may wish from time to time to employ coercive measures, these tactics are rarely employed on a widespread scale; rather they are at their most effective when they are employed in critical and symbolic situations such as punishment systems, and they are not effective as enduring weapons of mass control.

One of the most effective ways for a leadership to maintain its own confidence and the confidence of the mass of clients it rules is to formally coopt into its public structure representatives from groups which in some way reflect the sentiments, or possess the confidence of, the relevant public or mass it governs. This is because these new elements lend not only a substantial degree of public respectibility to, but also help to reestablish the legitimacy of, the group which is in control. This policy has obviously been and is still widely used, particularly when a leadership is responding to a potentially 'threatening' or 'revolutionary' situation. Thus, for example, colonial administrators typically coopt tribal leaders into the machinery of their imperial administration in order to gain the support and confidence of the mass of their dependent subjects. In West Germany industrial leaders have included representatives from trade unions on their managing boards for many years, and the evidence suggests that this has been a most effective means of gaining a wider support for their policies and also establishing the legitimacy of their rule at a time when in much of the remainder of Western Europe the legitimacy of the capitalist system is increasingly being called into question. In the same way this theory also offers us an effective means of making some sense of the complex social processes we have examined in Sheffield. Here again the leaders of many formerly disenfranchised and outsider groups — parents, auxiliary staff, pupils, and teachers — have now been incorporated into the formal administrative structure of nearly 300 local school systems. And, as we have seen, these administrative innovations have not only served to lend a substantial degree of democratic respectability to, but have also served to reinforce the authority of, these groups effectively controlling the city's school system.

However, formal cooptative tactics are not only a means for maintaining or even restoring the public's confidence in its rulers; they may also be used to solve quite different and essentially administrative difficulties. These typically tend to occur when the business of an organization grows so complex or extensive that its leaders' control is significantly weakened. This is because they find themselves swamped in a sea of administrative detail and have insufficient time or energy to continue to coordinate all sectors efficiently or to dominate their constituents effectively. This situation is most easily resolved if a substantial amount of everyday, detailed administrative decision making and minor policy execution is delegated to committees of clients, workers, or formerly disenfranchised groups. These essentially logistical objectives may again be achieved through the establishment of a series of new, formally ordered and publicly recognized procedures which incorporate the leaders of many subordinate groups into a series of self-governing structures set up within the general framework of, and under the overall control of, the wider organizational leadership.

The essential point about this latter type of participatory innovation is that it helps a leadership to substantially reinforce its dominant tactical position, and thus achieve three quite fundamental strategic objectives. Firstly, it helps to create a series of reliable and orderly mechanisms for communicating with a wider public or groups of clients. Secondly, it effectively devolves a great deal of burdensome minor administration, and thus gives a leadership more time to address itself to central policy objectives. Thirdly, it reinforces a widespread public impression that decision making has been substantially devolved and consequently the responsibilities for the successful achievement of policy objectives are no longer borne exclusively by one group, but are substantially shared with a variety of local committees and associations. However, these strategies are not usually intended to devolve substantial powers of decision making to subordinate participating groups; rather the latter are simply intended to be concerned with the details and responsibilities associated with the execution of a leader's policies. Once these basic premises are challenged and attempts are made to substantially question or influence a leadership's general policy, then character-istically one finds participatory policies are abandoned in favour of a more centralized, if less flexible, type of direct rule.

This type of cooptative strategy has been used in a variety of circumstances. Thus in many totalitarian states, trade unions are not independent bodies but essentially function as minor self-governing units of a centralized state machine, and are mainly used to maintain the efficiency, reliability, and morale of the labour force. Similarly, in the case of concentration or prison camps, where the problems of coping with large numbers of people are often very great, similar tactics are used and devices such as self-government, hut- or block-based committees, are typically introduced to ensure that prisoners organize most of the tasks of penal administration themselves, including minor punishments, maintenance of discipline, allocation of food, organiza-tion of recreational and educational programmes, and so on. In the same way, though obviously in a quite different cultural context, one might similarly argue that the kind of reforms we have been looking at in Sheffield are simply a more modern version of this ancient theme. In this case the establishment of many hundreds of local school-based executive committees serves to facilitate a substantial devolution of many minor administrative burdens and leaves a central administrative / political elite with more time and emergy to address central policy objectives. However, these committees are, as we have seen, essentially concerned with the implementation of policy, and once they step outside this administrative and coordinative role then their actions are likely to be tightly restricted.

Cooptation and the schooling system

It seems then that any formal act of cooptation offers the leadership of any large organization, including a school system, a number of very definite tactical advantages if it finds that its authority or right to rule is being called into question. These benefits may be extremely important in a social period when the total public educative process is itself increasingly being seen as problematic both by those working within it, disaffected groups of clients, and people in the wider community. Moreover, cooptation also has the added attraction that it promises to ease the work load within an administrative system which is generally growing more elaborate and burdensome to finance and give its leadership more time to think about central policy-related issues. This is because the type of 'people-oriented technology' implicitly associated with the cooptative processes tends to fulfil two analytically distinct if interrelated functions. In the first place, it may fulfil the important political function of restoring the wider public's sense of confidence in the policy of their ruler, and thus serves to legitimize their continued dominance in society. In the second place, it provide a ready solution to many key administrative problems, and provides a more reliable channel both for effective communication with, and maintemance of, control over a series of subordinate client groups. However, as we have seen, although formal cooptation largely allows a leadership to achieve these aims, it does not lead to a transfer of substantive power to either the workers, clients, or subjects involved within the school system. This situation largely explains why so many Sheffield governors appeared to be unsure of their duties and to have an ambivalent attitude to their new role; they were aware that they now occupied a conspicuous and status-giving office within their community, but at the same time they were acutely aware that they had little substantive power in the sense that their work was mainly symbolic and there was little tangible they could do either to mould their local school to their own wishes or alter the educational authorities' general policies. On those rare occasions when school boards threatened to challenge this opaque but nonetheless very real structure of power, then their formal constitution was quickly revised to divert this threat. Thus, although the original participatory scheme introduced in 1970 allowed the key office of chairman to be appointed by open election, the revised scheme introduced in 1975 substantially modified this procedure and specified that this office must be filled by a candidate chosen from a restricted list composed of local education authority nominees. Although the overt rationale for this change was never made very clear, one of the key factors at stake was the issue of power and ultimate control. The city's leaders were probably worried that if a school board's chairman was elected in a totally open contest, then in many areas of the city this key office might fall into the hands of people who were politically unacceptable to them or substantially critical of their policies. In the same way, when a key decision had to be made, such as whether to phase out a school or reduce the number of teachers in the city, then the city leaders also went ahead without consulting the relevant interests concerned. At the time of writing the Sheffield authority is facing a severe amount of criticism since it did not consult either the teachers' organizations or the schools concerned about its proposals to phase out twelve primary schools and 500 jobs from the city in the next ten years. Thus the local newspaper, *The Morning Telegraph,* of October 14, 1975, quoted one of the teachers' representatives on the education committee as saying,

. . . it was appalling that a decision appeared to have been made without any discussion with teachers.

I am obliged to say that the reaction of most teachers would be great indignation and the consequences of this decision are not something we are going to take lying down,' he said.

The local authority was seizing on the falling birth rate to suggest that a cut in teaching jobs was inevitable.

But he warned that any willingness to examine the problems posed by the dramatic fall in the birth rate had been badly damaged by the bald statements made yesterday by Coun. Peter Horton, the education committee chairman.

'This is back to the bad old days when consultation meant deciding a policy and then asking teachers what they thought about it, rather than a discussion of the problem together before minds were closed.'

The article went on to say that '. . . the managers and parents at three Sheffield schools said they were furious about the latest development, which appeared to confirm the impression they were being by-passed, despite promises by the education department of full consultations,' and concluded by noting, 'The managers are particularly angry because they have already had their term meetings and none of the questions about the future of the schools had been met by the education department.'

The iron law of oligarchy

It seems then that although participatory schemes often create a widespread public impression that the local community is 'fully involved', and 'a great weight of concerned manpower is now working for the school', in fact from a critical perspective these reforms do little to alter the locii of power within the local school system, and most key decisions are not made by the people ostensibly being served by the organization, but by its full-time coterie of officials, advisors, and professional managers. The reasons for these refractory tendencies are complex, but some of the key factors have been elaborated by Michels in his classic study — *Political Parties, A Sociological Study of the Olegarchical Tendencies of Modern Democracy.*[2]

In the first place, effective power remains in the hands of the full-time official, be he headmaster or school board clerk at the local level, or the administrator or adviser at the local authority level, simply because this group is in effective control of the school system's communication network. Thus, as we have seen, parents, teachers, or community representatives on governing bodies are often totally dependent upon their headteacher's cooperation if they wish to communicate effectively and rapidly with their constituents. This situation also means that the full-time officials are in a key position to decide which information to dispense or withold from the public, and most important of all, which issues to raise and which to omit from the agenda of public boards of control. In this way, a subtle but nonetheless censorial process takes place in the sense that, as we have seen, school boards tend to discuss those issues which trouble the city's caretaking elites and do not, of necessity, address those perhaps more critical issues — the private troubles of the clients, workers, or dependents of the local school system.

In the second place, the power of the full-time official is reinforced by his extensive, if not necessarily superior, knowledge of educational affairs. Their official role of necessity enables them to travel, visit different schools, read extensively, and conduct private research. In all of these ways they are able to build up such an elaborate and sophisticated rationale for their own actions that most lay people find it difficult to offer an effective critique of their policies. The root of the client's dilemma rests not in a fundamental intellectual inferiority, but in a unequal power relationship, for since the officials usually ultimately decide which educational issues are publicly addressed, which ignored, and which systematically devalued, then most of the public debate about educational policy is conducted from a dominant conceptual perspective, and thus even the most 'concerned' of diligent laymen finds it difficult to make an effective critique of or offer a substantial alternative to their policies.

Finally, the power of the officials is substantially reinforced by the general incompetence of the mass of the people they serve, and their own superior skills in writing, talking, and organizing. This is not to suggest that their clients are congenitally inferior; rather it is merely to state the obvious, that, in their case, the competing demands of work, leisure and family life leave them with insufficient time or energy to acquire the detailed knowledge or communicative skills necessary to build up an effective counterbalance, or act as a significant check upon the role of the expert. Ironically, even in cases where people do make great efforts to acquire these skills — through reading, attending adult education classes, talking to teachers or children — they may still remain ineffective since they are, by the logic of their situation, denied access to the internal and private communicative network of their local educational system.

The division of educational labour

It seems then that the social processes we have examined in the case of the Sheffield school board system may be seen as further examples which are generally consistent with the social law that the 'need to elaborate the division of labour', including educational labour, creates interests peculiar to itself. Thus, although as we saw in Chapter 1, effective power within the school system originally lay within the hands of the local bourgeoisie, the need to create a sophisticated structure of education in the late nineteenth century necessitated the growth of a complex national organization and a concomittant cadre of full-time officials, ideologists, and professional managers. This diffuse, but none-theless recognizable, status interest naturally possessed an intuitive set of characteristics which are commonly found within all organization structures, be they established to pursue military, religious, welfare, or in this case educational objectives, namely an instinct for self-preservation and the maintenance and, if possible, expansion of one's claim upon the wider society.

In the case of education, this task has become increasingly difficult in the context of wider economic and political developments during the late 1960s and early 1970s. In the first place a more general economic malaise has meant that society's resources are necessarily limited, and expenditure on education is constantly criticized since it is a labour-intensive and thus costly enterprise. Secondly, a more wide-ranging political crisis has developed in the sense that the postwar consensus between capital and labour has gradually broken down, and many politicians now view the school system as a mechanism which can be used to facilitate wider social changes, including the development of the first stages of a more meritocratic, if not egalitarian, society. Naturally, many other groups feel threatened by this process; they see state education as a machine which is not only transmitting 'socialism', but is also part of a wider process intended to undermine their class interests and traditional values. Largely as a result of this situation, the state of public education is both more socially visible and more widely discussed than it has been since the late nineteenth century. Thus, what evidence there is does seem to suggest that the demand for local control of schools, and greater democratization and devolution of power to school boards, does tend to be a primarily middle-class and professionally orientated movement. One convincing explanation for this group's awakening concern with the issue of 'Who controls the local school system?' may be found if one relates it to the gradual introduction of comprehensive education, and the phasing out of traditional grammar schools and, more recently, direct grant schools. Largely as a result of these developments, one powerful and articulate section of upper middle-class society has largely lost control over its children's education. Many families have suddenly, for the first time in their lives, found that they have little choice but to educate their children within the state system. This very new situation has naturally facilitated the type of reaction which is best summed up in the words of one anxious parent when he told me, 'We were not sure what these places (that is, state schools) were about, so we said let's set to and jolly-well tell them.'

In view of all these developments, it seems reasonable to assume that the leaders of the educational interest, both nationally and locally, are currently working out strategies for coping with two analytically distinct, if at the same time interrelated, problems. Firstly, how can they maintain their claims upon the wider resources of society in a period when many other well-organized interests, including the military industry, the social services, and so on, are also competing with them for their own share of a relatively finite total budget? Secondly, how can they effectively engineer a widespread public acceptance of, and belief in, the legitimacy of their policies in an age when education is no longer widely thought of in terms of consensual models, which tend to assume it is a neutral and independent area of activity, but is increasingly being perceived, both by providers and clients, as a process which may profoundly effect both their child's life chances, and ultimately the culture of the society we live in?

The gradual espousal of various types of cooptative devices, including the retrieval of a Victorian anachronism — the school board system — from the lumber room of educational administration, the gradual development of an allied and complex system of school's consultative councils, community groups and academic boards, may all be seen as one quite natural and largely managerially sponsored response to this quite new and delicate situation.

Thus, as we have already seen, it is extremely naïve to assume that the pressure for greater parental, worker, or communal involvement in the management or government of schools represents a genuinely spontaneous 'grassroots' activity in the sense that it might be compared in any meaningful way with a shop stewards' movement, a tenants' association, or a neighbourhood action group. Rather, it seems to be apparent when we analyse the aims, aspirations, and tactics of those groups currently pressing for school board reform, that most of the momentum has been generated by a diffuse, but nonetheless, in part, recognizable metropolitan intelligentsia, either employed directly or indirectly in elite roles within the nation's public educational industry. Similarly, and for reasons we have already identified, most of the mass support for, and responses to, these initiatives has been confined to the professional middle class.

Similarly, at the local level in Sheffield, most of the pressure leading to school board reform did not eminate from the community at large, but sprang from three fairly identifiable though closely related sources. Firstly, a district branch of the metropolitan intelligentsia which was primarily employed in, or indirectly involved with, the local educational industry, and which had formed local branches of such nationally organized pressure groups as the Campaign for State Education and the National Association of Governors and Managers. Secondly, a group of administrative officials who were dissatisfied with the city's extremely centralized system of organizing its educational service and who wished to see a greater degree of public participation and community involvement in the running of the city's schools. And finally, a group of local politicians, many of whom were employed in education or in other professional occupations and had grown increasingly influential in the city's ruling Labour Party.

All of these people, who may from one perspective be seen as members of Sheffield's new educational establishment, also tended to be generally critical of the city's long established paternalistic tradition of running its schools and were generally in favour of participatory democratic philosophies. They also, either overtly or implicitly, in their daily actions tended to question the conventional English tradition that public education was a politically neutral and value-free activity. In the main, they tended to support the view that the school system ought to be used as a tool to forge a more socially just and egalitarian society, while a few were proponents of a new radical orthodoxy and explicitly maintained that public education was an overtly political act which effectively maintained the continued oppression of the working classes.

Quite obviously an educational establishment which, either consciously, or implicitly, adopts this type of view is working within a potentially volatile political situation. It must not only address the central question of maintaining its claims upon the wider financial resources of society, but must also attempt to engineer a wide degree of client and worker consent for its policies, while at the same time working to effectively deflect, or neutralize, its critics or opponents. In other words, it may find it expedient to critically review the utility of maintaining the fairly centralized administrative and 'closed school system' traditionally associated with the traditional representational framework of local democracy, and think about the wisdom of employing new techniques to achieve its aims, including, of course, the rhetoric of participation and the machinery of cooptation. The old 'closed system' may well have been suited to a political climate in which there was a normative consensus about the aims of, and values to be transmitted within, a public educational system; however it appears to have less utility in a period when the national and local leaders of the educational interest are not only attempting to stimulate rapid social change but are also facing the challenge of an increasingly hostile environment.

Obfuscation and impression management

If one accepts the legitimacy of an alternative perspective which seeks to centrally question established conventions and ideologies, then one may perhaps see Sheffield's experiments in school board reform as an initial and still relatively crude response to changes which are taking place in the wider society. The city has become a 'test bed' for a series of ongoing experiments in the application of a new kind of 'people manipulating' technology which is effectively achieving two basic objectives. Firstly, the appropriate deflection or diffusion of groups who may be critical of, or actively hostile to, the policies being pursued by the educational establishment. Secondly, the engineering of an effective level of client consent for, and support of, the local educational system.

Most of the evidence seems to suggest that the new board system has been remarkably successful in achieving these aims. Although, as we have seen, these bodies have not facilitated any effective devolution of power to the community, at the same time their presence has helped to create, certainly amongst those groups most overtly interested in and vocal about education, the widespread impression that representatives of all concerned client and working groups are now intimately involved in the management of their own schools.

At the same time, the existence of the new boards also offers the local educational establishment a series of tactical advantages it lacked when it worked within a strictly and overtly centralized system of school administration. Today, if any of its policies generates bitter local criticism or violent public opposition, then it no longer occupies the kind of exposed and vulnerable situation where its leaders, be they politicians or administrators, must meet their enemies in a direct and damaging confrontation. Rather, in all but the most extreme cases of local discontent, these potentially troublesome and damaging conflicts are now likely to be deflected into a new '*decelerating* arena', the world of school board politics. These quasi-administrative bodies serve an invaluable obfuscatory function; this is because while in theory they can claim to represent local parental, worker, and other communal interests, in practice they tend, for reasons which should now be familiar to my readers, to identify themselves with and support the policies being advocated by the local educational establishment.

Consequently, if a contentious local issue such as a disputed catchment area, a school closure, or a discipline issue were to arise, then this is less likely to lead to the creation of local action group which will publicly seek to confront the town hall with a series of political demands. Under the new participatory system, two things may happen. Firstly, the issue may be deflected into the arena of school board politics, and in this way effectively deflected from a direct confrontation with the loci of power within the city. Secondly, the issue may still be serious enough to lead to the emergence of a local pressure group which seeks to publicly challenge the local authority. However, if this conflict does occur, then the tactical situation of the 'protestors' will now be a weak one, for the school boards in the area concerned are likely to support the local authority and call into question the action group's right both to speak for the local community and the legitimacy of the policies it seeks to advocate.

The new participatory structure also gives the leaders of the educational interest a number of strategic advantages in their fight to maintain what they see as their just share of public resources for the schools. This is because the new system effectively supplements the 'regular army' which is always fighting for the educational interest — the teachers unions, the education committee, the education officers, and so on — with a new 'volunteer force' which can be rapidly mobilized in a time of crisis, which usually means the threat of financial cuts to the existing service. Thus, when Sheffield introduced it's new board system in 1970, it not only effectively provided each school with its own board of managers; at the same time it formally enrolled the services of many hundreds of people previously unconnected with education, and familiarized them with all the problems and difficulties schools were currently trying to cope with. In other words, it created 300 public bodies which were nominally representative of the communal interest, which had become actively involved in education, and which were naturally prepared to fight energetically for their own school's interests in particular and the interests of education in the city in general. This additional reservoir of support was of particular importance to a leadership operating within the kind of social context existing in Britain in the mid-1970s. It provided them with more troops to fight against those who seek to question the burgeoning cost of education in general, or the usefulness of schools in particular. Moreover, at the same time the new board system also extends the depth of their power base, and this in turn gives them a greater degree of flexibility and manoeuvre within the new system of corporate management which was introduced into local government after the major reorganization of 1970-1971. This innovation threatened to effectively reduce the relative freedom and autonomy once enjoyed by senior officers and members of the education committee, in the sense that it sought to make them more accountable to people such as 'chief executives' and treasurer, and bodies such as finance or personnel committees not directly and intimately concerned about education or the day-to-day needs and interests of the schools.

The community school

However, although the new board system tends to provide the leaders of the educational interest with a number of tactical advantages in its struggle for survival, this is not to suggest that the new 'open system' of consultation was necessarily or consciously adopted with this end in view. Certainly many of the people who were responsible for taking a leading part in initiating these reforms, both nationally and locally, took the view that the new boards would offer a solution to one of the major paradoxes of the modern educational system.

The roots of this dilemma rest in the fact that, as more resources are devoted to education, schools grow into larger and more complicated institutions. They are increasingly able to offer their students a wide range of basic courses and subject options, while they are also able to employ a variety of teachers, each of whom is a highly trained and professional exponent of his own particular subject specialism. Largely as a result of these two trends, most modern schools are not only becoming quite large institutions, but also and partly because of this, they are also placed in locales which are geographically speaking quite remote from the people who make use of them. At the same time, partly because of the sophisticated nature of their curriculum, partly because of the social antecedents of many of their staff, parents, and other community groups, particularly in the working-class and 'downtown' areas of society, find it increasingly difficult to understand what goes on within their local school and gradually become more estranged from it. In short, the staff of many schools in present-day society find it difficult to maintain the sort of close, informal ties with their clients which were once possible when schools were small in size and served a definitive local territory, and their teachers were mainly 'craft-trained' generalists, who could, perhaps, because they were not sophisticated subject-bound specialists, communicate readily with the community they served.

For many people the reformed and representative school board promises to be an instrument which will break down this sense of estrangement and isolation and involve local people in the management of their own schools. Thus, in the case of Sheffield, as we saw in Chapter 2, one person took the view that 'It will be exhilarating, exciting and interesting to see every school with its own intimate little government, with local knowlege of both needs, and abilities, engaging in a democratic process of helping the children to integrate in an expanding, interdependent social grouping.' And in its booklet for Sheffield school managers, the authority specifically requested people to 'Try to strengthen the links between your school and the local community, between school and home and between associated primary ane secondary schools.'

Similarly the Taylor Committee also took the viewpoint that governing bodies have a potentially important role to play in improving communications and encouraging cooperation with the communities served by the school. Indeed, its recommendations are specifically intended to lead to the creation of school boards 'representing a wide cross-section of local opinion about education and the conduct of the school' (section 4.27). And the report suggests that in a place where schools draw their children from a wide area where a single community cannot easily be identified, then,

> a first task of the governing body is to survey the range and nature of the community interest. This task could usefully begin when the local education authority, staff and parent-governors meet to 'coopt' their 'community' colleagues, as the latter will be seen and will act as intermediaries between the school and the different elements of its community. (section 5.32.)

This being said, the report goes on to stress that,

> Whether or not it provides a community governor, any organisation or group operating in or connected with the community should be able to put questions, views or proposals to the governing body. Governing bodies should make known their readiness to consider representations from members of the community, perhaps looking to the local press and radio to publicise their intention to work in cooperation with the community. Another means of demonstrating this intention would be to encourage local people to attend school functions and to make the school premises available when practicable, for use by the local community. (section 5.33.)

However, as we have already seen in the case of Sheffield, it is often doubtful whether most people, particularly those living in the more deprived areas of urban England or Wales, find it either easy or very meaningful to relate to their local school through this form of close structural involvement. Most of the evidence suggests that, apart from a small, sophisticated and well-educated number of middle-class participants, most people prefer, if they relate to their local school at all, to rely upon an informal personalized series of contacts, and do not wish to involve themselves in the often formal and abstract world of school board politics.

Education and democracy

It seems then that the evidence I have examined in the course of my field work leads us tentatively towards the following general conclusions. Firstly, the kinds of participatory school governing structures which have been pioneered by such innovatory authorities as Sheffield in the early 1970s, and whose main features have now been incorporated into the Taylor Committee's proposals, offer many easily recognizable advantages to those responsible within the present statutory framework for the effective day-to-day administration of the local schooling system. Secondly, despite the rhetoric which is typically used to legitimate these innovations, these new kinds of participatory structures do little to reallocate power in favour of either groups of clients, students or workers, or even people in the wider community. Indeed, the perhaps unintended paradox associated with this type of reform is that all of the latter groups may suffer from an increasing sense of estrangement simply because the effective loci of power within the school system has not only become overtly collectivized, but is also effectively obfuscated.

In making their own assessment of how far this type of quasi-democratic structure is necessarily concordant with the long-term public interest or wider societal values, my readers may find it useful to distinguish between two very different types of initiative. The first of these, which we may reasonably classify as 'substantive reforms', explicitly seeks to involve representatives of clients, workers, and also the wider community in the determination of an institution's public policy. The second of these, which are in essence simply 'administrative innovations', are radically different in the sense that they serve, while giving the public a semblance of democracy, to enmesh those people who participate in these schemes into an essentially executive process serving the wider interests of a power elite.

Although many people often assume that the latter process is consistent with wider democratic values, a more critical inspection of these systems will reveal, as we have already seen, that the loci of decision making is not substantially altered. Thus, at best in most school boards, what tends to happen is a social process which we may label 'discrete manipulative cooption'. This means that although a process of formal and elaborate consultation now takes place with all interested parties, teachers, parents, students, community groups, local political workers, and so on, at the same time the differential knowledge of, or structural position occupied by, certain key actors — the headteacher, the chairman, the officers of the local authority clerking the meeting — means that in the main the responsible officials of the organization decide not only what issues are to be raised but also have a heavy influence upon the subsequent discussions and any final decision which is taken. Of course, in a minority of schools little attempt is made to maintain even the fiction of 'full and open' consultation, and power is openly exercised by a small subcommittee again typically composed of the clerk, the chairman, and the headteacher.

The reasons this situation develops are complex; however, they are perhaps best understood in terms of the unintended consequences of a complex number of social actions and not, as is often suggested, in terms of a Machievellian plot or a conspiritorial theory. This being said, this rather pessimistic overview of the current position and work of democratized school governing bodies, and by implication future 'post-Taylor' developments, does, I believe, offer a more satisfactory interpretation of the work of these bodies than the conventional eulogies written on this subject. Moreover, this conclusion does, I think, do much to counter the conventional assumption that economic and educational developments will, of themselves, help to create naturally a new highly articulate and self-contained class of people who will be able to form a natural counter to the cooptative techniques, and incorporative strategies, typically employed by the officials of all large organizations. This thesis, which was I think best elaborated by Bukharin in his classic work, *Historical Materialism*,[3] is an attractive one in the sense that it clearly consistent with our social hopes and ambitions, if not the realities involved in particular programmes of democratic reform. However, as we have seen in the case of Sheffield, where so many governors were typically highly educated, socially concerned, and selfless professional people, there was little evidence to suggest that as yet this group was any more likely than any other to resist the inexorable pressure to become incorporated into an existing and continuing power structure. Indeed, from one point of view one might well argue that generally those less well-educated and less overtly socially conscious members of Sheffield's working class were simply showing, by their general indifference to the new board system, a more acute awareness of the reality and nature of the distribution of power in the city.

Authority and the school system

However, partly because of the many short-term advantages it brings to the leaders of the educational interest in general, partly because of the present crisis of authority within the nation's schooling system, there seems every likelihood that the kind of radically democratized board system pioneered in Sheffield will be further refined and that following a national debate contingent on the report of the Taylor Committee, introduced more generally into the national educational system. However, this being said, it seems to me that there is an equal probability that in the long term these exciting participatory schemes will be abandoned, and we will once more return to the kind of authoritarian and centralized forms of educational government that have typified most of the urban English educational system for much of this century. My readers may well find this to be a surprising, and indeed highly contentious, note upon which to conclude a piece of research on participation and the schooling system. However, it seems to me that there are some very good technical and sociological reasons why this kind of unexpected 'revisionary development' is likely to happen.

Firstly then, let me run through some purely technical considerations. One of the classical dilemmas which always faces a political leadership when it considers the possibility of or even introduces participatory schemes which embody formal cooptative techniques is the potential danger that the technology may 'run away with itself'. In other words, the very people whom one wishes to coopt into a power structure; students, teachers, parents, community leaders, and so on, may in turn 'get out of hand' in the sense that they will attempt to encroach on those areas of decision making which have traditionally been the prerogative of the headteacher and local authority respectively. However, in what the Taylor Report notes 'may be a notable exception', the case of the

William Tyndale School, this development has occurred and gained a national prominence, precisely because it raises in an unequivocal manner the issue of 'Who controls the school?' Nonetheless, although Tyndale is an important and widely publicized case, from a wider perspective it may, in retrospect, be seen to be an exception to the general rule in the sense that the unique combination of circumstances which helped to precipitate this quite spectacular kind of crisis is unlikely to be replicated elsewhere. Thus, as the report of the public inquiry conducted by Mr. Robin Auld makes very clear, the school was situated in the inner London area, where at the time, late 1973 and 1974, there was a great turnover and shortage of teachers, since the high and increasing cost of living made it difficult for teachers to manage on their salaries. Moreover, the headteacher in question, Mr. Terry Ellis, had the misfortune to combine a quite overt class consciousness with a poor professional judgement which allowed him and other members of his staff to be influenced by strong ideological beliefs at the expense of more mundane practical considerations and the well-being of children in his charge. Finally, it seems, possibly because of the crisis of authority we have referred to in the last chapter, there was a reluctance by the local authority inspectorate to deal firmly with matters at an early stage in their development, and a surprising unwillingness to treat collectively with the managing body of the school as a corporate body, and a preference to negotiate informally with and to support a faction of the managers who were extremely critical of the work of the headteacher and most of his teachers.

In short, it seems probable that these explosive ingredients are not very likely and indeed may well not be allowed to ferment together again, and this process will be helped by the rapidly falling school roles in all of our inner urban areas, and the onset of a new phenomenon — teacher unemployment — which is leading to the growth of a far more stable labour force in schools in the late 1970s. In view of this, it seems to me that the type of technical malfunction which seems more likely to happen in reformed school board systems of the Sheffield and of the 'post-Taylor end' is not an open confrontation of the William Tyndale type, but a more subtle long-term process of factionalization. Thus, local people may gradually organize themselves into groups based upon ethnic, class, or local allegiances in order to mobilize the largely dormant powers presently exercised by school boards — general oversight of the curriculum, teacher appointment, direction of conduct, and so on. In turn this movement may be stimulated both by national developments such as the report of the Taylor Committee and the kind of radical analysis I have attempted in this study, in the sense that it may make people more conscious of, and thus prepared to challenge, the way in which school boards are presently used as instruments of impression managements and political obfuscation. However, for reasons I have already identified in past chapters, this movement when it finally develops is one which is very likely to be dominated by the professional middle classes, and largely because of this a revitalized school board system might well in the long term facilitate the development of a series of 'runaway' situations in which one articulate and politically sophisticated section of the community could capture control of the local comprehensive or primary school and seek to run it in the interests of a sectional, not a general interest.

This type of 'runaway' development might readily facilitate a new wave of educational parochialism which would not be in the best long-term interests of the children or the wider society. In some poor inner-city area this might lead to the widespread introduction of such dubious, if popular, concepts as the 'relevant curriculum', based upon the para-sociological assumption that poor white or black working-class children have different cultural experiences, and thus educational expectations, from their more materially privileged peers. In other, richer suburban educational settings this 'runaway' situation might lead to a different kind of development in the sense that the school board might favour the adoption of a particularly traditional, academic, and competitive curriculum, which effectively served to differentiate these middle-class children from their less privileged peers in the inner-city areas.

Obviously an author is treading on dangerous ground when he attempts to predict the future course of public events in the United Kingdom, for these developments are all obviously contingent on so many unpredictable and some still unrecognized factors. However, if as seems likely the major recommendations contained within the Taylor Committee's report are implemented nationally, then the kinds of situations I have simply schematized above may well develop and in their turn generate a counter-reaction leading perhaps to the re-introduction into the nation's educational system of tighter, more centralized systems of control, and the consequent downgrading of democratized school boards.

However, while this long-term development might well result from the inherent technical instability of cooptative systems of participation, it seems to me that they are equally likely to result from wider social developments. This is because, whatever framework of accountability, be it direct and local public participation or strict centralized state control, is eventually introduced into the nation's schooling system, the sociological reality is that these structures must be generally consistent with the philosophies and day-to-day practices which typically occur in other sections of with wider society. Because of this complex inter-relationship, it is always a useful exercise when one studies the overall structures of a school system, to relate its various subsidary elements and modes of control to the wider cultural context of the society within which it operates. Thus, in the same way that the Victorian school system we examined in the first chapter may be usefully analysed in terms of the radically different needs of three quite separate social orders, so is the current wave of interest in democratizing all aspects of social life, including the reform of school boards, usefully seen as part of a wider cultural movement which is at its strongest in the industrial sector of society. In turn, it seems reasonable to suggest that an analysis of some past and present help us to understand the likely future develop-ments of very similar kinds of initiatives within the field of education.

Participation and industrial life

During the last decade participation has become a fashionable term within the world of work, and various schemes for developing a more democratic industrial structure have been proposed, both by representa-tives of the management and the work force, and more recently by a government-sponsored inquiry — the Bullock Committee — in order to define more clearly how much, or how little, power should lay respectively in the hands of the employers and the workers. However, as Harvie Ramsden has recently pointed out, this current wave of interest in participation does not represent, as is so commonly assumed, one further experimental stage in a gradual evolutionary process which will gradually lead to the development of new forms of industrial democracy, in which our social arrangements are more consciously planned to respond to the exingencies of rapid technological develop-ment and economic change.[4] In contrast to this conventional interpreta-tion, Ramsden offers us an alternative and highly critical perspective, which suggests that the present fashion for participation, certainly in the case of industry, is but the latest in a series of such policies which can be traced back over a hundred years and include Whitleyism and the fashion of joint consultation after the Second World War. In each case it seems that these participatory schems were chiefly initiated by management, and were typically accompanied by rhapsodic eulogies written either by the employers themselves or by the consultants they had invited in to help them in setting up the new structures. At the same time, much of the evidence suggests that management decided to take this relatively unusual type of initiative simply because it was responding to a particularly challenging threat to its authority, and was consequently finding it extremely difficult to maintain an efficient and profitable level of industrial production. For example, Ramsden argues that the recent case of Chrysler U.K. was a typical case in point, in the sense that this company suddenly proposed 'a participatory offer on its workers in the midst of a negotiation crisis'.

However, what is perhaps equally interesting about these participatory cycles in industry is that they take place within the context of a dynamic value climate. In other words, there is a normative consensus which is generally supportive of these developments, typically on the grounds that they are resonant with wider democractive values. Largely because of the strength of this conventional and commonsense view of the world, the few alternatives and largely sociologically grounded accounts which may seek to puncture the myth of participation exert little influence, since they do not resonate easily with the dominant idealogical perspective which tends to assume the participatory movement is a 'good thing'.

The reasons both management and the wider ideological climate are generally supportive of participatory schemes in some historical periods and not at others is of course a complex matter. However, in part it would seem that one useful explanation for these initiatives may be offered in terms of the theories we have considered in this chapter. Certainly in the short term, participatory schemes may readily facilitate the deployment of the technology of formal cooptation into the field of industrial relations and in this way enable management to maintain its perogative, obfuscate the loci of decision making, and 'dampen down' any serious or avert challenge to its authority.

However, in the long term, the historical record suggests that once the direct challenge is averted, then the participatory scheme is either formally abandoned in favour of a return to direct negotiation or it is simply downgraded and merely becomes the focus for trivial and non-contentious discussions about such low key items as 'ten, towels, and toilets'. In short, as Ramsden suggests, 'I believe calls for participation may be more ideological than realistic. In fact, participation must not be seen as a blueprint of reform radically changing the existing arour, but merely as one aspect of the process and struggles of modern capitalism.'

Participation and education

In the same way, and though I can only speculate at this point, it may be useful to ask ourselves whether the current wave of interst in facilitating participatory democracy in all of our educative institutions, including reformed school boards, academic boards, liaison and consultative committees, and so on, may be viewed from the same critical perspective. Certainly if we attempt an initial and very crude comparative analysis, and look at some of the common elements present both in the movement to democratize industrial life and reform school boards, then a number of surprising parallels emerge. Firstly, in the case of industry, as we have seen in the case of schools, of development participation has not in the main been a 'grassroots' movement in the sense that most of the reforming initiatives came from management and the rank-and-file response to it was often ambivalent. Secondly, both in the case of industry and education, the new participatory schemes were typically accompanied by rhapsodic eulogies both from management, allied firms of consultants, and dominant intellectual groupings. Ironically, the few alternative accounts which served to show how these schemes worked in practice were generally ignored, and exerted little influence on the dominant view that their kind of initiative was a 'good thing'. Thirdly, it seems that, both in the case of education and industry, management decided to take the participatory initiative because it was responding to a challenge to its authority. In industry the employees were offered a place in industrial management in return for the implicit promise that they adopt a 'responsible attitude', including of course, safeguarding the firm's profitability. In the same way teachers, parents, and other interested groups were offered a place in the formal administration of the school system in return for adopting a similar 'responsible attitude', though in this case this meant supporting the policies adopted by the leaders of the educational interest. Finally, both in the case of industry and schools, despite the accompanying rhetoric, the participation schemes either tend to degenerate into discussion of trivia, 'ten, towels, and toilets' in the case of industry, 'broken windows, parquet floors, or leaking roofs' in the case of schools, or in the case of a serious issue the concerned party bypasses the participatory structure and resorts to direct negotiation with the representatives of the managerial interest.

Although this is an initial and still very tentative discussion of what may well turn out following more detailed research to be a merely speculative conjecture, it does nonetheless help us perhaps to end this chapter by making one or two long-term predictions about the future role and possible evolution of democratized governing bodies in the post-Taylor era. Firstly, it seems reasonable to assume that if, as is already happening, wider political events such as the 'recent call' by the Prime Minister in October, 1976, for a public debate on education leads to a nationwide reassessment of educational standards, what is taught in schools, and the training of teachers, then this may facilitate the emergence of a new consensus about the aims and ends of the state schooling system. It is significant in this context that the detailed proposals included in the Green Paper, *Education in Schools, a Consultative Document*, prepared by the Department of Education and Science and published in July, 1977, is specifically concerned with the means by which this new kind of consensus may be constructed.[5] This becomes very explicit when the Green Paper examines what is perhaps the most contentiously political part of the present schooling system, the comprehensive school, and it makes its position very clear in the following words:

> it is clear that the time has come to try to establish generally accepted principles for the composition of the secondary curriculum for all pupils.

And it goes on to say,

> there is a need to investigate the part which might be played by a 'protected' or 'core' element of the curriculum common to all schools. There are various ways this may be defined. Properly worked out, it can offer reassurance to employers, parents and the teachers themselves, as well as a very real equality of opportunity for pupils.

In short then, if current political events lead, as seems likely at the time of writing, to the emergence of a fair degree of consensus about the aims and ends of state financed education, then this development may in turn not only lead to the introduction of a more uniform 'core curriculum' into the schools, but also facilitate a more effective form of managerial control in the sense that it will be much easier to make teachers accountable for their actions to a reorganized national and local inspectorate. Secondly, if this situation does occur, then it will facilitate the task of professional management, both in the schools and at the local authority level, in the sense that headteachers and local advisors or inspectors will be working within a clear set of guidelines and will be less likely to suffer from the kind of ongoing crisis of authority which presently leads them to continually question and justify their everyday actions, both to themselves and to those people they manage. Thirdly, all of these developments, together with a new postwar phenomenon, the rise of a widespread teacher unemployment, may well lead to the reimposition of a stricter labour discipline within schools, in the sense that management will no longer be faced with the perpetual staffing crisis it has experienced for the last twenty years. Consequently, both headteachers and officers of local authorities will be in a stronger moral and tactical position to cope with incompetent, dissident, or radical teachers who wish to question their authority or right to rule.

If, as seems likely at the time I am writing this final chapter, January, 1978, all of these quite subtle social processes are gradually reshaping the landscape of the present schooling system, so that the nature and content of our children's education is no longer a matter for intense private concern or furious public debate, then the current wave of interest in participation and school board democracy may gradually subside. In this way, school governing bodies may once again, as they have for much of the twentieth century, be relegated to the lumber room of the educational system, and we may revert to something much more like the centralized and clearly defined control structure which operated in Sheffield and most other large urban areas before the quite unusual social circumstances of the late 1960s generated what may seem in retrospect as a series of brave, but ultimately temporary, experiments in school board democracy.

Postcript

We live in a society in which the ideals of a democratic culture — individualism, freedom of expression, equality of opportunity, public control over one's elected rulers, and public accountability of one's professional servants — are not only widely disseminated throughout the population, but are also consistently evoked by our leaders when they wish to mobilize us and enlist our support for their social actions. The most obvious corollary of this situation is that the social scientist has a continuing duty to this society to analyse not only the theoretical implications of democratic theory, but also the social behaviour of the various actors taking part in the democratic process itself. This pitiless exercise may of course be seen by many people, particularly those whose interests are most immediately affected, as regretable in that it illustrates, as we have seen in the last eight chapters, the often wide gulf which occurs between one's democratic ideals and the practice of every-day human affairs. However, it may also be seen positively as part of an ongoing therapeutic exercise which is necessary for the social health of all democratic societies. It offers us an effective means of taking democratic ideals seriously and exploring in a series of test situations the factors which tend to facilitiate their public expression, as well as those which confine and crib them in a complex web spun from strands of political opportunism, professional interest, and administrative convenience.

Notes and references

1. P. Selznick, *T.V.A. and the Grass Roots*, University of California Press, 1949.

2. R. Michels, *Political Parties*, Dover Publications, New York, 1959.

3. N. Bukharin, *Historical Materialism. A System of Sociology*, New York, International Publishers, 1925.

4. H. Ramsden, *New Society*, 30 September 1976.

5. *Education in Schools. A Consultative Document*, H.M.S.O., 1977.

Bibliography

Auld Report, The	*William Tyndale Junior and Infant Schools Public Inquiry*, ILEA, July 1976.
Bacon, A. W.	'Adult Education for School Government', *Adult Education*, Vol. 47, No. 1., May 1974.
Bacon, A. W.	'School Governors in Adult Education', *Adult Education*, Vol. 47, No. 5, January 1975.
Bacon, A. W.	'A Seat on the School Board', *Educational Guardian*, February 24, 1976.
Bacon, A W.	'School Systems and their Clients, School Governors in Sheffield', *Trends in Education*, June 1976.
Baron, G. & D. A. Howell	*The Government and Management of Schools*, The Athlone Press, 1974.
Becker, H.	'Whose Side Are We On?' in *The Relevance of Sociology*, edited by Jack Douglas, Appleton-Century-Crofts, 1970.
Bingham, J. H.	*History of the Sheffield School Board*, Northend, 1949.
Blumberg, P.	*Industrial Democracy*, Constable, London 1968.

Bullivant, B.	*The New Governors Guide,* Home and School Council Publication, 1974.
Bukharin, N.	*Historical Materialism. A System of Sociology,* New York, International Publishers, 1925.
Clegg, H. A.	*A New Approach to Industrial Democracy,* Blackwell, Oxford, 1960.
Gordon, P.	*The Victorian School Manager,* Woburn Press, 1974.
Green Paper, The	*Education in Schools — A Consultative Document,* HMSO, 1977.
Hampton, W. A.	*Democracy and Community,* Oxford University Press, 1970.
Hillary, G. A.	'Definitions of Community: *areas of agreement',* *Rural Sociology,* Vol. 20.
Hollis, P. (editor)	*Class and Conflict in the 19th Century,* Routledge & Kegan Paul, 1973.
Likert, R.	*New Patterns in Management,* McGraw Hill, New York, 1961.
Mandel,	'Workers' Control and Workers' Councils', *International* 2.
Maslow, A. H.	*Motivation and Personality,* 2nd Revised Edition, Harper and Row, 1970.
McGregor, D.	*The Human Side of Enterprise,* McGraw Hill, New York, 1960.
Maynard, A.	*Experiments with Choice in Education,* Institute of Economic Affairs, London, 1975.
Michels, R.	*Political Parties,* Dover Publications, New York, 1959.
NAGM Publications	*Policy Papers* Nos. 1 to 4 and *Discussion Papers* 1 to 4.
Plowden Report, The	*Children and their Primary Schools,* Vol. 1, London, HMSO, 1967.
Poole, M.	*Workers Participation in Industry,* Routledge & Kegan Paul, 1975.
Ramsden, H.	'Who Wants Participation?' *New Society* 30 September 1976.
Selznick, P.	*TVA and the Grass Roots,* University of California Press, 1949
Simon, B.	*Education and the Labour Movement,* Lawrence and Wishart, 1965.

Skeffington Report, The   *Report of the (Skeffington) Committee on Public Participation in Planning, People and Planning,* HMSO, 1969.

Taylor Report, The   *A New Partnership for Our Schools,* HMSO, 1977.

Appendix A. The Short Questionnaire

Survey of Sheffield School Governors/Managers

As you know, the new Sheffield system of school management and government has been in operation for over four years. In that time the new school boards have not only attracted a great deal of interest, they have also come to play an important part in the local educational system. However, in spite of this, surprisingly little is known about the experiences of the people serving on these boards.

In order to fill in some of these gaps in our knowledge, and to help us in planning for the educational needs of future school governors/managers, we are carrying out a small survey, in cooperation with Sheffield University, which is concerned with the experiences and opinions of people serving on Sheffield's school boards.

Ideally we would like to visit and talk to every governor and manager, but this is clearly an impossible task. Strictly as a second best we would like you to fill in the following pages during your meeting, and return the completed documents to the clerk of your board. Most of the questions can be answered by placing a tick in the appropriate place.

e.g., When does your board meet?

1. during the day ....

2. in the evening ....

3. sometimes day/
   sometimes evening ....

We know that some people serve on more than one school board, but for the purposes of this inquiry *simply relate your answers to your experiences on this school board.*

We are well aware of the limitations of this kind of survey, and because of this we have left a blank space at the end so that you may let us have any other ideas and comments which you feel have not been expressed in your other answers.

Thank you for your cooperation.

Yours sincerely,

1.   **How long have you served on this school board?**

    1. under six months   ....

    2. 6 months — 1 year   ....

    3. 1 — 2 years   ....

    4. 2 — 3 years   ....

    5. 3 — 4 years   ....

    6. 4 or more years   ....

2.   **Which type of school does this board serve?**

    1. primary/infant/first/junior/middle   ....

    2. secondary   ....

    3. special   ....

3.   **How local is your connection with this school?**

    Do you live:—

    1. within 5 minutes walk   ....

    2. within 1 mile   ....

    3. 1 — 3 miles   ....

    4. 4 miles or more   ....

4.   **Which of the following statements best sums up your relationship with your headteacher?**

    1. exceedingly friendly   ....

    2. just friendly   ....

    3. neither friendly nor unfriendly   ....

    4. unfriendly   ....

5.   **Which of the following people was most helpful when you first became a governor/manager?**

    1. the chairman   ....

    2. the headteacher   ....

    3. the clerk   ....

    4. a fellow governor/manager   ....

6.   **When you first joined your board, were you introduced to the teaching staff?**

1. yes ....

2. no ....

7.   **When you first joined your board, were you introduced to the children of the school?**

1. yes ....

2. no ....

8.   **Which of the following best describes your relationship with the other members of the board?**

1. close cooperation with all ....

2. close cooperation with most ....

3. easy with some/difficult with others ....

4. fairly formal ....

5. don't see eye to eye with most of them ....

9.   **How often are you able to attend your board's meetings?**

1. regularly (three or more times a year) ....

2. fairly regularly (twice a year) ....

3. infrequently (once a year or less) ....

10.   **When you were first appointed, how helpful did you find your fellow governors/managers, in 'showing you the ropes' of office?**

1. very helpful ....

2. helpful ....

3. not very helpful ....

4. don't know ....

11.   **Have you ever attended a training course designed for managers/governors?**

1. yes ....

2. no ....

12.   **How long on average do your meetings last?**

Hours   minutes

....

13.   **Do you communicate with, or inform people in your occupational/community/interest group, about your work on this board, and about the achievements/difficulties of the school?**

1. yes   ....

2. no   ....

14.   **If the answer to the last question was yes, do you find this process of communication**

1. extremely difficult   ....

2. fairly difficult   ....

3. easy   ....

15.   **Do you speak to any other meetings about the policy of the school?**

1. yes   ....   2. no   ....

If you answered 'yes', please write a few words in the space below giving details of this work.

16.   **Do you think that all school board meetings should be open to the public?**

1. yes   ....

2. no   ....

17.   **Do you think school boards ought to discuss the educational aims and objectives that their schools are pursuing?**

1. yes   ....

2. no   ....

18.   **Do you think that the main job of the school board is to look after the proper maintenance of the fabric of the school?**

1. yes   ....

2. no   ....

What do managers/governors discuss at their meetings? In order to pr[...]
some answers to these general questions please indicate below how of[...]
you discuss the following topics.

	Regularly (3 or more times a year)	Frequently (twice a year)	Infrequently (once a year or less)	Never
19. School Financial Allocation	....	....	....	....
20. The Curriculum	....	....	....	....
21. School Rules	....	....	....	....
22. Behavioural Problems	....	....	....	....
23. Vandalism	....	....	....	....
24. Zoning	....	....	....	....
25. Staffing/Appointments/ Resignations	....	....	....	....
26. Accommodation	....	....	....	....
27. Building/Repairs	....	....	....	....
28. School Expansion/ Closure	....	....	....	....
29 Reorganization	....	....	....	....
30. School Transportation/ Buses	....	....	....	....
31. Educational Research	....	....	....	....
32. Requests for the use of school property	....	....	....	....

33. Teaching Methods   ....

34.   **How did you become a governor/manager?** (e.g. were you elected
       to represent parents or teachers/coopted/appointed
       directly by the L.E.A.)

       Please specify giving full details below.

35.   **Why did you want to become a school governor/manager?**

36.   **Any other comments or ideas.**

Appendix B. The Extended Questionnaire

1.   How many schools do you serve as a manager/governor?

....

2.   How long have you served on the school board you have chosen
        to refer to in the rest of this questionnaire?

        1. Under 6 months   ....

        2. 6 months — 1 year   ....

        3. 1 — 2 years   ....

        4. 2 — 3 years   ....

        5. 3 — 4 years   ....

        6. 4 or more years   ....

3.   Which type of school does the board serve?

        1. Primary, Junior, First, Infant   ....

        2. Secondary   ....

        3. Special   ....

4. How local is your connection with this school? Do you live,

1. Within 5 minutes walk ....

2. Within 1 mile ....

3. 1 — 3 miles ....

4. 4 miles or more ....

5. What happened to you when you were first appointed to be a governor manager? (e.g. were you given a guided tour of the school by your headteacher?)

6. Which of the following statements best sums up your relationship with your headteacher?

1. Exceedingly friendly ....

2. Just friendly ....

3. Neither friendly nor unfriendly ....

4. Unfriendly ....

7. Which one of the following people was most helpful when you first became a governor/manager?

1. The chairman ....

2. The headteacher ....

3. The clerk ....

4. Fellow governors/managers ....

8. When you first joined your board were you introduced to the teaching staff?

1. Yes ....

2. No ....

9.   When you first joined your board, were you introduced to the
            children of the school?

            1. Yes   ....

            2. No   ....

10.   Which of the following best describes your relationship with
            other members of your board?

            1. Close cooperation with all   ....

            2. Close cooperation with most   ....

            3. Easy with some, difficult with others   ....

            4. Fairly formal   ....

            5. Don't see eye to eye with most of them   ....

11.   How often are you able to attend school board meetings?

            1. Regularly (three or more times a year)   ....

            2. Fairly regularly (twice a year)   ....

            3. Infrequently (once a year or less)   ....

12.   Apart from visiting your school for formal business meetings, do
            you visit your school on other occasions?

            1. Yes   ....

            2. No   ....

13.   If the answer to question is 'yes', would you please describe the
            nature of your visit to the school on these other occasions.

14.   How did you become a governor? (e.g. were you elected to
            represent parents or teachers, coopted, appointed directly by
            the L.E.A.)

15.   If you were elected by a particular group, e.g. parents or teachers, give details of the way in which you report back to them, and inform them of your activities

16.   If you were elected by a particular group of people, were you chosen because you represented a specific interest, issue, or policy?

1. Yes   ....

2. No   ....

3. Don't know   ....

17.   If you answered 'yes' to the above question would you please describe the nature of this interest, issue, or policy in the space below

18.   When you were first appointed, how helpful did you find your fellow governors/managers, in 'showing you the ropes' of office?

1. Very helpful   ....

2. Helpful   ....

3. Not very helpful   ....

4. Don't know   ....

19.   Have you ever attended a training course designed for managers/ governors?

1. Yes   ....

2. No   ....

20. Did you find any books, articles or other publications of particular help when you first assumed office?

    1. Yes ....

    2. No ....

21. If you answered 'yes' to the last question, please give details in the space below

22. How long, on average, do your governors/managers meetings last?

23. Do you communicate with, or inform people in your occupational, community, or interest group about your work on this board, and the achievements/difficulties of the school?

    1. Yes ....

    2. No ....

24. If the answer to the last question was 'yes', do you find this process of communication

    1. Extremely difficult ....

    2. Fairly difficult ....

    3. Easy ....

25. If you answered 'extremely' or 'fairly difficult' in the last question, write a few words about some of the problems you have encountered in this work.

26. Do you ever speak to any other meetings, or people about the policy of your school?

1. Yes   ....

2. No   ....

If the answer is 'yes', please write a few words in the space below giving details of this work.

27. Do you think a school board should force its views about an educational policy issue (e.g. streaming, school uniforms, exam. policies) upon a headteacher?

1. Yes   ....

2. No   ....

28. If you answered 'yes', or 'no' to the above question, please write a few words in the space below indicating why you take this attitude

29. Do you think all school board meetings should be open to the public?

1. Yes   ....

2. No   ....

30. Do you think school boards ought to discuss the educational aims and objectives their schools are pursuing?

1. Yes   ....

2. No   ....

31. Do you think the main job of a school board is to look after the proper maintenance of the fabric of the school?

1. agree   ....

2. disagree   ....

32. What do managers/governors discuss at their meetings? In order to provide some answers to these general questions please indicate below how often you discuss the following topics.

	Regularly (3 or more times a year)	Frequently (twice a year)	Infrequently (once a year or less)	Never
33. School Financial Allocation	....	....	....	....
34. The Curriculum	....	....	....	..............<
35. School Rules	....	....	....	..............<
36. Suspension/ Behavioural Problems	....	....	....	..............<
37. Vandalism	....	....	....	..............<
38. Zoning	....	....	....	....
39. Staffing/Appointments/ Resignations	....	....	....	....
40. Accommodation	....	....	....	....
41. Building/Repairs	....	....	....	....
42. School Expansion/ Closure	....	....	....	....
43. Reorganization	....	....	....	....
44. School Transportation/ Buses	....	....	....	..............<
45. Educational Research	....	....	....	..............<
46. Requests for the use of school property	....	....	....	..............<

47.   School Boards are often perceived as middle-class institutions; sometimes they are seen as simply puppet bodies with no real power. Obviously these assertions can only be adequately countered if we have detailed information about the political affiliation and social class of managing and governing bodies. In order that we may investigate this issue in more detail, I would like you to fill in the following schedule. In each case find out the relevant information and then simply enter a number in the appropriate space

	For example:	Born in Yorkshire	18
		Not born in Yorkshire	1
		Not known	0

Social Composition **Number on the Board** N = _____

48.   1. Men   . . . .

            Women   . . . .

            Total (N)   _____

49.   2. Professional   . . . .

            Businessmen   . . . .

            Housewives   . . . .

            White collar   . . . .

            Blue collar   . . . .

            Other   . . . .

            Not known   . . . .

            Total (N)   . . . .

50.   3. Conservative   . . . .

            Labour   . . . .

            Liberal   . . . .

            Other   . . . .

            Not known   . . . .

            Total (N)   _____

In conclusion:

51.   Why did you want to become a manager/governor?

52.   How long have you lived in Sheffield?

53.   Are you?   Male . . . .   Female . . . .

54.   At what age did you complete your own full-time education?

1. 15 years or under

2. 16—17 years

3. 18—19 years

4. 20 years and over

55.   Any other comments you wish to make

Appendix C. A Report From The University of Sheffield (Department of Extramural Studies) School Managers Study Group

Content Analysis of Minutes of School Managers' Meetings

In its booklet "Management of a County Primary School" Sheffield Education Committee states: 'In the belief that vigorous governing bodies would be of great value to their schools the Education Committee decided . . . to appoint individual managing and governing bodies to all their schools.' Elsewhere in the same booklet the functions of managers are listed, the most important of which is '. . . and through the agency of the headteacher, *to have general direction of the conduct and curriculum of the school.*'

It was thought that it could be instructive to find out exactly what was discussed at school managers' meetings by looking at the minutes of those meetings and grouping the points discussed under several broad headings.

The sample consisted of minutes of 30 meetings. These came from both primary and secondary schools within Sheffield, with a few from the West Riding. Some schools were represented by more than one set of minutes, but since the meetings of all schools appeared to follow such a similar pattern, it was thought that this would not distort the results.

Fifteen broad headings were taken though even this fairly large number necessitated the cramping of some tenuously related topics under one heading. They are as follows:—

1 *Procedure*. This covers the appointment of new managers, thanks, apologies for absence and so on.

2 *Fabric*. The maintenance of existing buildings, the provision of new buildings, complaints about structures.

3 *Safety*. This section was mainly concerned about Fire regulations, but it also includes complaints and suggestions about improving overall safety.

4 *Staffing*. This covered the appointment of both academic and non-academic staff. Short lists of suitable people were often discussed at the meetings but the actual appointment was often delegated to a sub-committee, and the make-up of those subcommittees is not known [i.e. particular managers were named, but it is not known what interests they represented — parental, local authority, teachers, etc.]

5 *Accommodation*. Shortage of space and places for more buildings.

6 *Special equipment and visits*. A "catch-all" including theatre visits, exchange visits, adventure playgrounds, as well as the purchase of kilns and similar equipment.

7 *Parent-teacher*. Liaison between the two bodies, either proposing that an association should be formed, or reporting on the activities of an already established one. This section includes in one or two instances relations between parents and managers.

8 *Reorganization*. Mostly the conversion of infant to first schools and junior to middle schools.

9 *School fund*. How to increase it.

10 *Behaviour*. Mainly discipline problem in secondary schools.

11 *Meals*. The inclusion of textured vegetable protein, etc.

12 *Social activities*. Outings, etc.

13 *Capitation*. Statements of what the capitation/child is, and (often) that it was not going to be increased.

14 *Curriculum* (and performance). Mainly restricted to discussion of exam results.

15 *Political*. One item only — a discussion of the noncentralization of teacher-training.

There were four items under "Urgent Business" and these were concerned with extra-staffing, National emergency (heating?) and reorganization.

One special meeting was called and this was about the reorganization of a particular school.

Conclusions

Most managing and governing bodies spend their time discussing accommodation, fabric maintenance, safety matters and other administrative details. They spend little time discussing educational aims in general, or the curriculum of their schools in general. Thus, although in theory these boards are seen as a means through which the professional educationalists are made accountable to a locally recruited lay body, in fact most managers and governors are reluctant to discuss the curriculum or other major educational objectives, and seem content to busy themselves with time-consuming, administrative matters.

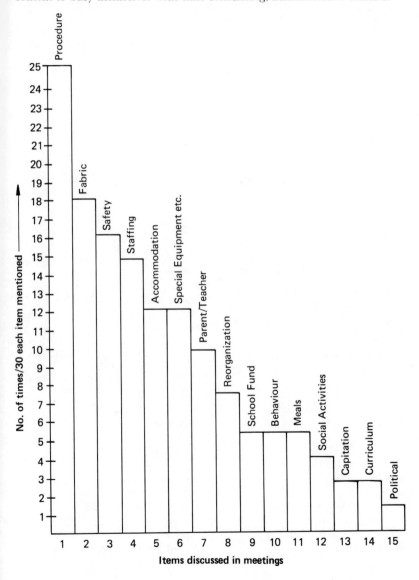

INDEX

Notes

Notes

Notes

Notes

Notes